for £1.50
D0811174

A HUNT AROUND THE HIGHLANDS

Col. Thornton breaking cover.
c. 1775 – SAM RAVEN – 1847

A Hunt Around the Highlands

(On the Trail of Colonel Thornton)

MICHAEL BRANDER

THE STANDFAST PRESS

1973

FIRST PUBLISHED 1961 BY DOUGLAS SAUNDERS
IN ASSOCIATION WITH MACGIBBON & KEE
© MICHAEL BRANDER 1961
REVISED SECOND EDITION 1973
THE STANDFAST PRESS
© MICHAEL BRANDER 1973

Text set in 12/13 pt. Monotype Bembo, printed by letterpress,
and bound in Great Britain at The Pitman Press, Bath

In memory of
Colonel F. W. Reid, M.C., T.D.
and many fishing days together

AUTHOR'S NOTE

Spelling is of the old variety when quoting from the original manuscript.

ACKNOWLEDGEMENTS

My thanks and acknowledgements for kindly allowing me access to family records or property, or in other ways materially assisting me to write this book, are due to: The Rt. Hon. Lord Moubray and Stourton; Lady Lawson Tancred; Lt.-Col. J. P. Grant, younger, of Rothiemurchus; Mrs. Mackintosh of Mackintosh; M. Campbell, Esq., The Captain of Dunstaffnage; Major Patrick Telfer-Smollet, M.C., D.L.; Sir Ivar Colquhoun of Luss Bt., D.L., J.P.; Major J. Fairfax-Blakeborough, M.C.; G. F. Willmot, Esq., B.A., Curator of York Museum; D. Wilson-Reid of Robertland, M.A., Archivist of Glasgow University, and A. Brown, Esq., Staff Photographer to the Scottish Tourist Board.

February 1961

My further thanks and acknowledgements are due to:

Lt. General Sir George & Lady Gordon Lennox; Ian Biggs of Culachy: G. Kenneth Whitehead, Esq.; E. Wain, Esq., Curator of Aldborough Museum; Mrs. M. Machin; Miss V. Turnbull; Father W. Bresslin, S.M.A.; The Revd. D. Dixon;

February 1973

Miss Ninetta Butterworth for the endpapers; Miss Mary Browning for the map; Vixen for the design of the cover; to Simon Grant Rennick for permission to reproduce the engraving of Heron Hawking.

FOREWORD

In 1958 I decided it would be of interest to follow the route around the north taken by Colonel Thomas Thornton in 1784 in his famous 'Tour through the Highlands and North of England', the first sporting venture of its kind. Accordingly in 1959 I followed his 'Tour' comparing the sport, scenery and people with his account written a hundred and seventy five years earlier. The first edition of this book was published in 1961 under the title 'Soho for the Colonel', 'Soho' being the old cry used to encourage hounds on a scent. The title of this edition is much more descriptive of the book, as a record of my efforts to establish the truth or otherwise of the Colonel's statements, which often seemed outrageous exaggeration. After such a time lag the scent was weak in places, to say the least, but it proved eventually a fascinating hunt spanning the centuries on the trail of a man who was certainly the greatest huntsman of his day and reputedly an even greater liar.

During the past decade and a half there have been many radical changes. Motorways now slice through countryside where all was once pastoral peace and quiet. Older roads have been broadened, straightened and even in places turned into dual carriageways. New towns have appeared, new sports centres have been built, as at Aviemore, and National Parks created. Sadly a number of people mentioned have died. Yet the book remains generally unaffected by these changes since it is dealing with the years around 1784 and 1959 as two isolated periods in time, comparing them with each other. The more obvious changes have been numbered in the text and noted in an appendix. In the last chapter on inns those no longer functioning have been deleted, being replaced by one or two previously omitted or overlooked, but the old 1959 prices have been left as of historical interest. The book remains a description of a hunt over the formidable barriers of history, time and place, with a faint answering 'Whoo-whoop' echoing back over the centuries.

PUBLISHER'S PREFACE

In an age of few sporting eccentrics, it is refreshing indeed to cast one's thoughts back over Colonel Thornton's exploits.

In those halcyon years, Colonel Thornton pursued all types of outdoor sports with the utmost enthusiasm, vigour and efficiency and, so we are told, he had his moments indoors as well!

A falconer of great renown, together with Lord Orford he founded what is now The British Falconers Club. He was famed for his flight at Heron as well as excelling at all types of Game Hawking.

A great patron of Coursing, together with Major Topham he founded the Old Yorkshire Coursing Club,—he owned, among many others, the celebrated greyhound MAJOR who won him a 1,000 Guinea Stake at Carshalton. Dog breeder of many varieties and crosses he bred milk white terriers, the famous pointer DASH, spaniels, beagles, foxhounds and greyhounds.

A tireless horseman, he hunted packs of hounds, rode for wagers, etc. An outstanding shot, famed for his 7 Barrelled Gun, he was equally good with a rifle.

Fisherman of great efficiency his 64″ Pike fairly startled the fishing world of those days.

Connoisseur of wines, patron of the arts, he commissioned paintings by Sawrey Gilpin, Reinagle and other fashionable artists of the day, and on his Sporting Tour he took with him George Garrard the engraver (pupil of Sawrey Gilpin) who later became an R.A.

The first property tycoon. The fantastic figure he obtained for his house would make the speculators of today green with envy!

Traveller in the grand manner and greatest luxury, his Sporting Tours of the Highlands and later France are famous not only for their exploits (some of which are doubtful) but also for the variety of the entourage.

For example as shown by the endpapers is his 'caravansarai' when he moved from Thornville Royal in Yorkshire to Spye Park in Wiltshire—'Led by a huge vehicle known as the boat-waggon, formerly used for taking regiments of Yorkshire voters to the Polls. Packed with dogs, luggage, guns, rods, otter-spears and sporting gear. Draped with skins of stags, roe-buck and large game, drawn by four cream-coloured Arab horses of royal breeding. There followed a dog-cart of a load of terriers in clothing embroidered with records of their triumphs, then the huntsman and his whippers-in in charge of a mixed pack of 100 couple of foxhounds, stag-hounds, otter-hounds, beagles. Next in order came a string of thoroughbred horses, each one clothed in deerskin and led by a groom in livery; liveried keepers leading the Thornton pointers, a green and silver clad Falconer in charge of various hawks and a 'brace' of Cormorants broke to fish-hunting; and a garde-chasse with two wild boars. The rear brought up by a line of waggons loaded variously with red deer, roe-buck, Asiatic deer, white muscovy ducks, ferrets and other animals, to say nothing of the collection of works of art and old master paintings and a large collection of exotic hot-house plants. Finally, there were nine waggon loads of vintage wine and ale'.

This is a brief resumé of the character whose sporting tour of the Highlands is the subject of this book.

Opinions vary about this extravagant extrovert but none can deny that life with Thornton can never have been dull.

Richard Grant-Rennick
GLOUCESTERSHIRE 1973.

CONTENTS

ILLUSTRATIONS

A HUNT AROUND THE HIGHLANDS

Chapter 1

A STIRRUP CUP

> He was a huntsman of renown,
> He was a man about the town,
> He shot, he fished, his bag he filled;
> He hawked and talked and lady killed.

Colonel Thomas Thornton's heyday was that brief period towards the end of the eighteenth century when the rich were able to indulge to the full their varied zests for living, unaffected by wars abroad or taxation at home. It was the age of new ideas, of experiment and expansion in agriculture, the age of the individual, of the bucks and the eccentrics, the prelude to the industrial revolution of the next century. In his own chosen sphere Thornton was an outstanding example of this age of originals, even if in the following century he seemed something of an anachronism.

He was undoubtedly a paradoxical character. Colonel of the West York Militia, which was founded by his father to assist in quelling the '45, he was educated at Charterhouse and Glasgow University at the time of Adam Smith. Bon viveur, gourmet and womanizer, athlete and sportsman, classical scholar and patron of the arts, soldier by title and humanitarian in theory, author and versifier, Whig and Francophile, he was a lavish entertainer and open-handed host, as well as something of a showman who enjoyed the limelight.

Latterly considered eccentric, even in an age of eccentrics, he was also openly immoral, judged by today's standards, although perhaps not outstandingly or viciously so, if judged by those of his own era. Yet, in spite of his excesses in later life, he had the moral courage and good sense to forbid excessive gambling after dinner under his own roof in an age when fortunes were frequently lost in this way.

When the Duke of York, the self-seeking son of the mentally deranged George III, tried to cheat the ebullient Yorkshire Colonel out of £5,000 on a property deal he was ignominiously exposed. Subsequently Thornton claimed, almost certainly with justification, that the Duke used his influence as C.-in-C. of the Army to have him court-martialled and reprimanded for a trivial offence. The Colonel gave his side of the case in a vigorous pamphlet entitled: 'An Elucidation of a Mutinous Conspiracy entered into by the Officers of the West York Regiment of Militia against their Commanding Officer. Dedicated (Sans Permission) to H.R.H. the Duke of York'. He then resigned his commission 'in disgust'.

Shortly afterwards, during the war with France, Colonel Thornton was involved in an acrimonious correspondence with ministers of the Government following his friendly treatment of two French Commissioners in this country. In spite of all this, prior to the turn of the century, he had few equals in hunting, shooting, fishing and, above all, falconry, and not even his enemies, led by the Duke of York, could deny that he was the leading sportsman of his day.

By way of example the programme for a week's sport he intended holding in Yorkshire in 1803 was announced as: 'Monday, Stag hunting followed by Coursing. Tuesday, Wolf, Stag and Fox hunting and Beagling. Wednesday, Stag hunting and Coursing. Thursday, Wolf, Stag and Fox hunting. Beagling and Coursing, to meet every day at Falconers' Hall, where there will be a sportsman's breakfast provided for all the Company.' In 1805, in the presence of vast crowds at York, his mistress, Alicia Meynell, riding as 'Mrs Thornton', won a gold cup worth seven hundred guineas in a flat race against the champion jockey of the day. 'Mrs Thornton' is the only woman listed in the jockey Club records to this day as having won a flat race against the opposite sex.

About this time he had two country seats and a considerable acreage of land in Yorkshire. He was also a member of the notorious Savoire Vivre Club in London and he had a pied-à-terre in Westminster blatantly named 'The Boudoir', which he subsequently sold for fourteen hogsheads of claret. At the age of forty-five he was capable of writing: 'As the race of man is but of short duration, I am still solicitious to skim the cream of the existence, and leave the blue milk for such as may happen to prefer it.' It may well have been possible to dislike such a man, but it must have been difficult to remain indifferent to him.

As well as various pamphlets, he wrote *A Sporting Tour of France* in the form of letters to the Earl of Darlington, which still makes interesting reading, but we are primarily concerned with his book entitled *A Sporting Tour through the Northern Parts of England and Great Part of the Highlands of Scotland, including Remarks on English and Scottish Landscapes and General Observations on the State of Society and Manners*. This was first published in 1804 and in 1805 was reviewed, rather unkindly, by Scott, then an unknown young lawyer. It was republished, as a classic of its kind, with a foreword by Sir Herbert Maxwell, in 1896.

Judged purely as a work of literature it was not good, as Scott hastened to indicate. The unusual thing about it, as Scott also noted, was that it was written at all. Few sportsmen of that day ever put pen to paper and recorded their impressions at length. In this also Thornton was exceptional.

Having at some time or other been over most of the country he covered I was particularly interested when I came across his book. My first conclusion after reading it was that he must have been an inveterate optimist and something of a liar. After checking one or two points it seemed to me that he was the greatest liar since Munchausen.

It was then that it occurred to me that it might be interesting to follow his route, trying to check on some of the more glaring discrepancies and, as far as possible, shooting and fishing where he shot and fished. To start with I read his other works and delved into his background and life as far as possible. Very soon I found the trail both fascinating and rewarding. There must always be a certain bond between hunter and hunted, even when the hunt spans the centuries, and Thornton, the leading huntsman of his day, would have been the first to appreciate my feelings as I followed the 180-year-old scent through his tangled narrative.

The solution ultimately proved simple enough. Thornton had tried to condense too many expeditions into the one 'Tour'. A full third of his book is devoted to various expeditions to Speyside, where he had a shooting lodge for some years. It was probably a source of considerable pleasure to him that no critic, from Scott onwards, ever noted this, for it was the sort of deception which would have appealed to his mischievous sense of humour. But whether his 'Tour' covers one year or several is really immaterial except in so far as it affects understanding of his book.

Apart from being in diary form, which makes confusing reading at times, there is no doubt that some parts were written from memory about twenty years after the events. He was also guilty of plagiarizing whole pages at a time from Pennant's *Tours of Scotland*. His accuracy was certainly questionable on occasion and he was undoubtedly liable to exaggerate, but his observations were often shrewd and of especial interest today. There is also a lively humour and human interest in his writing, not always to be found in the drier works of Pennant.

Making due allowance for all its shortcomings, Colonel Thornton's book is still of interest, as a chronicle of the times, as an account of travel in those days less than forty years after the '45, and as the first general sporting survey of the Highlands.

Following his route, checking it very thoroughly and going over parts of it a number of times, it is only fair to admit that where I had thought him wrong, he frequently proved, on double checking, to have been correct. As a travelling companion he was seldom dull and his remarks often proved exceedingly apposite. Even if I had not been looking for them, it would have been difficult not to find parallels with the present day, nor to be struck by the contrasts between the scene as he described it and as it is now.

In a way therefore this description of my hunt after Thornton is two-dimensional in that it is an account of travel round Scotland and the North of England both in the past and in the present.

It is certainly not intended as an accurate economic or historical survey, although where I have given facts or figures I have tried to check their accuracy from reliable sources. Nor is it intended as just another traveller's guide, although a list of sporting inns is included. Following the Colonel I had little time for shooting, and throughout that extremely hot summer of 1959 I caught no fish, which was hardly surprising, but Thornton provided plenty of sport and I found it, as I have indicated, a fascinating and enjoyable 'chace'. I can recommend the route and I hope others will share something of that fascination and enjoyment in pursuit of the Colonel, either in reality or through the ensuing chapters.

Soho* for the Colonel.

* Soho, from Sohowe, old term of encouragement to hounds picking up a scent.

Chapter 2

DRAWING THE HOME COVERT

The dusky night rides down the sky,
And ushers in the mourn:
The hounds all join in glorious cry,
The huntsman winds his horn;
And a-hunting we will go.

HENRY FIELDING: 1707–54

Boroughbridge to Darlington

On reading Thornton's 'Tour' one is at once struck by the tremendous change in the tempo of life between then and now. The first sentence strikes a quiet leisurely note which contrasts sharply with the jet whine and roar of travel today. Meeting his friends Messrs Parkhurst and Serle in London in the spring he told them of his previous year's sport and added that he intended 'again traversing the mountainous regions of the North'. A refreshing change from the annual influx of people 'doing' the Highlands. No one could surely 'traverse' in a hurry.

There is also an aura of an age of gracious living about the fact that Mr Serle 'lamented' his inability to leave at once, but promised to join him later, while Mr Parkhurst, 'not being particularly engaged', and all unaware of what he was letting himself in for, agreed with apparent alacrity. From subsequent remarks it is clear that Thornton regarded Mr Parkhurst as something of a butt, and the comparison which inevitably springs to mind is that of the playboy millionaire who suggests to a couple of his sycophants that they should join him on a big game safari. One can readily imagine the agitation of secretaries, the wiring of cables, the book-ing of planes and other arrangements which would follow such a decision.

In his day, Thornton was the equivalent of a millionaire without the drawbacks of super tax, and all his arrangements were, accordingly, on an extremely lavish scale. His immediate reaction was to go on a shopping spree, ordering two boats '(in order that Mr P.'s plans and mine might not interfere; a mode which in like cases I would recommend every sportsman to adopt implicity)' a portable kitchen, which failed to arrive, and sundry other articles, which he had sent up to York by boat before leaving London.

At first sight he seems to have taken a vast amount of equipment with him, and his critics, from Scott onwards, have often sneered at him on this account. Certainly he prepared himself for every contingency, but, examined carefully, it does not seem an unduly excessive amount for the sports he intended to pursue. It was not for him a question of simply hitching a caravan on to the back of his car and setting off without further preparation. He had, in effect, to arrange for the transport of a considerable part of his household to the Highlands for several months at a time when conditions there were still primitive, by the standards to which he was accustomed, so that they had to be virtually self-supporting.

Arriving in Yorkshire with Mr Parkhurst at the end of May, he hired a cutter at York to take his boats, tents and equipment, nets, six falcons, four setters, six pointers and a deerhound, two double-barrelled guns, one rifle, three single barrels, eighty pounds of gunpowder, eleven bags shot and sufficient flints, along with hams, bacon, reindeer and other tongues, smoked beef, pigs, countenances, pickles, sweetmeats, etc., enough to serve until the end of October. Also on board were his falconer, wagoner, groom and boy, as well as Mrs C., a housekeeper. Going on down the Ouse the cutter was to stop at Hull and take on biscuits, flour, corn, beans and oatmeal, as well as porter, ale and small beer, '(the latter being a necessary I had found great want of)'. The cutter was then expected to take ten days to reach Forres, the nearest port to Raits, on Speyside, where he had rented a house.

In his party travelling by land the Colonel included Mr Garrard, an artist, whom he chose because he was a good animal painter and because his 'age, constitution and acknowledged rising genius would admit of no comparison; added to which he was an excellent walker'. He also appears to have had at least two servants, presumably a valet each for himself and Mr Parkhurst, at least one groom, five horses, a setter and sundry fishing rods and guns, as well as a light carriage. Altogether quite a party to assemble.

By contrast my party never consisted of more than one companion on my various expeditions, usually two dogs, three fishing rods and tackle, two double-barrelled twelve bores and a few boxes of cartridges. Apart from that we had suitcases with various changes of clothes and a sack of biscuits for the dogs, all of which was transported in a 1926 Rolls-Royce. This stately yellow vehicle with the dogs, fishing tackle and guns in full view in the back, conveyed, without a word being spoken, that we were on a sporting tour. Like Thornton we intended putting up at inns on the way, and that is just about where the resemblance ended.

The Colonel was probably up in Scotland in 1782 and almost certainly 1783 and 1784 were the main periods of the 'Tour', but there are points which indicate other years. Sir Herbert Maxwell, who edited the reprint of Thornton's book in 1896, mentioned the year 1786, although he gave no reason. Certain correspondence indicates that Thornton was there in 1788, and from 1789 to 1794 he rented a lodge, which he had built on Speyside. It may well be, therefore, that a number of years in the 1780s were involved in his book. Various duplicate dates, the necessity of sending the servants home twice, and many other contradictions, all point to several years condensed into one.

Having the advantage of the internal combustion engine, albeit a venerable machine, I felt that it was not unreasonable to make as many expeditions round the route, or parts of the route, as I felt necessary in the one year to cover the ground adequately. Accordingly I canvassed amongst my friends and promptly ran into the same difficulty Thornton had in getting people to join him. It was not the terra incognita of the Highlands that put them off, but rather that they simply could not spare the time in the rush of modern living. Several agreed, but like Mr Serle, failed to come up to scratch when it came to the point. However, I was fortunate enough to rope in three old friends eventually, a scientist, a farmer and an importer, who each in turn covered some stages of the route with me.

It is worth adding that although I tried to match his dates as far as possible I did not try to emulate his records or methods. It has only to be pointed out that he cheerfully netted various rivers and lochs and thought nothing of catching fifty or sixty trout at a time to explain why. Furthermore one of his favourite methods of fishing was to bait half a dozen cork floats, or trimmers, of different colours, each named after a favourite foxhound, and then lay bets on which would catch the largest fish. Needless to say this now is also illegal.

Following his trail assiduously, however, I made a series of excursions into the countryside between York and Boroughbridge where Thornton was brought up. It seems that he sold his paternal estate in 1789, after his Scottish Tour, and bought Allerton Maulserer from the Duke of York for £110,000, promptly re-christening it Thornville Royal. This was the deal mentioned in the first chapter over which the Duke tried to cheat him of £5,000 and was ignominiously exposed. Subsequently, when in need of money, about fifteen years later, Thornton sold the estate to Lord Stourton for £226,000.

Allerton Mauleverer is still owned by the present Lord Mowbray and Stourton and in the grounds he has some of the descendants of the park deer of Thornton's day, as well as a flock of St Kilda's black sheep. The only part visible from the Great North Road is the folly known as the Temple of Victory, which Thornton described as 'an elegant structure, of stone', though perhaps elegant is not the adjective which would be applied to it today. The house and grounds are not opened to the public, which must now be the exception rather than the rule. However, its only real connection with this book is that the 'Tour' was written there in 1804.[1]

To return to Thornton; having sent his heavy luggage off by sea, he then had dinner with the Lord Mayor of York. The following day he set off with his party by road. Unable to find much to say about the very attractive rolling countryside between his home and Boroughbridge and not apparently crossing the old toll bridge over the Ouse at Aldwark, which still stands, he 'arrived by the old Roman Road at Aldborough'. Here he mentioned especially a Roman pavement, 'the most perfect one hitherto discovered', dug up in 1750 in the house of a Mrs Dorothy Ellers 'when intending to make a cellar'. He noted that she 'has ever since taken care to preserve it in the best manner'.

Stopping at the local inn I inquired tentatively if they knew of a Roman pavement anywhere locally. Somewhat to my surprise I was told that there were two, 'Up at back of garden, beyond the hens'. Duly walking up between two enclosures of somnolent Rhode Island Reds I came to a couple of small outhouses where on opening the doors, I saw two tessellated pavements which the Ministry of Works had padlocked and barred from injury. Neither tallied with Garrard's illustration nor merited the praise Thornton gave his. Slightly disappointed, I returned to the inn and inquired as a cross check when they had been discovered. Without a moment's hesitation the reply came:

'1850.'

In view of the obvious discrepancy I asked if there was another pavement. There was some hesitation about admitting the presence of a rival pavement. Finally I was told to speak to Mr Simpson, down the road, opposite the Village Institute.

'You can't miss it.'

This other pavement, I gathered, was the property of Lady Lawson Tancred, and, having obtained her permission to view it, I went down the road to the Village Institute. Mr Simpson had, fortunately, just finished his lunch. In his dark waistcoat, dark breeches and this gaitered legs stretched at ease in his corner seat he might have posed for Mr Emmett's conception of a village beadle. When I had explained my business he was very helpful and led me past a fine display of roses in front of his house to the potting shed at the back. Here were all the appurtenances of a keen gardener, rakes, spades, hoes, brooms and a lawn-mower. Seizing a broom he set about sweeping the sawdust off the floor to reveal 'the' Roman pavement It is no longer, I fear, looked after as well as in Mrs Dorothy Ellers's day, but it is still, undeniably, as good as the two which the Ministry of Works, have taken such care to preserve.

Having duly admired it and given Mr Simpson the wherewithal to drink to his benefactor, Mrs Dorothy Ellers, coupled with Colonel Thornton, we withdrew. This was certainly the pavement Thornton mentioned. I am no expert, but having been in hospital during the last war opposite the ruins of Pompeii, round which I used to walk on crutches every morning, I can appreciate a good Roman pavement when I see it. I would be the last persons to deny that Mr Simpson makes good use of it, but he must be the only person in the country with a Roman pavement in his potting shed. It seems surprising that the Ministry of Works cannot provide him with another shed and make some effort to preserve this pavement before it is too late to do so.[2]

Our next stop was the inn at Boroughbridge called the Three Arrows. This we decided must have been the house where Thornton stopped and 'took a little refreshment with my worthy and intimate friend Captain W., who accompanied us to take a view of those great curiosities, the three pyramids in the adjacent fields, vulgarly called the Devil's Arrows'.

I had often stopped at this inn on my way north or south, but had never before appreciated that it must at one time have been a rather charming private house, or that, in fact, there were 'Three Arrows' close behind it. As it was the week-end the bar was full of parents taking their children out from schools within range. Snatches of conversation surrounded and submerged us.

'The headmistress is a termagant, I can tell you. Old Major Carruthers arrived back with his daughter twenty minutes late last week and she had him up on the carpet . . .'

'Don't spill your Coca-Cola on the carpet, darling . . .'

'At Hilary's school they all roll up in Jaguars and Rolls-Royces . . . .'

'I'm not interested in your excuses, Major, she said. You must

have known there would be extra traffic on the roads. Kindly
don't let it happen again . . .'
    'John's headmaster once said . . .'
    'There, darling. All over the carpet . . .'
    No one seemed to know anything about the 'Three Arrows'.
The barmaid, inevitably, was 'new there herself' and the manageress was obviously harassed, so we moved quietly round the
corner by ourselves. It was then that I experienced my first distrust
for Thornton's accuracy, for he gave the measurement of the
girth of the largest pillar as eighty-four feet. Even from a distance
this looked wildly wrong. Walking carefully through a field of
growing corn I measured it myself and made it only approximately
twenty-eight feet. Either the 'light refreshment' had so affected
the Colonel that he was pacing round not one pillar but three,
or else it must have been a printer's error. The logical conclusion
is the latter.
    Apart from his mistake about this measurement his detailed
description of them appears to be reasonably accurate. They are, I
gather, probably part of a large Neolithic, or Early Bronze Age,
avenue or circle, such as that at Avebury. Standing as they do in
cultivated fields, next to modern houses and near to telegraph
wires and electric cables, they have that peculiarly out-of-place
and apologetic air of most ancient monuments caught up in the
spread of civilization today. The proper place for such things is
open grass land or a 'blasted heath'.
    At this point Thornton developed a trick which was not easy to
detect unless the route was followed carefully. As far as I can
make out he used it only in his home county to bring in points of
interest, so that it may almost be counted as a legitimate device.
The convincing minor details he used to supplement it, however,
make one wary of accepting anything he wrote without a check.
In this instance he claimed to be heading for a friend at Northallerton and then brought in a neat detour of some sixty miles or so,
which obviously, must have been complete fiction. In a motor-car
it was both practical and pleasant. On horseback it would have
been impossible, at least as a prelude to a long journey.

He went on: 'Bedale, a small bad town, through which we now passed' (but, as this is in the opposite direction to Northallerton, he really did nothing of the sort) 'is only remarkable for a tolerably spacious street and very slippery pavements. Adjoining to it stands Hall House, the property of Mr Pierce, a good family mansion with a hall sufficiently roomy to form a commodious barracks for soldiers, for which purpose it wants nothing but the addition of a second fireplace.'

For some reason he disliked Bedale, which seems a pleasant enough little town. The main street is still extremely wide and the cobbles, no doubt, slippery to horses. The hall is now owned by Sir Henry Beresford Pierce, the forestry expert, who used to be a neighbour of mine, and who now lives in a bungalow in the grounds. Looking at the house one can still see what Thornton meant and the delightful part of it is that his joke actually came true, since the hall was used as a barracks during the last war and, no doubt, was as draughty as he suggested. It is now the district urban offices, being a good deal too large for occupation by modern standards.

From there, in theory, Thornton went on to Spenningthorne and mentioned the 'prospect much heightened by the fair town of Middleham'. This is still true. Apart from one or two late Victorian additions and some corrugated iron roofs, which stand out like chromium plate on a stage coach, Middleham remains much as it must have been in his day. A small and most attractive village perched on a hilltop, it is a charming sight, especially from below Spenningthorne. From there the stone houses, weathered into the landscape by centuries of Yorkshire winters, look more like a stage backdrop of a village than the real thing.

Below Spenningthorne is an interesting old arched bridge with crenellations, or pockets, for pedestrians. Turning right there it is not far to the market square of Middleham itself. The notable feature about it is that nowadays it would be termed at best a village and by no stretch of the imagination could it be called a town. Of course in Thornton's day the population was mainly agricultural and there were only eight million people in England

and two million in Scotland, so that towns and villages were all on a much smaller scale. On the other hand those houses owned by the rich were, in themselves, inevitably, one of the local sources of employment and, as such, kept a large staff busy throughout the year. For this reason, probably, they tended to be larger than was strictly required, sheltering as they did not only the owner and his numerous family, but a flock of servants as well. It is noticeable that the trend then was towards new and larger houses, few of which have survived intact and unaltered.

The route next led by Stanton Moor, which was not mentioned, but where, no doubt, he had often hawked and hunted. According to the warning notices it is now a tank drivers' training ground. Fortunately, being the week-end, we did not meet any learner tank drivers and continued safely on past Halfpenny House, a small castellated house standing above the Swale valley with such really splendid views that it is surprising Thornton did not mention them, even in a piece of fiction. In fact this is another indication, if it were needed, that he never made this journey as part of the 'Tour' at all.

After Middleham the next place he mentioned was Marske, 'a very Gothic, old mansion'. The house can be seen on the left of the road after a winding hilly approach with some more excellent views over the Swale valley. The 'Gothic, old mansion' he referred to seems to be still standing, empty, behind a more modern building, which was, presumably, erected after the 'Tour' was published. With crumbling terrace and broken stone balustrades, not to mention holes in the walls covered with tarpaulins, it is another example of a house too large for modern purposes, which has suffered from years of neglect.[3]

'Having tasted some beverage here', although apparently his imagination could not stretch to visualizing exactly what he drank, Thornton continued, theoretically, towards Richmond. The road lies over the High Moor and the views are very fine indeed, only marred by the ever-present power pylons stretching their wires as far as the eye can see in sagging lines of glistening steel. It was up here that I made the mistake of deciding to exercise the dogs. We had with us a sensible old bitch and a wild youngster recently taken back from the man I had sold him to, whose only idea of exercising him had been to open the kennel door in the morning and allow the dog to roam. He then wondered why the dog chased a sheep and was thinking of having him put down.

The dog had chased sheep with me once, but I had put him in a pen with an old black-faced ewe and her lamb and she had butted him so nearly insensible that he no longer evinced any real interest in them. He still, however, had to learn that he was not out on his own. Self-hunting, that particularly insidious form of vice in a gun dog, was his besetting sin. It was in order to try to cure him of this that I had suggested taking him with us in the car to strange places where he might hesitate before going off on his own. So far there had been a marked improvement, but now he took it into his head to go and simply disappeared over the moorland out of sight.

Thornton said at one point that there is no worse feeling than that of the falconer who has lost his hawk, or the huntsman who has lost his hounds. Anyone who has had to do with either will agree with him, and I would add the dog owner who has lost his dog. How I cursed the man who had so needlessly spoiled a good animal. However, short of reporting to the nearest police station there was nothing to do but take my own line across country and try to intercept him. Fortunately after a mile and a half over dykes and ditches I saw him looking somewhat lost and decidedly pleased to see me, so thus it was, I think, with a mutual feeling of relief that we returned to the car together, trousers muddied but none the worse.

Passing a series of notices warning that racehorses might be encountered we came eventually to Richmond, still a charming old town and, from the length of his digression on it, the main object of Thornton's detour. It is not to be recommended nowadays on a Saturday afternoon. The cobbled streets are precipitous and winding and it is surprisingly easy to lose one's way. By the time we had circled the market place for the third time the Rolls was beginning to be greeted with cheers by the populace and the police were probably getting tired of finding a way for us through the seething mass of humanity round the stalls, reminiscent of an Eastern bazaar.

From there, without apologies, Thornton took over again as from Boroughbridge. 'The road to Topcliffe is excellent ...' (it is now an airfield) '...and lies over Clutton Moor...bounded to the North East by the Hambledon Hills...but nothing of any consequence occurring we encouraged our cavalry and soon arrived at Northallerton.'

If he had gone via Richmond he would have had no need to mention Topcliffe and neither would he have been able to see the Hambledon Hills to the north-east. Perhaps he did not feel that he had enough to say at the start of his travel book and simply added in this detour as a makeweight. As he seems to have been guily of using this trick only in Yorkshire, however, it could be explained, in part at least, by local pride.

After spending a short, but apparently enjoyable, time with his friend at Northallerton, Thornton took his party on to Darlington, where he noted they arrived in time for a late supper. In other words their first day's journey consisted of forty-two miles with a number of stops for refreshment and sightseeing, rather than the hundred miles marathon he happily set down on paper.

Chapter 3

TALLY O

And O! in all their angling bouts,
On Coquet, Tyne or Read,
Whether for Maidens of for Trouts,
May Anglers still succeed.
THOMAS DOUBLEDAY: 1829

Darlington to Lauder

Before we reached Darlington the weather broke and a slow drizzle started. Although this was disappointing in a way, there was no doubt that it was long overdue. Wilting crops and pastures burnt brown by the sun were badly in need of it. They could have done with forty-eight hours' steady rain, although whether the townsman out for a week-end jaunt in his motor-car would have appreciated this point is a different matter.

This essential division between town and country, which is so obvious today, scarcely existed in Thornton's time. We had then an almost purely agricultural economy, and everyone, perforce knew something about the country. Even from London it was a simple matter to walk out into the surrounding countryside towards the villages of Chelsea, Walthamstow or Dulwich.

It is difficult nowadays to appreciate how enormously the towns have expanded during the past century and a half, or the staggering speed at which the process still continues. About 35,000 acres of good arable land, the equivalent of nearly sixty Kensington Gardens and Hyde Parks combined, are swallowed up annually by mechanical grabs and bulldozers, with their attendant concrete mixers. Whereas in Thornton's day the towns were separate and distinct communities surrounded by country-side, now the time has already come, in places, when the country-side has been reduced, by the spread of the towns, to a series of isolated green patches surrounded by concrete.

Yet in spite of the vastly increased population today there is still a tendency to cling to old district divisions and loyalties. Anyone who has ever lived in London will almost certainly have noticed how the old village boundaries have survived to an amazing extent in spite of the ever-increasing outward growth of the amorphous mass. Thornton noted, after leaving Darlington early in the morning, that, as they approached Durham, the people they passed were swarthier and spoke with a more guttural accent; 'but found, from some shrewd remarks, that they were by no means deficient in sense'.

Even today there is a clear distinction between the Yorkshireman and the 'canny lads' around Durham, or farther north in the Newcastle area. There are probably few places in the country where local rivalries flourish as strongly as in this north-east corner of England. The mining villages and shipyards still breed tough individualists and sportsmen. Yet they are a friendly and generous people too.

As a case in point I was once going to a field trial near Consett, not far from Durham, when the half shaft of my car broke. Coasting to a standstill in front of a farmhouse I knocked on the door. A voice said, 'Come in'.

The farmer was having breakfast in his shirt sleeves.

'You're a North Country man', I challenged him, without preamble. 'Therefore you're a sportsman. My car has broken down outside and I've only ten minutes to go before I get to a field trial five miles away. If I don't get there on time I'll probably be all day looking for them. What about it?'

I had hardly finished speaking before he was out of his chair and pulling on his coat. Ten minutes later he delivered me at the meeting place. A more helpful and friendly attitude it would be hard to meet anywhere, and, although this is only one instance, it is typical of the generous sporting spirit of the average North Country man.

Today the tendency is to follow the Great North Road and to bypass Durham. There must be many people who have been deterred, by glimpses of unattractive pitheads and slagheaps and by the grime of Newcastle, from visiting this fine old cathedral city. Thornton remarked on 'the inequality of many of its streets, owing to the hill on which it stands' and indicated that it was better viewed from a distance, or explored on foot. To some extent this is still true today. Like those of Richmond, the streets are narrow, steep and winding and a Saturday afternoon is not the best time to arrive. One can only be impressed by the way in which the police manage somehow to cope with modern traffic in spite of single-track bottlenecks.

There may be finer examples of Norman architecture than Durham Cathedral, but certainly none can be so well sited and it is well worth a visit. Even Thornton, who referred to it as 'an aged and stupendous pile', was impressed by it, although his description is a little sketchy. Considering how much he quoted from Pennant's *Tours* farther on it is surprising that he failed to include Pennant's story of St Cuthbert, the misogynist saint, who was buried there. Women were not allowed in his shrine, as, according to the legend, a princess once wilfully accused him of seducing her, and although the earth promptly swallowed her up and returned her conveniently to her father, he remained a misogynist thereafter.

Having often been in Durham before, we decided, in view of the crowded streets, to move on rather reluctantly towards Newcastle. Via the dual carriageway on the bypass[4] we were soon on the outskirts of the city, which always reminds me forcibly of its counterpart on the west of Scotland, Glasgow. The Tyne and the Clyde, shipbuilding and commerce, industry and coalmining, cobbled streets and trolleybuses, grime and smoke; the 'Geordies' have much in common with their opposite numbers in Glasgow, even down to large and friendly policemen. Both tend to be good friends and bad enemies and I have always found them to be cheerful and friendly.

All the same, Thornton's description of the approach into

Newcastle still proves apt today: 'The descent to the bridge
...certainly is a most abominable entrance.'

Although the races were on at the time of his visit he was not
impressed with the facilities for visitors and after dinner at half
past three and 'a few glasses of wine' he pressed on with his party
to Morpeth, where he described the inn as 'a good old fashioned
one, not very showy, but containing all the necessary requisites'.
There is generally a strong relationship between the means of
travel and the inns, whether conscious or unconscious. This
'horse coping' description conjures up an inn smelling of old
leather and horses, with oak panelling, ale and inglenooks,
whereas today, with chromium-plated motor-cars everywhere, it
is scarcely surprising that we get chromium-plated bars and cock-
tails like high octane fuel.

At this inn Thornton sent for an old 'dog-breaker' from whom
he had bought setters on his way to Glasgow University in his
student days. There is a familiar ring about: 'Found him uncommonly well for a man of his years, which proves that air and exercise
tend not only to preserve health, but, by that vigour which they
give the constitution, promote longevity.'

'Dog-breakers' may seem out of date nowadays, but I have met
one at a field trial in this part of the world. A thin, wiry figure of
indeterminate middle age, he had an inexhaustible fund of stories
of his 'dog-breaking' experiences. His account of the 'breaking
of the sharp dog' was typical.

'I were looking for a sharp dog, like, to stop tramps bedding
down for the night in t' kennel loft and mebbe setting place on
fire, when a lad comes up to me and says, "Would you like
a sharp dog?" When I says, "How much?", he says, "He's too
sharp for me. If you don't take him I'm going to have to shoot him".
So I had a look at him and he were nothing special, nobbut shaggy
ole dog, and I claps him all over and don't have no trouble with
him, so I takes him and ties him in loft doorway for the night.
In the morning there he is standing in doorway wagging his tail,
but when I reaches down hand to clap him he nearly takes arm off.
So I says, "You need more than clapping, you do," and I picks up

stob which is lying handy and clouts him one behind ear'ole. Then I looks down at him to see he's still breathing, like, and goes and does t'other dogs. When I comes back, mebbe forty minutes later, he's standing up shaking his head, groggy like. And after that I don't have no more trouble with 'im.'

This sort of attitude is of course the exception rather than the rule today. The outstanding difference between Thornton's day and now, in matters relating to dogs, is that, whereas then breeding was uncontrolled in any way, the Kennel Club now exercises what is sometimes referred to as 'supreme authority in dogdom'. If the Kennel Club has grown large since its inception in 1874 it is basically because the number of dogs in the country has increased enormously. That saturation point must be reached eventually should in itself prove a limiting factor to the application of Parkinson's Law on 'dogdom's civil servants'. In practice the latter, while comparatively few in number, perform a very necessary and useful purpose, not least in checking and controlling the standards of each breed of dog.

In those days dog breeding was largely a haphazard business. Thornton, one of the foremost breeders of his day, laid down his principle as trying 'to bring a large quantity of bone into a small compass' and he was very concerned with 'the distemper', which had first appeared in the 1760s. Although nowadays we have an entirely different set of problems to cope with under the aegis of the Kennel Club, with new diseases, new breeds and sub-divisions of breeds and apparently ever-increasing numbers of dogs, we no longer have to worry about what seems to have been a hazard of travel in Thornton's day, namely the savage dog.

After leaving Morpeth on the road to Mindrum the Colonel's favourite pointer was attacked by 'a large and furious mastiff, which rushed forward apparently with intent to destroy him; we immediately interfered and the attack, on an instant, was changed from the pointer to us'. In spite of stones thrown by Mr Parkhurst, the mastiff 'was in the act of flying at my friend, when I gave him the severest crack I could with my gig whip. This changed the attack to me. I had no defence, but parrying as skilfully as I could with my whip and my hat; the latter I took off to allow him to seize it when he had broken the whip, which he soon did....' Fortunately Mr Garrard summoned the owner, who called his dog off in time.

Thornton then quoted Sterne: 'They manage these things better in France.' He went on to record a time when his carriage horses were attacked by a similar 'large ungovernable mastiff' while travelling in France, whereupon he shot the dog near the heart with an air-gun, a much more powerful weapon than those of today, capable of killing a roe deer at eighty yards. In spite of this 'my companion, Mr Pierce and myself were obliged to fire a brace of pistols at him, before he would let go his hold; he was desperately hurt and must have died soon after of his wounds, all of which were apparently mortal'.

Nowadays admittedly dogs are the cause of considerable numbers of accidents and near accidents on the roads each year. In the course of my journeys in search of Thornton I saw a typical case. A young Alsatian dashing out of a side road straight into the middle of the Great North Road was run over and killed instantly by a man I had already noted as a bad driver when he had passed me on a blind bend just previously. I saw the dog run out and prepared for a reacting swerve or brake, but the driver's speed was too fast for his reactions. He braked yards too late without pulling into the side. Fortunately there was no oncoming traffic. Had there been and had he reacted quickly, by swerving or braking, there could have been a major accident. If only people would keep their dogs under control near main roads or traffic of any description, such accidents would not arise.

When Thornton reached Edinburgh he 'bought an additional quantity of fishing tackle, with six or seven excellent rods, from that ingenious maker M'Lean'. Such a fishing enthusiast today would hardly be likely to miss the opportunity of visiting Messrs Hardy's factory at Alnwick.[5] It is a fascinating place, where every employee is first, and foremost, a keen fisherman. Certainly Thornton would have been amazed at the precision with which modern rods are produced, even though in his day he had the best that were obtainable.

If we had taken the Alnwick route we could have been certain of a good dinner at that old coaching inn, the White Swan. As it was, we made the mistake of stopping for dinner at a pleasantly placed wayside inn. The meal served us was deplorable. The menu began with 'iced melon', which arrived after a long wait, straight from the tin and still warm. There followed an indifferent steak, without the advertised mushrooms and with quite uneatable vegetables. The whole was served to the accompaniment of highly audible altercations amongst the female kitchen staff. We did not wait for the last course. If it has not already done so, it is certainly time that the brewery which runs this inn took appropriate action.

Thornton noted at one point that 'it has always been a rule with me to defer giving my opinion of an inn until I have examined the most useful part, I mean the inside'. This is all very well, in theory, if you are intending to stay, but if you merely want a meal and some idea of what it will be like it is usually worth asking for the wine list with the menu. If there is no wine list you may well get a good meal. If there is a good wine list you will usually get a good meal, but if there is a poor wine list, or the wine list is clearly a fraud, then the food will almost certainly be indifferent.

On many occasions Thornton drank 'very good claret', which, in those days, was a popular wine in Scotland. Nowadays unless the inn is known it is inadvisable to order a claret, or a burgundy, as, too often, it is run under a hot tap, or shaken, and arrives tasting like warm vinegar. White wines travel better and it is usually possible to ensure that they are chilled if necessary. The best answer of all, if in doubt, is to stick to beer or water.

There are plenty of excellent inns and good inns at all prices, and one can simply avoid indifferent or thoroughly bad inns. When I find myself in surroundings that have been polished and oak-beamed and pewtered and bronzed and brassed, where beer is either not served at all or is twice the price it should be, then I depart as soon as possible.

After this extremely bad meal we went on with all speed towards Wooler, which, even on a Saturday evening, is a dull town with, however, the merit of at least one good inn, where we regretted we had not dined. Our experiences over the previous stretch matched Thornton's here to a surprising degree. He noted: 'Got in good time to Wooler-Haugh-Head, an uninteresting town and the inn as dreadful as the surrounding scenes are enchanting.'

Beyond Wooler, Thornton and Mr Parkhurst went fishing. 'I raised and killed a few tolerable trout; my companion was not so fortunate, and blamed his bad luck; when, desirous of seeing his cockney mode of fishing, I perceived that he fished with a fly as he would with a worm. I was polite enough to look as grave as any fly fisher could be supposed to do.... As soon as I conceived him fairly out of hearing I gave vent to my hitherto-stifled emotions and, laughing immoderately ... I had nearly gone headlong into the river. He heard me and very good naturedly came and asked me what the d——l I was laughing at and whether I had seen a female or any other cause of such extraordinary mirth. I begged he would forgive me and plainly told him my mirth was occasioned by his style of fly fishing. He looked rather disconcerted, and, after clipping off a considerable quantity of his best flies, the number of which he carefully concealed, was readily induced to give up and fish with worm and killed, in the course of the evening, as many trout as made him, who had never killed a trout before, the happiest man living.'

All of which adds point to the Colonel's return of fish caught for the day: 'Killed thirty nine trout—Mr P. three.'

They must have enjoyed their sport here, for they spent the next day fishing by Mindrum Mill. Colonel Thornton caught a pike of eleven pounds and a trout of two pounds, but saw many larger. He noted that the day was hot, still and sultry, which probably explained his poor results.

On the following day, June 10th, they crossed the Cheviots, although he described them as 'those uncommonly beautiful hills, the Teviot ... covered with sheep and all they want to make the prospect the most charming imaginable is wood and water'. As Scott in his review of Thornton's book was quick to point out, the Colonel's geography was not always accurate. In practice this could have been merely a slip caused by the twenty-year delay in writing up his diaries. However, in view of subsequent date discrepancies, it may well be that this part was pure invention, or else was entirely from memory. Joining several journeys into the one 'Tour' must have led to some confusion in Thornton's mind at times. In the circumstances such mistakes are understandable.

He next noted that Mr Parkhurst shot 'several beautiful white birds, which proved to be kittiwakes. The young of this bird are a favourite whet in North Britain, being served up a little before dinner to procure an appetite; but, from their rank smell and taste, they seemed to me more likely to have a contrary effect. I was told of a stranger who was set down for the first time to this kind of relish, as he supposed, but, after demolishing half a dozen with much impatience, he declared that he had "eaten sax and didna find himself a bit *more* hungry". A similar story is told of a late duchess, who having ate a Soland goose, found no advantage'. (A Soland goose, more generally known as a gannet, must be an extremely fishy dish.)

In those days, of course, there was no Protection of Birds Act and Thornton had few inhibitions about shooting at any strange bird he saw. At one point he went after an osprey on Loch Lomond, which he saw 'make some noble dashes into the lake after her prey'. He noted even then that 'these birds are very rare'. But 'she rose long before we got near'. On another occasion Mr Garrard informed him that 'he had seen a very uncommon bird'. It turned out to be a night jar when 'shot at, and accidentally killed. He also shot a raven on one of the islands of Loch Lomond, although this was a very aged bird, 'all his joints rotted, the consequence of extreme old age'.

Yet the Colonel was by no means a gun-happy butcher. It would have been difficult to be so termed, anyway, in those days, when flintlocks and muzzle-loaders were still in their experimental stages and when shooting flying was still regarded as a feat. Reflecting the times, Thornton's views on double-barrelled guns were: 'I look upon all double-barrelled guns as trifles, rather nick-knacks than useful.'

Elsewhere he described an illuminating incident. 'Joseph Manton, the gun smith, was of the opinion, that he could make a double-rifle gun sufficiently stout to carry seven balls each barrel, and that they could do more execution than one of my seven barrelled guns, which were only stout enough to carry three balls each, i.e. twenty one from the seven barrels. This piece carried very small balls about the size of what is called buckshot.

'Great pains were taken in hammering the barrel of the new gun, and when it was finished, I went to witness its execution and resigned to Manton the honour of making the first experiment, which was to take place in a narrow passage adjoining his shop. He loaded the piece with the utmost exactness, and, by his appearance, he would cheerfully have relinquished the *honour* to me; but I thought it no more than justice that the inventor should be the first gratified. Accordingly he placed himself and took exact aim; but the subsequent concussion was so great and so very different from the firing of any other gun, that I thought the whole shop was blown up and fully expected, when the smoke dispersed, to find that the piece had burst. This however was not the case; it appeared that the whole force of the powder, being insufficient to drive the balls, had come out through the touch-holes, and, what was very extraordinary the gun was uninjured.

'This circumstance affording an indisputable proof of the excellency of the metal, and the firmness of the touch-holes, we took out the breech, and then gently forced the balls, which had only moved six inches. It was now, therefore, sufficiently obvious, that to use this in competition with a seven barrelled gun was quite out of the question. . . .

'I determined to have it bored out as a shot-gun. I resolved to have the best borer that could be engaged, and as I had seen guns made by Fisher, of Greek Street, shoot so as to surpass all others . . . I thought I could not give it into better hands.

'It had stood proof after boring and had shot very well at a mark. . . . As the gun, with respect to its neatness, appeared a mere

bauble, several sportsmen. . .seemed inclined to doubt its utility
except with small shot as snipes or woodcock. But in the present
instance it was to be tried with No. 2 shot as waterfowl. I killed the
first bird, a large gull, which fell at about fifty yards distance, with
which we were all very pleased. Seventeen subsequent shots took
effect at very great distances, one of which was supposed to have
been upwards of a hundred yards. . . .'

There cannot be much doubt that the tendency in those days
was to take shots as greater ranges than is the custom today. Even
so a hundred yards is most improbable. Even allowing for the fact
that it might have been bored between ten and eight bore, seventy
yards was probably the maximum killing range. A lucky pellet on a
light bird, such as a gull, when using heavy shot and an extra charge
of powder, might have had effect at greater range, but that is all.

During a visit to France, however, the Colonel gave a revealing
description of the power of his air-rifle. 'I now thought fit to take
my air-rifle, of whose powers my companions had no conception;
and conceal myself in cover. The hounds being brought up, a
young wild boar passed me, when I got a fair shot at him about
fifty yards, and heard the ball hit him, though he did not seem to
feel it. However at about thirty yards he began to stagger, and I
followed, my gun being re-loaded instantaneously. The keepers
now advanced, when we perceived the boar stretched on the turf,
and so effectually wounded, that it seemed unnecessary to shoot at
him; but in order to try my gun, I took aim at his skull, and he
immediately expired. On examining the first wound, it appeared
that the ball had passed through his heart; in consequence of
which, Colonel Marigny placed a hat in a tree, and requested me to
trot his Hungarian horse, and endeavour to hit it at about sixty
yards distance. I did as he desired, and very luckily took my aim so
true, that the ball passed through the centre of the crown. The
colonel was highly gratified, and, having heard me extol his
Hungarian horse, as the surest footed animal I ever rode, begged
that I would recollect this shot, by accepting his horse, which he
pressed to strongly upon me, that it was impossible to refuse the
present.'

These two incidents, although taken from Thornton's other works and not from his Scottish 'Tour', give a very clear idea of the powers of the guns and the extent of the knowledge of the sportsmen and gunsmiths of the day. Although shotguns were in their very early stages of development air-guns were far more powerful then than now. Incidentally the Colonel must have been no mean shot if he could hit a target at some sixty yards from the back of a trotting horse. Some of our modern sportsmen who appear to have every scientific device built into their rifles would be hard put to it to emulate this feat. Yet there is no real reason to doubt it, as a trotting horse can be a steady enough platform for an experienced rider and there would be no recoil with an air-gun. Nor does the Colonel deny that an element of luck was involved.

To return to the Scottish 'Tour': we continued on beyond Wooler towards Mindrum, but we also stopped to admire the views of the Cheviots 'unequalled in verdure...covered with sheep'. The hills are still conspicuously dotted with grazing sheep, and as there are now plenty of trees, which Thornton noted were lacking in his day, the views from here in the evening sunshine were superb.

On the road towards Mindrum I thought I had run over a small laggardly lapwing and saw it flutter towards the ditch by the roadside. Stopping the car I went back with one of the dogs to put it out of its misery. As we approached I saw the lapwing fly off apparently unhurt, but the dog came firmly on point. Further investigation revealed a healthy looking rabbit which bounded away into the hedge. There is no doubt that they are on the increase all over the country.

One wonders how many young birds of all species must be killed in the spring and summer months by careless motorists. It is almost impossible to drive at all during these months without killing one or two, however careful one may try to be, and the annual toll of young birds and small mammals such as hedgehogs must be almost unbelievable. The annual toll of dead and injured human beings on the roads is astounding enough in itself; some 87,000 in 1959;

more than any major action during the last war. The hazards of savage dogs pale in comparison with other road risks today.[6]

Passing Mindrum Mills and the river where Thornton fished, which is still beautiful, we nearly lost our way, until, crossing the stream he mentioned, we found ourselves at last in Scotland without any border signs marking the boundary. This is the part of the Border country which he termed 'totally denudated of trees, which must have been occasioned as well by its natural poverty as by the consequences arising from the constant state of warfare between the Borderers who...mutually destroyed the least vestige of woodland. Though the northern men of rank have exerted themselves more than their southern neighbours in prosecuting every scheme that could tend to improve their estates...it takes a very considerable period to make those improvements...added to this the infant plantations not protected...make slow progress'.

It is difficult nowadays to visualize this fat, sleek and obviously prosperous, well-wooded, farming land as it must have been when Thornton saw it still showing signs of the ravages of constant border raids. It would now be very difficult to choose between this and his own Yorkshire dales as far as beauty is concerned. There is not much doubt that Thornton would be very pleasantly surprised by this change in the appearance of the countryside since his time. There must be few places indeed where the same can be said today.

Thus, on June 10th, four days after leaving Darlington, Thornton made his leisurely arrival in Scotland. He recorded that on stopping at the turnpike above Kelso they had 'a very favourable opportunity of admiring a healthy, well made, *sonsy lassie*, whose appearance gave Mr P. a very favourable impression of Caledonian beauty'. They also discovered a view of the descent to the bridge, which Mr Garrard noted as particularly beautiful.

'Proceeded to the inn and just got fairly housed when it rained most heavily and gave a set of florists (whose annual feast it was) a most complete soaking. The inn here is large, but not incommodious; we found it however a palace to our last quarters. Here we got well refreshed, as did the cavalry, who had suffered greatly at Mindrum, where, notwithstanding the bad accommodation, they knew how to make a very handsome bill.'

He continued: 'From the shower, we had flattered ourselves with sport in the Tweed, and set off with great hopes, after a very good dinner...and fished up the river. Killed several small trout, but had no great sport, as the water was...too clear.' This must mean that he fished the well-known Junction Pool, where the Teviot joins the Tweed, just above Kelso, from which notable bags of salmon have been recorded.

Apparently he was not interested in salmon, but the probability is that there were no salmon there then, anyway, for it is really only since just prior to the first world war that there has been a regular spring run of salmon on the Tweed. Before 1910 there were occasional clean-run spring salmon recorded, but they were the exception rather than the rule. Since then it is an interesting fact that there has been a regular run of spring salmon and, whereas the average weight of the autumn fish is around twenty pounds, the average weight of the spring fish is usually around ten pounds. Quite why this should be the case is one of those salmon mysteries to which no one has yet found a satisfactory answer. My own conclusion is that there might well be a connection between this and the increased pollution of the Tyne about the same time.

It is worth noting in any case that the fishing on the Tweed has undoubtedly improved very considerably since Thornton's time. Then the river was netted to an absurd extent, right up to the spawning grounds. Leistering, or spearing, parties were common and there was little or no control over the fishing. Today six to eight times the number of salmon are caught compared with records of seventy years ago. This is an example of what can be done by common-sense measures, and in it lies hope for the future.

The time to fish the Tweed for trout is in April when sizeable bags can still be made. I tried for them myself that evening, but June is a bad time and the water was too low and clear. It was irritating to see trout of a pound or more examine the fly, however cunningly cast, and turn about with disdain. Had I waited until dusk I might have been successful. As it was, unlike Thornton, I failed to catch even one 'small trout'.

One point he noted, however, which is still true today. 'This river is a very dangerous one to the fisher, being full of shelves and rapid streams.' Fishing the Tweed in waders can be a dangerous occupation, unless you know the river bed well. There are pot-holes for the unwary and a strong current. Salmon fishing on the expensive beats is generally conducted from the bank, or from boats of a kind I have only seen on the Tweed, with a revolving stool for the fisherman mounted in the stern. Outboards are not used, though the current can be fierce, and fish are netted, not gaffed. In spite of this precaution the bed of the river in April is usually littered with dead kelts lying belly up.

In almost every way the Tweed is a river with a character and a pattern of its own. Yet, though some beats are very expensive indeed (£300 to £400 a month or more), it is not necessary to be a millionaire, like Thornton, to fish there, and the sport to be had, even on the stretches of Association or public water, can be very fine. It would be foolish to deny this, just as it would be foolish to compare it with other rivers, equally attractive in their own ways but in totally different settings. The Tweed is unique.

Thornton, no doubt, would have been astonished at the commercialization of a sport which, in his day, was apparently free to all who wished to indulge in it. He continued: 'June 11th. We had this morning a thunder shower, which soon wet me, much to my wishes, to the skin; but I was sorry to find it made no impression on the water, which was uncommonly low.' Altogether his visit to the Tweed, on this occasion, like mine in similar weather, was a disappointing one. He made up for it, however, by returning to the inn, where he drank 'a couple of magnums of very good claret' with dinner. After which, at half past three, they set out on the road to Lauder.

He recorded: 'We had a very tedious drive.' Since they did not arrive until after nine o'clock this sounds like an understatement. Five and a half hours for seventeen miles is slow going by any standards. I have ridden this road myself and three hours is taking it easily whereas four hours would be positively dawdling. It is admittedly something of a switchback road and the two magnums of claret may not have helped, but the only real explanation is that the road must have been heavy with mud. The wheels must have been almost sinking to the axles in places and the horses were probably beginning to flag.

Since he later noted a drive of thirteen miles in the Highlands which was accomplished in fifty-nine minutes this stage must have been exceptionally slow even then. It is difficult for us today, with good metalled roads almost everywhere, to appreciate the difference they have made to journeys, or how tiresome and 'tedious' travelling must have been in Thornton's time. Even in our elderly Rolls this journey only took half an hour.

'Got to Lauder by nine o'clock; house only tolerable, which gave my friends but an indifferent opinion of Scotch accommodations; however they were soon silenced, on my desiring them to compare it with Wooler-Haugh-Head and Mindrum Mills.'[7]

The journey that had taken Thornton six days, according to his version, had been comfortably accomplished by us in less than twelve hours at a speed and in a manner which would certainly be termed leisurely by today's standards.

Chapter 4

GONE AWAY

By yon bonnie banks and by yon bonnie braes,
Where the sun shines bright o'er Loch Lomond.

LOCH LOMOND

Lauder, via Edinburgh and Glasgow to Tarbet

After leaving Lauder early next morning, June 12th, Thornton and his party ran into a heavy rainstorm on Soutra hill. 'Such a downfall of rain I think I never yet saw.' His subsequent description of the view over to the coast of Fife and beyond therefore reads somewhat unrealistically. Giving him the benefit of the doubt, however, it is just possible that the weather cleared temporarily, as he suggested it did. Certainly the views from Soutra and from above Dalkeith especially, over the Pentlands and Arthur's Seat to one side, over the Forth and as far as the Bass Rock and May Island on the other, can be very fine on a clear day. He did admit that 'the rain prevented, in great measure, that noble effect I had observed, the former year when the day was favourable'.

Beyond Dalkeith he was more forthcoming. 'Continual showers of rain involved the whole surrounding countryside in such a density of vapour as totally to preclude all perception of distant objects, whilst the extreme heaviness of the roads added a weight to every step we took.' This sounds like a more honest description of a thoroughly wet day when the roads must have been something like ploughed fields.

Apparently the carters of Edinburgh were a species of road hog. 'The carters, a set of men, who affecting English liberty, drive against the carriage of every peaceable traveller they meet, are...

a perfect nuisance. . . . It is fortunate that the carts they drive are but small and lightly laden, otherwise his Majesty would annually lose a greater number of his subjects.' It is doubtful if Thornton would have even been able to visualize the number of her Majesty's subjects who are lost annually on the roads today. Six thousand five hundred and twenty, or about an eighth of the population of Edinburgh at that date.

Arrived at Edinburgh at Duns Hotel (no longer in existence), 'the cleanest, neatest and best furnished in any country', he first set a blacksmith to examine the carriages. Then he 'ordered in two large chests of biscuits, several Cheshire and Gloucester cheeses, together with a number of Yorkshire hams, reindeer and other tongues, hung beef, etc., in order to be amply provided for a large party. Also laid in some seventy pound weight of fine gunpowder, shot, etc. . . . and having provided divers portable gun cases, plaids, and other necessaries, the baggage wagons were ordered to be ready to set forward in a few days by Stirling for Raits'.

On top of the arrangements made and supplies already laid on this seems quite superfluous, and the logical conclusion is that Thornton, by an oversight, is including arrangements made for another expedition. He was already well supplied with reindeers' tongues and provisions, as well as gunpowder. Also he started with one carriage, but now required his 'carriages' repaired. All points to another year and another expedition.

Fortunately Thornton himself supplied us with a perfect date check. He mentioned intending to breakfast with the King's Own Dragoons at Dalkeith, but his servant, who had been sent ahead, informed him that they 'were marched to Edinburgh to quell some riots, the causes of which he could not explain'. Thornton himself did not explain the cause of the riots but he did mention that they were at Leith, then a mile outside Edinburgh and that there was another outbreak three days later. He also mentioned a friend of his in the King's Own Dragoons being particularly implicated. All of this indicates the riots of 1784.

According to the report in the *Edinburgh Weekly Review* Mr Haig's distillery at Leith was attacked by a mob on the evening of

June 4th, 1784. Two servants left to protect it opened fire and killed a man. The riot grew serious, and the King's Own Dragoons under Captain Sykes were called from Dalkeith to take the two men into custody in Edinburgh for their own protection. The troops were noted as behaving with admirable restraint. Subsequently on June 7th the mob rioted again and the Dragoons were again called out. The matter appears to have been settled finally by Mr Haig paying compensation to the family of the man killed, but not before there had been a sizeable disturbance, which today reads like an account of riots in the Middle East.

Thornton also mentioned Mrs Siddons acting in Edinburgh at the time, which provides a cross check. The *Weekly Review* noted that Mrs Siddons was playing in Edinburgh for eleven days from May 22nd to June 11th, leaving on the 12th for Dublin. (Incidentally she earned £50 a performance and £350 on her benefit night, clearing £1,000 on the eleven days she appeared, not to mention an 'elegant inscribed silver tea service'.) This proves that instead of being in Edinburgh from the 12th to the 17th, as he claimed, Thornton must have been there from the 5th to the 10th of June, 1784.

Already there were at least two expeditions joined together, but here the seams were showing. Farther on yet other visits are dovetailed neatly into each other to make up the 'Tour' and it becomes almost impossible to disentangle the years with any accuracy. All that can be done is to note each discrepancy as it arises.

The one thing in common that any of our various visits to Edinburgh seem to have had was that we each bought fishing rods. I was taking my favourite Hardy's Traveller's Rod, a very useful combination fly and light spinning rod, and a very fine presentation Martin's medium fly rod which I had inherited, but I wanted a powerful spinning rod. Accordingly I decided to spread my favours evenly and bought it from Dickson's the gunsmiths.[8]

Of Edinburgh itself Thornton did not say much. He did however comment on the 'fashionable affectation of feeling' shown by the audience watching Mrs Siddons. Apparently Edinburgh audiences have always been notable for their reactions, although according to the critics of the present series of Festivals they are inclined more often nowadays to stint their applause.

Thornton's description of Edinburgh from what is now the West End is amongst the best pieces of descriptive writing in his book. 'On the left hand extends Princes Street, a long continued line of regular stone houses forming the Southern side of the New Town, a most elegant vista of magnificent new buildings. To the right, rising as it were from the depth of a vast *fosse*, called the North Loch, stands the old city, fantastically piled on the summit of an immense rock, nearly two miles in length, and abruptly terminated by the ancient castle, which impends in sullen grandeur, like the stronghold of some giant of romance.'

One can see from old prints of Princes Street what a fine spectacle it must have been. It is even possible by looking at the upper stories of some of the shops which have not yet been completely rebuilt to conjure up a picture of what it must have been like before the multiple stores stepped in and did their best to turn it into yet another garish main street. On the other side the 'vast *fosse*' resounds to the chuffing of trains and brass bands. The romance has been all but killed by the advances of civilization. Yet, if her face and dress are those of any modern wench, her proportions remain those of a classical beauty, and, especially when silhouetted by clouds or gathering darkness, the Castle still lends a splendour and a touch of grandeur to this street which can never be entirely lost.

Thornton then went on to describe the road to Glasgow, via 'Kirk of Shotts', where he 'found the inn so bad and the whole house so inebriated, that we did not take off the horses'. He also noted that 'the soil at Kirk of Shotts is the most naked and barren imaginable', and he referred to the 'very bleak and dreary country'. With the addition of the twin girders of the BBC and ITV television masts, which are suspended skywards, as if in defiance of gravity, and not omitting the red and grey masses of the bing heaps from the mines, this description still holds good today. It is a dreary countryside at best.

Contrary to Thornton's time, when the road was 'superior to any between Edinburgh and London', it is now a miserable three-lane type where a dual carriageway should surely be an essential. The surface is bad and the road is in every way inadequate to meet the considerable demands put on it. It is certainly the scene of numerous accidents.

We saw one happen on one occasion as we drove towards Glasgow. A car overtook us and drove on past the lorry in front of us, unable to allow much clearance because of oncoming traffic. The lorry swayed on the uneven surface and the two scraped together. Nothing very much, it is true, and very little damage done, apart from crumpled bodywork, but if their wheels had locked, or if it had been a greasy surface, there could have been a major pile-up with the pair of them skidding broadside-on into the oncoming traffic. By any standards this road is a disgrace today and as the communicating link between the two major cities of Scotland it is pathetic.[9]

I would strongly recommend any traveller who can spare the time and who is looking for beautiful scenery to take the route via West Linton and Carnwath. This is an extremely attractive road on a fine day, between the Moorfoot and the Pentland Hills, although the last few miles are through the industrial suburbs of Glasgow. On one of my journeys round the route, my companion and I set off via Carnwath for a day's shooting on the moors, and though the sport was rather spoiled by the heat we had a very pleasant drive.

On his arrival in Glasgow, Thornton seems promptly to have been involved in a series of parties with old friends of his student days. At the first of these, a supper and ball, 'my companions agreed that handsomer women, or, in general, better dressed, were not to be met with; their style of dancing however, quite astonished these *southrons*, scarce able to keep sight of their fair partners. At twelve the supper-rooms were opened, and supper ended, and a few general toasts drank, the ladies retired about three; the gentlemen, as is usual in the north, remained to pay the proper compliments of toasting their respective partners, and I was detained, contrary to my wishes, till *six* in the morning'. The following morning, alone of his party, he was up by eleven and was apparently out until the small hours again.

It is the exceptional supper and ball today that lasts till six in the morning, but the chief difference in this emancipated age is that I cannot imagine the ladies retiring without their partners. This particular function, according to Colonel Thornton's dates, took place on Wednesday, June 19th, which, by reference to the perpetual calendar, would make it 1782, but we have already proved that his dates are inaccurate, so that this is not a reliable guide to the year. However, he later mentions crossing the 'great canal, which was intended to join the Firths of Forth and Clyde... which is completely finished within a mile of Clyde'. Since the canal was finished in 1790 this would seem to place the visit in 1789, or thereabouts. In any case it seems likely that this visit to Glasgow took place in a different year to the rest of the 'Tour'.

Inevitably he conducted his party round Glasgow. They 'were much astonished with the regularity of the streets and the universal magnificence of the buildings'. Later he 'took a walk round what is called the Green... here the gentlemen resort to follow their favourite amusement, the game of golf, which is universal throughout Scotland, as well as Holland.... It is a wholesome exercise for those who do not think such gentle sports too trivial for men, being performed with light sticks and small balls, and is by no means so violent an exertion as cricket, trapball, or tennis'. After such scathing comment one wonders what he would have had to say on the subject of motorized caddies and other modern refinements of the game.

With a proper pride in his Alma Mater, Thornton went on: 'The plan of education at Glasgow is better arranged than at any other college I am acquainted with; the incentives to vice are infinitely less, owing to the judicious regulations and restrictions; whereas the opportunities at Oxford and Cambridge are so great as to make it next to an impossibility for lively young men to resist temptation.' This was certainly a reasonable statement of fact at the time. Oxford and Cambridge were then at very low ebb, and this was probably one of the reasons why Thornton was sent to Glasgow.

At no point does the Colonel make any comparisons between Glasgow and Edinburgh, since in his day Edinburgh was the capital city and the centre of literary and philosophical thought of the country, whereas Glasgow was still only, according to Pennant, a 'well built second-rate city'. The industrial and commercial activities of the West of Scotland were only just beginning to shift towards Glasgow as the centre. It would have been difficult then to visualize the enormous growth that was to take place during the next hundred years.

Only one point strikes a familiar note. On June 24th Thornton referred to a 'very thick fog' which obscured his view of Clydesdale and Glasgow. This sounds exactly like the Glasgow weather of today, as seen from the East of Scotland.

The following day was spent 'in hopes of sport' on Bardowie Loch. They netted four trout and used them to bait the trimmers, or 'fox-hounds', finally killing a pike of eleven pounds. Today Bardowie Loch is a yachting centre for keen dinghy sailors and, apart from being illegal, such 'sport' would not be popular.

Leaving Glasgow at last a couple of days later and stopping only to inspect 'the ironworks at Dunnotter' on the way, Thornton went on to Dumbarton, 'a small, indifferent town'. He noted 'the face of the river here appeared much altered since I saw it last, nearly the whole extent of the north side being taken up with bleaching grounds, by which means the noble trout and salmon fishing there has been greatly hurt'. Mr Garrard took a sketch of the 'fantastic, bold rock of Dumbarton'.

It is inadvisable for a stranger, I found, to try to take the old road out of Glasgow on a rainy day. I lost my way in the cobbled, slippery streets, which make driving unpleasant and dangerous. Trams and tram lines are another hazard for those unaccustomed to them. Leaving Glasgow by the Great Western Road is easier. By degrees the monotonous and depressing rows of houses are left behind and the countryside opens up and improves on the right of the road. On the left there is a conglomerate succession of gasworks, graveyards, filling stations, stagnant ponds, petrol and oil storage tanks and refineries merging finally into warehouses of bonded whisky, with occasional fleeting glimpses of Dumbarton Rock in the distance growing gradually nearer.

As Dumbarton itself is approached the Rock disappears alto-gether from sight, blotted out by its industrial surroundings. It is only finally by turning off the road through sordid streets of near-slum tenements and past depressing factory buildings that it is possible to find it. The final approach is down a long narrow road reduced to the proportions of alleyway by an immense factory wall on the left which almost seems to dwarf the Rock in the foreground. The 'bleaching-grounds' and the 'iron-works' were the thin end of the wedge indeed. Let those who condone atomic stations in National Parks take heed.[10]

If Thornton could see this same area today he would undoubtedly be lost for words. The 'noble trout and salmon fishing' has been very nearly completely ruined. The Clyde itself is little more than an open sewer in places. Returning at dawn one hot August morning from a journey round the route, I was appalled near Bowling at the unhealthy sewage-laden stink that rose and almost choked us through the open window of the car.

Beyond Dumbarton towards Loch Lomond the industrial out-skirts of Glasgow are mushrooming. New towns and new factories are springing up on the banks of the Leven. Yet on reaching Loch Lomond itself there is no denying its beauty. It remains a most attractive loch, almost in defiance, one feels, of all that has been written about it and even though it is inevitably one of Glasgow's playgrounds.[11]

Such are the techniques of modern advertising that one is seldom prepared for anything to be as beautiful, or as super-colossal, as the publicists suggest. Like most of the Highland scenery, Loch Lomond exceed any verbal superlatives or written eulogies. Small wonder that Thornton enthused over it when he saw it unmarred by bed-and-breakfast signs and cars and trippers at every halting place.

Yet allowing for all these, its beauty remains remarkably un-affected. Almost the only jarring feature I noticed was the intrusive bed-and-breakfast sign displayed by nearly every house or cottage. It would surely not be difficult for the Scottish Tourist Board to produce an attractively designed sign as a substitute for these throughout the Highlands. Appropriately a thistle could represent bed and breakfast, two thistles supper, bed and breakfast, and three full board. Apart from implying a certain standard some such recognized design would be much less of an eyesore than the botched products of amateur signwriters.

As regards the fishing it is really remarkable that there are any fish left in the loch. Salmon, sea trout, pike and perch, as well as powans, a species of whitefish peculiar to the loch, are still caught there. Considering how much it must be fished, both from boats and from the shore, not to mention the disturbances caused by pleasure boating, water ski-ing and swimming, quite apart from pollution and organized poaching, the Loch Lomond Angling Association, the river watchers and the police must have an uphill task. Twice in the spring the entire run on the Leven was poached by cyanide poachers and on one occasion the police found twenty-two fresh-run salmon in the boot of a poacher's car. Needless to say no water can stand up to this sort of punishment for ever.

Thornton's remarks in this connection are very revealing. 'June 30th—Recollecting the salmon I had observed to leap yesterday, though I prefer trout-fishing, I was inclined to see what might be done, and accordingly rose by five and rode sharply to the Moss of Balloch ... began my operations and, before eight o'clock, killed five, to the no small surprise of Mr Garrard. One of them weighed forty-one pounds; the others from twenty-two to nine pounds. Having put up my tackle, and perfectly satisfied with my success, I returned home as expeditiously as possible.'

Five salmon, including a forty-one pounder, inside two and a half hours means that he must have had a fish on his line almost the entire time. In these circumstances it is possible to see why he preferred trout fishing. This was too easy and probably too much like murder; simply a case of casting a fly and hauling out a fish. In case anyone should imagine that this was a highly exaggerated account it is worth pointing out that Pennant, only a few years earlier, mentioned the water of the Leven 'animated' with 'Parrs' in May, and that Richard Franck, the Cromwellian fisherman, caught as many as he wanted at this same spot in the previous century. Only the cyanide poacher succeeds in these numbers today and by his very action ensures that there will be even less fish in the future.

Unfortunately there two features which encourage this deadly form of wholesale poaching. The first is the extreme simplicity of it. Cyanide in certain forms can be obtained very easily on the pretext that it is for grassing rabbits. As the law stands at present it is almost impossible to keep any check on the vast quantities which are used throughout the country. The second prime cause of this form of poaching is the high price which unscrupulous dealers and hoteliers are prepared to pay for salmon. This again is understandable when it is appreciated that even kelts, copper-coloured, spent, uneatable fish, on their way back down the river after spawning, will fetch five shillings a pound for smoking. Simply because of the demand for smoked salmon in London restaurants and elsewhere the rivers are being denuded of their fish by unprincipled and foolish criminals, for they are no less. They are cutting their own throats and spoiling other people's sport without a thought for the future.

Thornton's description of a poaching gang he saw at work on the Spey in September and his comments are both interesting and to the point. 'I saw the fire moving, which made me enquire into the nature of this strange nocturnal party and I found that they were poaching for salmon by *blazing*. This they effect here in the following manner:—They run a net across the stream and then going up it in a boat, they drive the salmon, which avoid the light, down into the net, having also a spear, with which they occasionally strike the fish. By this mode many fish are killed at this time of year, when they are black, out of season and spawning; and the fisheries are thereby greatly injured. It would answer their purpose very well if those who rent these fisheries would employ proper persons to detect and punish the offenders.' Unlike Scott and Scrope, who romanticized 'leistering', as it was termed, Thornton disapproved of it as the evil it undoubtedly was.

Unfortunately the 1951 Salmon and Freshwater Protection Act, although allowing for confiscation of the car and apparatus, as well

as the imprisonment of proven poachers, left plenty of legal loop-
holes and proved no deterrent to those who receive poached fish.
It should be understood that there is nothing in the very least
glamorous about this sort of poaching. It is organized vandalism
as well as theft, for once a river has been poisoned all the young
fish and plant life are destroyed and it may take up to ten years to
recover. The poachers themselves are the sort of riff-raff who
would probably turn their hand to other petty crimes if poaching
were not so easy and so profitable. The regrettable feature hitherto
has been the reluctance of many sheriffs to punish the offenders
heavily enough when they have been caught. Only when the courts
deal strongly with them will this sort of thing stop.

A policeman put it to me this way: 'These lads would be off to
the burglaries and sheep stealing, if there were no fish to poach
or deer to shoot.'

There is not much doubt that the same gangs have also been
guilty of some of the shocking cases of indiscriminate slaughter of
deer, which have roused the public conscience in recent years and
led belatedly to the Deer (Scotland) Act. It is to be hoped that this
will prove more effective than the 1951 Act has been.

Even if these modern gangsters from Ullapool and Aberdeen do
take to sheep stealing, they are unlikely to prove more than pale
emulators of a rogue named Kennedy, mentioned by Thornton.
'One of the most daring fellows ever known.' His gang stole 'no
less than between six and seven hundred sheep in the year 1783.
When he was brought up for trial, the witnesses were so brow-
beaten and threatened by his party, that they durst not appear; by
which means he got off, though there was not the least doubt of
his guilt'.

It was not until long after Thornton's day that the salmon fishing
in the Highlands became generally popular. It is only today that
the stage has been reached where over-fishing, over-netting,
pollution and organized poaching, water abstraction, or hydro-
electric schemes, or a combination of these, have, in many cases,
almost completely ruined the fishing. There is still time for drastic
measures to have effect, but it should be more widely appreciated

that we are in danger of losing a national heritage through neglect.

After his salmon-fishing expedition Thornton and his party continued up Loch Lomondside, and he went on to describe how he shot a mallard and a cormorant. From his description it seems that he must have stalked them and shot them on the water. Of interest today is his remark that his setter was an excellent water dog, 'as eager as any Newfoundlander'. The Newfoundlanders of those days were particularly prized as water dogs and were amongst the ancestors of the modern Labrador.

Thornton continued: 'We showed him [Mr Garrard] the duck and afterwards the cormorant, with which he was quite delighted and joined in opinion with Mr P. that it would make an excellent repast at a Highland inn.' I know people who claim to have eaten cormorant, but they are welcome to it as far as I am concerned. This appears to have been Thornton's view also, as he added a footnote: 'The Southern gentlemen, particularly those in the vicinity of the metropolis, never see game of any kind without expressing, instantaneously, their inclination for a roast.'

Poor Mr Parkhurst was already finding 'yon bonny banks' more than he had bargained for and Thornton was by no means sympathetic. 'Mr P., not an extraordinary good walker, was a long time before he had made the summit, which, however, he gained just when, tired with waiting for him, I was going to descend. He was pretty well exhausted, and execrated the Highland hills, not considering that, from a southern education, spent chiefly in luxury, his youthful nerves, instead of being strengthened, had become more relaxed and effeminate.'

The first day ended at Luss, where 'great complaints were made by the servants and Mr P., who had the care of superintending the cavalry, that the stables were not divided, the hay bad, but little straw and no coach house. All this I had guessed would happen very soon, but not at Luss; however...he was soon pacified. Our beds were, all things considered, very comfortable'.

They were not so fortunate as we were in August when we arrived at Loch Lomondside after a very hot day on the moors.

Hungry, thirsty and weary, in a travel-stained old Rolls loaded with bored and hungry dogs, we arrived on the doorstep of the Lomond Castle Hotel. Mr McCowen, the owner and manager, took us in his stride and even made us feel that he was pleased to see us, which, in itself, was quite a feat. In a comparatively short time the dogs had been fed and we were sitting down to an excellent meal accompanied by a very satisfactory Montrachet. This is the sort of hospitality and management which one would like to meet more often.

As I have indicated, I made a number of sorties round different parts of the route, in order to check various points in Thornton's narrative. My first visit to Loch Lomondside, as near his date of June 30th as I could manage, was during one of the few heavy and prolonged downpours of the year. Even seen thus, in a mist, with rain pouring down the windscreen and only a few hundred yards of water visible at a time, Loch Lomond still impressed us with its beauty.

This was the only occasion when it might have been worth fishing the water, as later, in August, it was hopelessly sunny. However, even if I had done so, it is certain that I would not have equalled Thornton's efforts. Amongst other fish here he caught a perch which, he claimed, weighed seven pounds three ounces. The British record today stands at five and a half pounds, but before disbelieving Thornton automatically, it is worth noting that there are reasonably authentic records of a nine-pounder caught in the Serpentine and a ten-pounder taken in Loch Bala, in Wales. Thornton's own remarks carried conviction. He pointed out that 'though from its size a great curiosity to us, [it] was no rarity here'. Unfortunately I have not been able to find any game records of that period which might confirm this.

It was while at Luss that Thornton and his companion met the Duchess of Gordon travelling incognito. As far as I am aware, we met no Duchesses on Loch Lomondside, incognito or otherwise. While taking refreshment in an inn there, however, my farming friend and I did have cause to note that Mr Butler's measures following the Wolfenden Report had effectively driven the prostitutes off the streets of London. Two painted hussies at our elbows conducted their conversation in Tottenham Court Road accents, thinly overlain with Mayfair, so that we could not help hearing.

'It is naice to hear a civilized accint again ahfter orl this Scotch ock aye bisniss, isn't it, dahling?'

'Yers, dahling. Fraightfully naice, and a spot of civilized company is just wot we need in our carivan ahfter a fortnight of this lark, traipsing round these 'ills.'

'Oh, dahling. Do look at that dahling old Rolls.'

This was our cue, but we did not take it, though the question of a bed for the night was still unsettled. After surveying the wenches we could only reflect that a fool and his money are easily tarted. No doubt Thornton would have scorned us. It would not have been in his nature to have turned down such an offer. He was not, as Scott indicated, a 'fastidious gallant'. The occasion when he was stranded in a bothy in the Highlands after a day of rain shows that clearly.

'My landlady (perfectly ignorant of any language but Erse) might be the wrong side of forty-five, much wizened and dried by the smoke, but had a cheerful countenance and, as is usual with most ladies, a prodigious desire for conversation, which was, for the reasons already given, totally denied us.

'At length an itinerant soldier, driven from these wild moors by the weather, came in, and acted as interpreter, and by him I made my proposals to become this lady's guest for the evening. . . . Matters thus adjusted she procured me a bowl of her best milk to which I added a flask of very strong Jamaica rum; turned out of my canteen some ham and chicken, biscuits and Cheshire cheese, and, with fresh fuel, we became very merry. . . . The punch, and other causes (probably the fire not a little contributing) occasioned my landlady to come much nearer to me, and we became very familiar. I shall never forget the state of the house, its furniture, etc., but, nevertheless, I found some charms I had not expected.'

At this point the weather eased and his baggage train came to fetch him unexpectedly. His comment was enigmatic. 'Except

Colonel Thornton
From a painting by Reinagle

Taymouth, circa 1784, by Garrard

Taymouth, 1959 (note afforestation)

Hawking

from some private reasons, I was not dissatisfied.' What exactly his 'private reasons' were is perhaps better left to the imagination.

Leaving Luss, Thornton took a boat up past Tarbet and fished from the opposite shore at Inversnaid, where a garrison of troops was still stationed. Thornton considered this quite ridiculous; 'the causes that first rendered it necessary, namely to subdue the spirits of these northern mountaineers, being long since removed'. He felt sorry for them, 'immured in a recess, at the base of Ben Lomond . . . when, should it be the lot of an officer not particularly partial to sporting or reading . . . what a dreadful life he must lead!' With modern amenities, wireless, TV and film shows, boredom on similar stations, such as South Uist, is not so likely today, although the same factors are still involved for all ranks.

He ended the day at Tarbet, where they prepared to fish yet again, but 'the boatman, a man apparently turned of seventy . . . jumping about like a schoolboy . . . there remained no doubt of his inebriety. In spite of all my admonitions . . . the old gentleman . . . jumped upon the fourth piece of the rod, and broke it'. It seems that even the 'ingenious Mr M'Lean' of Edinburgh had not evolved the idea of spare tips for rods in those days. Compared with today's light rods a four-piece rod, probably some sixteen feet or so of greenheart, spliced into an ash handle, must have been a formidable weapon to wield.

Thornton continued: 'Without being a warm man, it would have been excusable to have thrown him overboard . . . however . . . looking at . . . his vessel very much resembling a condemned west-country barge . . . [we] acknowledged the accident an intervention of Providence, and left the old gentleman not a little disappointed at the loss of the *siller* he had expected, and of the different libations it would have afforded him of his favourite whiskey.'

After 'whiskey' Thornton added an explanatory footnote: 'A spirituous liquor, extracted from oats.' Sir Herbert Maxwell, in his revised edition, added in brackets, '(The Colonel passes an unmerited slight on John Barleycorn.)'. As I I often found myself, when I thought him wrong, Thornton was in fact correct and Sir

Herbert Maxwell was mistaken. In those days whisky was made from barley, or barley and oats, or oats, or even potatoes. The methods then employed were probably more reminiscent of an Irish shebeen than a modern distillery.

Thornton concluded his anecdote of the broken rod with a sardonic touch: 'Passing the boatman's house, two matrons came out and asked the cause of our sudden return . . . and feeling themselves also baffled in their expectations, they met our old gentleman, and seemed in most excellent humour to make him pass a very pleasant evening.'

He and Mr Parkhurst then retired to the inn, which he praised: 'The rooms here were small indeed, but they were clean, and we wanted nothing more; better linen I never saw, and every attention was shown us that the most finical traveller could wish for . . . and on visiting our beds, we found them very comfortable indeed.'

We did not stay at the inn there ourselves, because, as it was August, all the inns on Loch Lomondside were full. We moved on instead to Crianlarich, where we spent the night with the local policeman, who, in common with everyone in these parts, puts people up for the night, although, in his case, there was nothing so indiscreet as a bed-and-breakfast sign at his door. Like Thornton at his inn, we also spent a very comfortable night.

Chapter 5

IN FULL CRY

From Kenmore to Ben More the land is a' the Marquis's,
The mossy howes, the heathery knowes, and ilka bonny park is
his.

J. L. ROBERTSON: 1903

Tarbet to Dunkeld

Leaving Tarbet in the morning Thornton noted: 'Arrived at Glen Falloch; inn very bad; passing through a pleasant vale . . . proceeded for Cree in La Roche'. In his review of Thornton's book Scott scathingly wrote: 'There is scarcely a Gaelic name properly spelled.' It is obvious, however, that the Colonel was using a purely phonetic spelling. 'Cree in La Roche' for Crianlarich is a perfect example. No doubt the lilting cadences of the Gaelic pronunciation made it sound very like that to his Sassenach ear. Most of his mistakes are on the same principle, but it is worth noting that the maps of the day had very considerable variations and there was little uniformity of spelling. Pennant also made numerous mistakes, like Avymoir for Aviemore, but the landowners of the day were not themselves reliable, or even consistent, so that it is difficult to blame a stranger for such errors.

The road to Crianlarich still remains extremely pleasant save for an eyesore erected by the Hydro-Board on the roadside not far beyond Tarbet. This enormous mausoleum of a place, illuminated at night like some vast chocolate factory, and standing out during the day as an ugly monstrosity, is entirely out of keeping with the scenery. Pumping stations may be necessary, but there is no need to thrust them into view. They can surely be hidden discreetly like drains, or other necessary devices of a similar nature. Whatever authority was responsible for this blunder should think again before spoiling other beauty spots. This is planning without foresight, or even common-sense.

Thornton finally reached 'Cree in La Roche', where he dined. He noted that Mr Garrard, who had stayed behind to paint, 'from the meanness of the inn, had really rode past it'. From his descriptions it is apparent that in his day the Highland inn was generally a shabby affair, although there were some notable exceptions. Thornton himself was not over-fastidious about his comfort, and in general the standards of the day were not exacting, at any rate in matters of hygiene. Even he, however, was seldom able to describe them as very good. They were usually placed at convenient stopping places for the traveller, at ferries and cross-roads, and their purpose was simply to provide shelter and refreshment and little more.

It was only during the Victorian era, when the railways opened up the Highlands, that another type of inn began to develop, which catered especially for the sportsman, whether fisherman, deer stalker or grouse shooter. Then, after the first world war, tourists and sightseers in ever-increasing numbers started to discover the Highlands, and some inns began to cater especially for this seasonal trade. But it was only on the lifting of petrol rationing after the last war that the boom years of tourism began.

Climbers, hikers, pony trekkers, caravanners, sightseers and tourists turned their faces northwards to the Highlands. In winter there was ski-ing as well. The fishermen, the stalkers and the grouse shooters were in a minority. Inns decorated with antlers, stuffed birds and fish in glass cases, where the leather-covered arm-chairs by the fire were flanked by eighty-year-old bound volumes of *Punch*, suddenly blossomed forth with chromium; plated 'American' bars, or added hastily built extensions to cope with this increased trade. Until they adapted themselves this resulted in some odd juxtapositions of ancient and modern.

The situation has now become more or less stabilized. Some inns, which rushed to take advantage of the tourist trade, have merely succeeded in alienating their old clientele and at the same time failed to cater adequately for the demands of the new. Others, the majority, have successfully adapted themselves to both worlds by modernizing and improving their premises and retaining efficient service. Yet others, a conservative minority, have remained faithful to their regular sporting visitors and have not altered their interiors or lowered their high standards of comfort and personal service over the years. Making due allowance for occasional eccentric plumbing, these last are usually my favourites.

As the five-and-a-half-pound brown trout in its glass case in the hall testifies, the inn at Crianlarich has at one time been a small and comfortable fishing inn. From its strategic position at the junction of the roads to Lochs Lomond, Awe and Tay it was bound to expand with the increased tourist trade. It is not fair to judge any inn on one meal during crowded August conditions, but my general impression was that they were bearing up remarkably well under the strain of very heavy holiday traffic. It is in such conditions that the less well-managed inns go completely to the wall.

After our comfortable night with the police we had breakfast at the inn, finding our way through the small and crowded sitting-rooms to the large dining-room annexe. It was a good breakfast, with a wide choice, from which we selected grapefruit, bacon and egg, toast and marmalade and coffee. Thornton also fared quite well here as he noted: 'Uncomfortable as the house was, we found good eggs, fresh barley bannocks, and tolerable porter, together with some smoked salmon.' Whether we would have preferred this for breakfast is another matter.

Thornton then fished the Dochart. 'I raised some fine trout, killed about ten or a dozen pretty tolerable fish, and really expecting very good sport ... ordered the carriage and horses to be detained an hour longer; I had scarcely sent the message, when the fish seemed to rise very tardily, and in two hours I had no further success, though I tried every fly I had and also trolled with a minnow.' This sounds like a very familiar fishing story, and, if spinning were substituted for trolling, could have taken place today.

We left Crianlarich fairly promptly after breakfast in order to try to avoid meeting too much traffic on the attractive but rather narrow and winding road to Killin. Passing Loch Dochart and then Loch Lubhair, which are really the headwaters of Loch Tay, we followed the river Dochart down the glen until we reached the very pleasant inn at Luib, which has the fishing rights on all these waters.[12]

Stopping here on one occasion I had an interesting conversation with a gallant elderly sportsman, who, though he had lost his sight completely four years earlier, still continued to fish, with a line stretched along the bank to act as his guide. Owing to the state of the water he had had no luck, but, although I had not fished the Dochart myself, I was able to assure him that this was a widespread complaint. The prolonged drought certainly ruined the fishing very effectively between June and October in most parts of the country.

On this road to Killin, Thornton broke one of the springs of his carriage when a wheel slipped into the ditch. 'No trap for *springs* could be better conducted, about two feet deep and two broad.' It is a feature of many Highland roads today that they frequently have a well-concealed ditch, just broad enough to catch a tyre and sometimes deep enough to break an axle. Rolls-Royce axles, even thirty-three years old, do not break, but it is as well to be careful. It is still a trap for the unwary and one to look out for on all occasions.

After walking the rest of the way Thornton's party arrived in Killin in the dark, 'about nine o'clock, passing over a bridge from whence we saw, by the faint glimmerings of the moon some singularly broken rocks, over which the water breaking had a very extraordinary and pleasing effect'. In the morning he examined this again and noted: 'The bridge is very well, but the rapid Lyon, dashing over these obstructions, has a wonderful effect.'

When we were there the water was so low that the usual spectacle of the water tumbling in white foam over the boulders was rather lost. It can be a fine sight and makes an impressive entrance to Killin. It is, however, the Dochart, not the Lyon, as

Thornton called it. This and a number of other discrepancies between here and Dunkeld, though slight in themselves, strengthen the impression that this part was written from memory without the aid of diaries some twenty years after the event.

He approved of the inn at Killin, which, by a coincidence, was run by a Yorkshireman who had frequently hunted with his hounds and was extremely pleased to see him. It was this man who suggested that he should take a boat down the loch and send his carriage on to Kenmore, where 'there was said to be the most ingenious whitesmith [i.e. tinsmith] in the country'. Thus 'Mr P. and myself could fish, and Mr Garrard draw; and, by the baggage being stowed in the boat, the springs of the carriage would be most completely eased'.

Thornton asked Mr Campbell, Lord Breadalbane's factor, to breakfast with him, 'as I had the honour to be a little known to this nobleman', and, in due course, Mr Campbell did him 'the honour of a visit and insisted on my making use of his yatch, which proved to be a very handsome one'. In the circumstances one feels that Mr Campbell had remarkably little choice in the matter. This is just one of the many instances of the power of the limited 'Society', or the 'Establishment', of the day, which infuriated Scott, 'angry young man' as he then was.

After indicating his own sporting inclinations in his review of Thornton's book* Scott went on: 'But we are doomed to travel in a *style* (to use the appropriate expression) far different to that of our worthy author. Having in our retinue nothing either to bribe kindness, or to impose respect—having neither two boats, nor a sloop to travel by sea, nor a gig, two baggage wagons and God knows how many horses for land service—having neither draughts-men, nor falconer, Jonas, nor Lawson, groom nor boy—above all having neither crowns and half crowns to grease the fists of gamekeepers and foresters, nor lime punch, incomparable Calvert's Porter, flasks of champagne and magnums of claret to propitiate their superiors; all of which Colonel Thornton says he had. In our mind he should have given God thanks and made no boast of

* See Appendix.

them.' Thus speaks a definitely envious as well as an 'angry' young man.

Not having the loan of a 'yatch' ourselves, we took the south road round the loch, which, though narrower and more winding than the other, is, I think, much the pleasanter of the two. Having fished most of the loch at one time or another I was not so depressed by the fine weather, which made fishing virtually hopeless. Loch Tay fishes best in April, May and June, or September. July and August are never likely to be very good months. As with most large lochs the water requires knowing, but good bags of trout can still be made, and prior to June this year the salmon fishing had been exceptionally good.

Half-way along the south side we stopped at the very attractive little inn at Ardeonig. Like most fishing inns in the Highlands there is a farm attached to it as a source of fresh eggs and milk. With good boats and outboards, as well as comfortable beds and good meals, what more could a fisherman want? Or anyone else in search of a quiet restful holiday in beautiful surroundings, come to that.

Apparently Thornton had an idyllic sail up the loch, trolling and fishing with fly all the way and catching a very satisfactory bag. 'After sailing eight miles we anchored; went to dinner, and regaled ourselves very pleasantly; and a bottle of rum, made into milk-punch was given to our attendants, who would easily have been prevailed on to have dispatched more, if we had had it to offer; they also showed no dislike of some good bottled porter.'

Going on from Ardeonig towards Kenmore we stopped briefly at Acharn to look at the hermitage there, which Thornton sent Mr Garrard to draw: 'To bring to my rememberance what had once pleased me so much.' The reason he gave for not going to see it himself was strangely inadequate and unconvincing: 'As I knew I should see it often in the course of my travelling through this country I rather wished to defer my curiosity till I should have more leisure thoroughly to examine it.'

The remains of the 'herritage', approached through a tunnel perched opposite and above the waterfall at Acharn, are quite worth seeing. The Colonel's explanation of lack of time to see it and other contradictions, as well as the fact that for the first time he started to quote freely from Pennant, without acknowledgement, all points to memory failing and lack of diaries twenty years afterwards. For instance, at Killin he noted: 'No situation ... could be more desirable for the seat of a great man, and here we are told the Breadalbane family had once thoughts of residing ... what were the motives for giving preference to Taymouth I have yet to discover.' Yet on arrival at Taymouth he completely contradicted himself by continuing: 'This place, from my first visiting it, which I did when I was at college in this country, had made such an impression on me, that whenever I thought of anything extremely pleasant Taymouth constantly presented itself to me.'

The latter reads more like an honest statement of fact. Taymouth is still delightful. The village of Kenmore must be very little changed since his day. The Breadalbane Arms there is probably the one clearly identifiable inn that Thornton stayed at, which is still standing and functioning as an inn; its exterior not greatly altered since his visit. Although from its position naturally involved in the tourist traffic, the inn has remained much the same since the first time I visited it before the war. My recollections of this part of Scotland have always been very similar to Thornton's.

On his arrival at Kenmore there was a scene with the boatman: 'Unwilling to give what might not be thought adequate, I consulted the landlord, whose opinion was that three shillings for the boatman, as they had been found in provisions, would be very handsome, and two to take him back, and that I might give the attendant what I pleased ... but, unwilling to disappoint even his most sordid expectations, I gave him what silver I had, which was nine shillings and sixpence; when to my no small mortification he was dissatisfied and behaved very unhandsomely. I therefore recommend it to every gentlemen to make a previous agreement with every countryman, whose services they may want, but particularly with a Highlander; many of whom have but one idea, which is that an Englishman is a walking mint. ... They really fancy that no person understands the value of money but themselves.'

This complaint has a familiar ring about it. During the Victorian era it was the cry of the English tourist abroad. Now the Highlands are one of the few places left where anyone might be found who still imagined it to be true.

It is interesting to note that though the 'wages of this part of the country were at sixpence a day' Thornton cited a comparison with a man he employed to walk hounds in Yorkshire, whose 'constant pay is three shillings and sixpence a day'. The wages differential between the Highlands of Scotland and the North of England seems to have been considerably wider than today.

The following day they explored Taymouth Castle and the park, walking down the river bank. Apparently, keen pike fisherman though he was, Thornton failed to notice any, although today large pike are to be seen rising lazily at intervals just beyond the large sandbank opposite the boathouse below the inn. At any rate here he only claimed to have caught trout in the loch. 'Such a weight of fine fish I never saw taken in one day.'

We also walked down the river bank to Taymouth Castle, which I knew well of old. When sold by the Breadalbane family it was first converted into an hotel, with a fine nine-hole golf course in front of it, exactly where, in Pennant's print of 1771, figures are depicted with raised sticks, apparently in the act of playing golf.

During the last war it was converted into a camp for the Polish Forces. I remember watching a Polish officer receiving lessons in English from an evacuee girl.

'Ma hond,' she said, in broad Scots, holding out her hand.

'Ma hond,' he repeated after her, holding her hand firmly in his.

After the war it was taken over by the Civil Defence as a training establishment and it is now the site of one of the more extraordinary pieces of folly that modern peace or war can produce. In the beautifully wooded grounds, bordering a glorious stretch of the river, is a complete miniature 'village', which has been solemnly built and as solemnly blown up for the sole purpose of training civil defence recruits how to approach ruined buildings. Agreed it may be necessary, but in itself it is certainly an indictment of the age we live in. We may be probing for the secrets of outer space, but, as this epitomizes, mankind still has a lot to learn on earth yet.[13]

After surveying rows of emergency cooking stoves and other paraphernalia and looking sadly at the low, unfishable state of the river, we turned to try to discover where the picture by Garrard had been painted. We showed it to a likely looking local man, with the air of a gamekeeper or water bailiff about him.

'Where was this view taken from?' we asked.

'That'll be from the old look-out tower. I'm thinking,' he said, studying it carefully, 'Aye. Yon's the place. Up the hill there, above the road. You'll find a track leading to it.'

'Does anyone live there?'

'No. You would not find anyone staying there in a hurry. There was a Pole murdered a shepherd's wife there, just after the war. You may remember the case?'

We explained that somehow it had slipped our memories.

'Ah, well. That may be so. It was in all the papers at the time and the place has not just what you might call a savoury reputation these days.'

We thanked him and went on our way. Following a rough grass-grown track up the hillside above the road we eventually arrived, the Rolls puffing but triumphant, at the top, beside the old tower. In spite of its local ill repute we found that a shepherd must have been using it as his bothy, for, although he was not present, there were signs of habitation and two attractive collie pups greeted us wholeheartedly.

The view from this tower is magnificent, although it was only on a subsequent visit that I realized that the angle was wrong and that in fact Garrard's picture had been drawn from the 'Fort', much lower down. This is the other side of the road and at one time would have been in full view of the Castle below, although now largely hidden by trees. It consists of two small towers joined by a single castellated wall. The whole is reminiscent of a crumbling Hollywood film façade.

Thornton mentioned: 'We reparied to the Fort, ordering a cold dinner to be sent to us from the inn; for we meant to dine in one of the bastions, which had been fitted up as a banqueting house.' It is clear from this that the 'Fort' was merely built to enhance the view from the Castle, and, like the 'hermitage', to act as a convenient place for a picnic, or as a sort of glorified summer-house. It could never have been intended for serious defence in spite of the cannons in Garrard's picture, which again must have been merely ornamental, or for ceremonial salutes. Now roofless and decrepit, the two 'bastions' are the haunt of owls and bats and the view is hidden by the growth of trees on the hillside below, amongst which, on one visit, I counted no less than half a dozen red squirrels in almost as many minutes.

Thornton's description of the view from here, though slightly flowery, is accurate, and, although elsewhere he included several unacknowledged paragraphs from Pennant, appears to be his own. 'To the West . . . the very elegant subordinate village of Kenmore, and the bridge, over which is seen the noble loch Tay, its banks covered with wood and cornfields. Through these are indistinctly viewed the two excellent roads leading to Killin, meandering on either side of the lake. At the end of this noble sheet of water is seen very faintly Ben More, and, following the northern shore, arises the hill of Lawers. Looking across the park and appearing to arise from the river lost in foliage, rises . . . the smiling hill of Drummond, and above it . . . is seen the cloud-capt Shehellion.'

The changes here are mainly in the growth of the trees and in the work of the Forestry Commission on the hillsides. I have a proprietary interest in those on Schiehallion, having helped in the planting and clearing of some of them on one occasion in my school holidays. Even before then I had pleasant memories of days on the loch acting as boatman to my uncle, who had early implanted the 'fishing bug' in me and to whose memory this book is dedicated.

It is a common thing for the keen river fisherman to decry loch fishing as an old man's sport and purely a matter of 'chuck it and chance it'. But if you are relying on oars and not an outboard and acting as your own boatman it is no old man's sport. There is also far more to knowing your water and knowing where and when and how to fish than meets the eye. Keeping the boat steady on a drift and fishing at the same time requires skill and practice in itself. Comparing it with fishing a river is like comparing shooting over dogs with shooting driven game. It is a different sport, but good bags are certainly not a matter of luck and it has a fascination all its own. As with different rivers so each loch has its own problems and characteristics, be it a small hill lochan or a large inland loch.

One point that those who have never fished such a large Highland loch may not appreciate is the amazing swiftness with which the weather can change. It is no joke being caught on such a loch in a storm, as Thornton obviously knew when he thanked Providence for not sending them out with a drunken boatman on Loch Lomond 'in the furious tempest that blew on the lake'. Winds funnelling amongst the hills reach gale force with surprising rapidity. As an example, a well-built timber summer-house had been blown clean off the shore into the middle of Loch Tay by a sudden gust shortly before one of my visits. It is easy to be swamped in a small boat, and if it starts to become rough it is advisable to row for the nearest shore.

It is interesting to note that Thornton and Pennant both mentioned, with identical wording, that the park 'is one of the few in which fallow-deer are seen'. Some of the descendants of these same 'fallow-deer' are still to be seen on occasions in the forests and on the hillsides round about. With these and roe deer and red deer, as well as pheasants, wildfowl and other game on the low ground and grouse on the moors, quite apart from the fishing, both in the rivers and the lochs, this is still a fine centre for sport.

Mr Cameron, owner of the inn at Fearnan, on the north side of the loch, whose grandparents were tenants of the Breadalbane family in the last century, told me an amusing story about a famous white stag of this herd, which was particularly prized by the Lady Breadalbane of the day. Apparently she ruled the estate and her husband in an almost mediaeval fashion, which it is difficult to credit now. In particular she had a habit of entering the house of a tenant or employee without warning and going straight through to inspect the contents of the pots cooking on the fire. If there was any game, or venison, the family was packed off the estate instantly, bag and baggage, regardless of explanations.

Yet naturally the deer, then as now, could be a nuisance raiding the farmer's crops in the winter and breaking down his walls and fences. One dark January night Mr Cameron's grandfather heard them crashing around in his cabbage patch close to the house. In exasperation and more to scare them than anything else he opened the window of his bedroom and fired his rifle blindly in the direction of the sound. To his satisfaction he heard them stampeding off and thereafter there was silence. Shutting the window he went back to bed.

When he went out in the morning to inspect the damage, he found, to his horror, the famous white stag lying stone dead in the middle of his cabbages with a bullet through its heart. Needless to say, the family was hastily summoned and a hole was quickly dug in which the carcass was furtively buried. Thereafter he lived for some weeks in terror of being found out, but, fortunately for him, although Lady Breadalbane mourned the unexplained disappearance of her much prized white stag, she never discovered that it was buried beneath his cabbages.

In a footnote Thornton mentioned that 'Lord Breadalbane has introduced a breed of Tee-side, or Yorkshire cows, brought from the vicinity of Thornville, where they are of immense size. My predecessor paid great attention to them'. These must have been the early improved shorthorns, which were first bred in Yorkshire. By his 'predecessor' he presumably meant the Duke of York.

To illustrate their size he referred to a cow which 'weighed ninety eight stone . . . exclusive of hide, head, feet and tallow', or about a ton live weight, roughly the size of an average bull of the breed today. During the eighteenth century agriculture was making great strides forward in the South, but Scotland, from having been extremely backward, was catching up fast by importing new stock and new methods, as this indicates. Today matters have so far swung in the other direction that an East Anglian farmer friend of mine insists that his county is now largely farmed by Scots.

On leaving Taymouth there is another unexplained hiatus in the journey as Thornton went on: We drove through the park, taking the road, which follows the Lyon, to Invar . . . meaning to dine at the Duke of Athol's Hermitage on this side of Dunkeld. The views, in general, on this road are as beautiful as various; the road itself is a pretty good one, but might be improved, being full of large cobbles, and, near Dunkeld, rather sandy.' Apart from the fact that again it is not the Lyon, but the Tay, he makes no mention of Aberfeldy, or General Wade's bridge there, over which he probably passed. Again the conclusion must be that he had no diaries of this part and memory and invention failed him.

It is a pleasant road, following the Tay most of the way. The fisherman's eye is constantly catching sight of likely looking places to fish. Aberfeldy itself is a sleepy little town, possessing several hotels, one cinema, some good fishing and McKercher's garage, run by a very efficient and courteous Yorkshireman, paradoxically named Jones.

Some years ago Mr Jones was extremely helpful to a five-foot-two friend of mine who, while on a fishing holiday with me, had persistent mechanical trouble with his two-litre M.G., which was identical to one I had at the time. We visited the garage hopefully each day, but the engine had to be stripped completely and re-assembled three times before the fault was found to be due to the negligence of a previous garage. Not altogether surprisingly in the circumstances we became known to the mechanics as 'The long b—— and the short b—— with the b—— M.G.s'.

Farther down the road to Dunkeld the inn at Grandtully has a likely stretch of water. Not far beyond this on two separate occasions I met a large black tom-cat stalking proudly down the side of the road with a rabbit in his mouth. Either there are a lot of rabbits here or there are a lot of black cats rabbiting in this area.

The side road to the hermitage is signposted, but is at an awkward angle to enter from the Taymouth direction. It is only a narrow single-track lane and a great deal of reversing is required if another car is met. Thornton's description of the building is very apt: 'The Athol hermitage is, in my opinion, much too elegant, and takes from the beauty of the waterfall. The room is highly finished, and adorned with a fine transparent painting of Ossian, which, in any other place, I should admire, but here is quite out of character. The residence of an anchorite should undoubtedly be plain and simple, and had this building resembled that in Lord Breadalbane's park, it would . . . have infinitely better answered its destination than at present.'

As it had just been newly decorated in 1783 and Thornton probably visited it the following year, it must have been rather dazzling, with newly gilded pillars and panelled with glass. Subsequently it had a somewhat chequered existence. In 1821 an attempt was made to set it on fire and in 1869 it was actually blown up, although the reasons for both attacks are somewhat obscure.

In 1952 it was taken over and restored to some degree by the National Trust for Scotland. Although the interior is now bare of decoration, the pillars inside showing only faint traces of their former gilding, it is still a sufficiently elaborate edifice, with a curved slate roof and a veranda overlooking the falls, for anyone to appreciate what Thornton meant. In view of the number of visitors it is probably a pity that the 'transparent painting of Ossian' failed to survive. The dramatic effect of the Acharn hermitage, whereby you enter a tunnel into darkness and come out suddenly into an open, once roofed, platform facing the falls is much greater, as Thornton indicated.

He continued: 'Invar—On approaching the inn . . . I immediately discovered the mistake I had constantly laboured under, in taking this place for Dunkeld. Invar is only divided from the village of Dunkeld by the river Tay, over which there is a ferry, and, consequently, a traveller may easily conceive them to be the same town. The outside of this inn has a comfortable appearance enough.'

At a bend of the road just beyond the track leading to the hermitage there is an attractive old building with a cobbled courtyard open to the front, built round on the three sides. This we decided was obviously at one time the inn Thornton mentioned, and following the small burn, called the Brann, we came to the site of the old ferry. On the other side of the Tay, at a slight angle, lies the old quarter of Dunkeld, parts of which have also been restored by the National Trust for Scotland.

Just beyond Invar, which now consists of just a few cottages and the old inn, there is a camping site by the roadside. This rather detracts from the beauty of the place. One wonders what will happen when, as they inevitably will, such sites become fouled by successions of caravanners. Presumably in this instance they will move to an alternative site, but such alternatives are not always available. Nor does it seem much escape from a town existence to line up cheek by jowl with one's fellows in the close proximity usually required by such camping grounds.

The result must too often be the sort of disturbed night that Thornton suffered: 'The landlord . . . informed us, that, there being a meeting of surgeons, to examine and decide on a particular case, he feared we should be incommoded. . . . We went to bed . . . but our ears were, for a long time, stunned by the noisy mirth of this scientific body, without being able to enjoy their jokes.' This sounds more like a medical convention than a serious meeting, but it is still one of the odder aspects of the medical profession to a layman that when they meet together socially they can often revert to the behaviour of medical students. Psychologists might term it 'over-compensating'.

It is a pity that Thornton made no mention of hearing any fiddling at Invar. Perhaps this 'meeting of surgeons' was the cause. For Invar was the birthplace of the famous Neil Gow and his sons, whose compositions form the Gow Collection. It is really due to them that the old Scottish airs were not lost to posterity. Neil Gow himself and his four sons would all have been alive at the time of Thornton's visit in 1784, and to have heard them playing in the cobbled courtyard, which was the scene of many of their gatherings, would have been a memorable and noteworthy occasion.

Chapter 6

A CHECK

By Loch Tummel and Loch Rannoch and Lochaber I will go,
By heather tracks wi' heaven in their wiles.

THE ROAD TO THE ISLES

Dunkeld to Speyside

After 'a comfortable, solid breakfast' the next morning the
Colonel continued: 'We soon came to the ferry, but were prevented
from crossing for some time by a number of wild looking horses,
and their owners, little less wild than themselves, who were waiting
there for a passage. . . . The men pulled and hauled in their horses,
accoutred, in general, not with bridles, but *branks* (two pieces of
wood, through which a halter runs) which, when the rider or conductor wishes to stop his steed, he pulls, and consequently,
pinches the animal by the nose. This happening to several of
the shelties at the same time, a great confusion ensued, attended
with much kicking from men and horses, and more noise . . .
the oversetting of the boat was prevented . . . by three of the
horses leaping into the river and dragging one [driver] . . . with
them.'

The hazards and hilarity of the modern car ferry, involving
merely a certain amount of gear changing and reversing and curs-
ing, are nothing to this. It has admittedly been known from time
to time for people to engage reverse instead of forward gear and
to back off into the water. This is something to avoid, as, surprisingly enough, it usually seems to result in the deaths of the occu-
pants, although how it can happen in the first place I have never
quite been able to understand.

It is interesting to note that Thornton recorded: 'The High-lander . . . might have run the risk of being drowned, had not a friend caught him by the kilt.' This is the only time he mentioned the kilt directly, and it is a reasonable assumption that whenever he referred to a 'Highlander' he meant someone wearing Highland dress, which must have been sufficiently common for it not to have been worthy of note.

There has occasionally been a certain amount of controversy about tartans and the kilt. Highland dress was forbidden after the '45, by Act of Parliament, as part of the process of subduing the Highlands. Considering the area involved the Act must always have been difficult to enforce and there is good reason to believe that after the first few years it was generally ignored. Pennant certainly noted 'a most singular group of Highlanders in all their motley dresses' in Inverness in 1769, which indicates that it was not being enforced then.

His descriptions are intriguing 'Their *brechan*, or plaid, consists of twelve or thirteen yards of narrow stuff, wrapped round the middle, and reaches to the knees; it is often fastened around the middle with a belt, and is then called *brechan-feill;* but in cold weather is large enough to wrap round the whole body from head to feet; and this is often their only cover on the open hills during the whole night. It is frequently fastened on the shoulders with a pin, often of silver and before with a brotche [i.e. brooch].

'The *feil-beg*, "i.e. little plaid", also called *kelt*, is a sort of short petticoat, reaching only to the knees, and is a modern substitute for the lower part of the plaid. . . . Almost all have a great pouch of badger and other skins, with tassels dangling before. In this they keep their tobacco and money.

'The stockings are short and are tied below the knee. The color of their dress was various, being dyed with stripes of the most vivid hues; but they sometimes affected the duller colors, such as those of the Heath, in which they often reposed.

'The *truis* were worn by the gentry, and were breeches and stockings made of one piece.'

Thornton included in his book a picture by Garrard of Loch

Laggan in which, out of seven men shown netting the loch, six appear to be wearing the kilt and two also have plaids and bonnets. As the Act proscribing Highland dress was repealed in 1782 and this was probably 1784 they were not breaking the law, but it is fairly obvious that by this time the kilt was being generally worn in the Highlands again.

Although Thornton subsequently noted the complete disappearance of Highland dress in the area around Forres the kilt is such an eminently suitable garment for the hills and moors that it is doubtful if it would ever have disappeared completely, even if it had not been popularized by Queen Victoria. The custom that the 'gentry' wore 'truis', except on ceremonial occasions, was gradually changed, due to the example set at Balmoral. Nowadays, as the kilt is an expensive item to buy, it is no longer the garb of the average 'Highlander', although there are still plenty to be seen in the Highlands. As for tartans, there is an infinite variety, as there probably always was. From local or clan significance it has degenerated to a general Scottish trade-mark abroad. There is tartan, tartan everywhere.

The ferry at Invar was replaced by Telford's bridge over the Tay in 1809, which now carries the main Perth–Inverness road into Dunkeld. The oldest part of Dunkeld lies to the left. The square is an attractive place with an original tailor's ell measure still on one wall. Most of the old village was burnt, when it was besieged after the battle of Killiecrankie, but the National Trust for Scotland has done some good work in renovating the old houses and it is worth visiting.

Beyond Dunkeld I was fascinated to notice the behaviour of an assorted group of carrion crows and black-backed gulls gathered round a large refuse basket at a convenient lay-by. They were systematically extracting the contents in search of food. The resulting scraps of paper and rubbish were being blown about all over the place. Although I had already seen several lay-bys in a similar disgusting state I had previously put it down to human agency.

It is one of the odder aspects of human behaviour today that so many people seem to be content to stop at the side of a busy main road for their wayside meal or siesta, within a few feet of passing traffic and exhaust fumes. At week-ends they will even drive out of town for that express purpose. Presumably the effort required to find a suitable side road and a comfortable quiet place of country-side is too much for them. Or possibly it would be too quiet for them and they actually enjoy the bustle, the noise and the fumes of traffic to which they are accustomed. As such unimaginative people are usually responsible for littering the countryside with tins and paper, in any case it is perhaps just as well that they should not venture farther afield.

There is no doubt that nowadays the whole problem of litter in the Highlands is becoming serious and it is difficult to suggest a solution. There can be no easy one. This is essentially a modern development, and it is not a question which could have arisen in Thornton's day. It is not, however, that human nature has changed. It is merely that there are more people than ever before travelling through the Highlands and modern methods of manufacture and packaging ensure more rubbish.

The next obvious stop on the route today is Pitlochry. In Thornton's time it was not even marked on the maps. There was literally nothing there. It was only in the middle of the last century that it began to be developed as a health resort. Now it is the largest small township between Perth and Inverness and is a noted centre for 'doing' the Highlands. It is in a beautiful setting, is widely known, much publicized and has all the usual tourist attractions; added to which it has its own theatre. The Pitlochry Festival Theatre, founded in 1951, is a noteworthy venture. Any extension of the live theatre in this television age deserves encouragement and success and this is a particularly worth-while achievement.

Pitlochry is also the site of the Hydro-electric Dam, where, through a plate-glass window, the salmon can be watched climbing the fish-pass. Unfortunately it has proved almost impossible to get the smolts to return. After several years' painstaking research, however, the Brown Trout Research Laboratory there has proved conclusively, as was suspected, that brown trout, like salmon, also return to their place of origin to spawn. It is to be hoped that the problem of the smolts will also be solved in time.[14]

Thornton's next entry after Dunkeld was Fascally. Here an entirely new loch has been formed by the Hydro-electric Dam. Although it has been assiduously stocked with trout it is, unfortunately, rather too steep-sided and deep for good trout fishing. While not unattractive, this part has changed radically since Thornton saw it and commented: 'The situation of this place is extremely romantic.'

He added: 'A scene near the bridge is particularly fine and I could not help wondering how it had escaped Mr Pennant, for it is certainly superior to his view.' He then added insult to injury by misquoting the poor man without any acknowledgement. He continued: 'The road from thence to Blair we found excellent . . . made entirely at the expence of Lord Breadalbane, who . . . has erected a great number of stone bridges; Mr Pennant says as many as thirty-two; but I did not count them.'

This was one of the Colonel's worst slips. Except for his interpolations the whole of this last paragraph was quoted word for word from Pennant's description of the road on the north side of Loch Tay. This was a piece of gross carelessness, as he must have known that the Breadalbane estates were to the west and that this was all Atholl land. In fact the bridge over the Garry, to which, in the first instance, he was presumably referring, was built by public subscription in 1770, to replace a ferry that had capsized. As Thornton was quoting, or rather misquoting, from Pennant's Tour of 1769 it is hardly surprising that a view 'near the bridge' was not included.

Today the road is a narrow and winding one by modern standards, especially for the heavy traffic that it has to bear. A modern road is being driven through alongside the old one, which is being straightened, and eventually the two will constitute a dual carriageway. This should be an improvement.

The proprietor of the inn at old Fascally House, a retired captain, was inclined to be rather gloomy at the prospect of having a road driven across the fields in front of his windows. I am inclined to agree with him that it will spoil his view, but I would have thought that it would almost certainly increase his trade. His present winding and rocky approach is not exactly conducive to visitors, I should imagine; nor is the presence of an ancient burial mound behind the house, surmounted by a ruined chapel containing a tablet to the dead of the Clan Robertson, likely to excite the interest of any but historians, archaeologists, or morbid-minded Robertsons.[15]

Yet it is also easy to appreciate his feelings. With the introduction of dual carriageways, with the building of a Forth Road bridge at last, and with the increased power available from new hydro-electric schemes the character of the Highlands must inevitably change. New industries, new towns, or the fresh growth of old ones are bound to follow. The tourist trade is likely to boom to an even greater extent. Something, however, is bound to suffer in the process. Unfortunately experience has shown that far too often natural beauty is marred, or historical landmarks destroyed, by short-sighted planning. It is only to be hoped that it will not happen here.

It is understandable that the innkeepers should be hesitant and dubious of changes. The proprietor of the Killiecrankie House told me that he had given up his lease on the Garry as the fishing had been completely ruined by the hydro-electric schemes. Admittedly it was a dry year, but in places the riverbed was merely a trickle and farther up it was absolutely bone dry.

The reason for this, I was informed, was not primarily the Pitlochry dam itself, but the complex series of tunnels and channels connecting Lochs Garry, Ericht, Rannoch and Tummel, which have diverted the flow from its old course and, in effect, turned each of these lochs into a reservoir. The general result, since these were all waters flowing into the Tay, has been, to quote one rather bitter comment: 'To hydro-electrocute the Tay.' While some fishing has inevitably been adversely affected, this may, however, where there is a large and resilient enough fish population, result in improved fishing elsewhere. It is possible that improved catches on the Tay are not unconnected with this scheme. It is still, however, too early to assess all the effects of this and other similar schemes.

Our next stop was at Blair Atholl, where Thornton noted: 'Having arrived at the inn, which we found tolerably comfortable and despatched a hasty dinner, we walked towards the castle. . . . The walls are wonderfully thick . . . but have been much reduced in height since the rebellion in 1746, when it was strongly fortified and held out a close siege. I have heard many circumstances of this event when conversing with Mr C., a lieutenant, who attended my father's volunteers in the year 1745.'

This was the last castle in the British Isles to stand a siege, and after the '45, as Thornton noted, the second Duke of Atholl had the entire building remodelled on the lines of a Georgian house. The walls were 'much reduced in height' and the main tower lowered and windows inserted in the walls. The interesting point is that in 1869 the seventh Duke had the main tower rebuilt and the whole building recastellated, so that it once more resembled its original outward appearance. There have been changes in plenty to almost every building Thornton saw, but this must be the only instance of one that was modernized when he saw it and today is virtually back as it was before then.

He quoted Pennant, without acknowledgement: 'The most singular piece of furniture here is a chest made of broom, most elegantly striped in veins of white and brown. This plant grows to a great size in Scotland and furnishes pieces of the breadth of six inches.' There is today a room, called 'The Derby Dressing Room', almost entirely furnished with this type of furntiure. It is a matter of taste, but I cannot say that 'elegant' would have been my choice of adjective. The furniture, except for a hideous money-box, modelled as a temple, is pleasant, but the wood is not attractive.

I am inclined to doubt if Thornton ever saw the 'chest', but he certainly added a distinctive note, all his own: 'We saw several guns belonging to his Grace, chiefly rifles, which we thought, in general, too unwieldly.' They are, no doubt, still hanging on the walls somewhere. There appeared to be complete armouries displayed. This is now one of the many 'stately homes' competing for the 'half-crowns' of tourists. It is well organized and worth a visit. There are no juke-boxes, or roundabouts, and the guide book enables one to stroll round without a guide. I would have liked to have spent more time there.

Thornton added a footnote: 'Pennant says that the culture of rhubarb under the auspices of the Duke of Athol, with an intention of reducing the price for the benefit of the poor, has met with great success. However I may admire the plan, I fear it has been Utopian, as I could not trace the least reason to believe it ever existed.' This was an unkind cut at poor Pennant, whom he had already quoted and went on to quote, at length, all unacknow-ledged. It was perhaps as well for them both that Pennant died in 1798, prior to the publication of Thornton's book. As it is, he was probably turning in his grave like the propeller shaft of a racing engine.

After a night at Blair Atholl accompanied by 'a few bottles of our landlord's best claret' the Colonel and his party went on their way via the Falls of Bruar, where he noted: 'To gain a drawing was not only difficult, but exceedingly dangerous. Mr Garrard was very shy, but after gently reproaching him for his timidity, he was at length persuaded to follow me to a stone overhanging a precipice where, had his foot slipped, it would have been his last sketch.' Scott seized on this and commented: 'We do not recognize Colonel Thornton's humanity, elsewhere displayed . . . , in his treatment of Mr Garrard.'

They next stopped at the inn at 'Dalnacardock', where they found 'Liquor and provisions of all kinds . . . were plentiful and excellent'. As it had been General Wade's headquarters when building the roads this was perhaps not altogether surprising.

Fishing there, possibly on Loch Garry, Thornton was surprised to catch a char on fly and noted: 'It is a very uncommon circum-stance to kill char, either by fly, or worm; nor did I, during my stay in the Highlands, hear of any fishers having been so fortunate before.' It is admittedly uncommon, but it does happen occasion-ally on various lochs. Loch Moy is one and there are several others where it has happened in recent years.

On their return from the fishing expedition he noted their dinner:

'Hodge Podge,
Pudding—Greens,
Trout and Char,
Roast Mutton, excellent.
Second Course.
Brandered Chickens,
Cold hams,
Snipes,
Cheshire Cheese—biscuits
Wines.
Limes, Jamaica rum and
Incomparable Porter from Calvert's.'

They certainly did themselves well, but one could expect as good a meal at any really good hotel today. The probability is that the average man would be unable to eat, or drink, his way more than half through it, although, after a day on the hills, or on the loch, it is likely that most people could make a better attempt at it than they might imagine.

The following day they set off on the last stage of their journey to Speyside. Thornton was trying to transport some perch he had obtained at Blair Atholl, 'with which we hoped to be able to stock some of the lochs in Badenoch, where as yet, they are unknown'. He had them 'in a tin kettle brought from London, having this object always in view'. Unfortunately it was 'found very inconvenient, on account of the water splashing at every jolt, which was unavoidable'. At last, 'at Dalwhinny', he hired a soldier to carry it, whom he carefully instructed to replenish the 'kettle' at every brook. They then made the last thirteen miles in one minute under the hour.

As they might have expected, the soldier disobeyed orders. He arrived not long after them and they 'were greatly mortified to find them [the perch] all . . . dead'. So ended Thornton's somewhat inefficiently conducted biological experiment. According to biological theories perch should in any case be found in most of the eastern waters of Scotland. Whether in some cases they have been introduced subsequently by similar private experiments is now almost impossible to tell.

Following Thornton from Blair Atholl, we did not investigate the Falls of Bruar, because of the drought, but went straight on. The road from here onwards is amongst the most forbidding and bleak of the whole 'Tour'. On the left, not far beyond the falls, are the remains of an old Army camp fallen into a state of disrepair, which makes it a depressing eyesore. Apart from occasional pill-boxes, also hangovers from the war years, and the usual scattering of tents and caravans by the roadside, the bareness of the country-side is broken only by glimpses of the railway line beside the road. The moors, purple and black, stretch unrelieved to the horizon, giving the hills on either side an air of brooding desolation.

The 'excellent' inn at 'Dalnacardock' no longer exists. The next possible stop for travellers is at Dalwhinnie, where the Loch Ericht Hotel is the inn for fisherman. From this point northwards the fishing and the inns improve as the barren countryside gives way to the fertile valley of the Spey.

In Thornton's time neither Newtonmore, which is the next village, nor Kingussie, existed. He only mentioned arrived at the inn at 'Pitmain', where he 'took a cup of tea with my old landlord, M'Lean, of whom I made enquiries concerning those families I knew'. There is then another serious hiatus in the text. The most obvious discrepancy is that Mr Parkhurst is scarcely mentioned for some time, except for occasional cryptic references to him as an 'invalid'. Perhaps it had all been too much for him.

In effect the 'Tour' stops abruptly here, and the next three months, nearly a third of the whole book, are filled with extracts from game books and diaries kept over a number of years. It is impossible to say with any real accuracy which entries were made in which year. The best we can do is accept that he was certainly there in 1784, probably also in 1783 and 1785. Above Loch Alvie in 1789 he built a house which he gave up in 1794, so possibly extracts from records kept during those years may also have been included in his 'Tour'.

There is an inevitable similiarity about game books, which,

while fascinating to their author, is liable to be boring to the reader, and this is true whether they were written yesterday or a hundred years ago. After a while they tend to repeat themselves tediously. It may be that it was Thornton's eagerness to reach this part that caused him to skimp the latter portion of the route and quote at length from Pennant, or it may merely be that without diaries his memory had failed him. This section is almost entirely his own and we can only try to follow his route as far as possible in a coherent and logical manner and note the more interesting points he raised.

From the 'Book of the Roads' it is possible to check some of the families he mentioned. There was Mr M'Lean, landlord of the inn at Pitmain; Mrs M'Intosh of Raits, where he stayed a large part of the time. There was Captain M'Intosh of Kincraig; Captain Sir Aeneas Mackintosh of Mackintosh of Moy; Mr Grant, the laird of Rothiemurchus; Captain J. MacPherson of Indereschy and Captain McPherson of Balacroon, to name but a few. (The last-named was the local recruiting agent and was killed in the notorious 'Guiack disaster' of 1800, when an avalanche killed him and three companions in a shooting lodge.)

As Thornton frequently mentioned these people, or their numerous relations of the same name, simply in the Scots' style, by reference to their property (i.e. Captain McPherson, or Balacroon) it is often difficult to follow him, more especially as he admitted that he was sometimes confused himself. Furthermore he now suddenly introduced hitherto unmentioned friends, who came to stay at intervals; namely Mr Whitaker, Captain Waller, Mr Dreghorn, Captain Fleming of Barochan and Captain Monteith.

Raits was his base, but he also appears to have made a number of expeditions from there and to have had two, if not three, separate camps in the hills; one near Raits and the other above the Dulnan river. It is surprising that no one else seems to have noticed the prize error he made in this connection, although a number of his critics, as late as the 1930s, seem to have realized that he might have made other visits to Speyside. He actually made the mistake of including duplicate August 26ths. The first is 'Raits—August 26th', the second follows at 'Dulnon Camp'. The probability is that they were separate years, although there is no way of proving that it was not somehow just a printing error.

His idea of camping, by the standards of the day, was luxurious in the extreme. As his ideal he quoted a mediaeval French writer, Jacques du Fouilloux, and although my French is rusty the gist is clear enough. After suggesting every imaginable food and wine in idyllic surroundings he went on: 'Le Seigneur doit avoir sa petite charrette, là où il sera dedans, avec la fillette de seize à dix-sept ans, laquelle luy frottera la teste par les chemins. . . . Et si le temps se trouve un peu froid, il pourra faire porter son petit pavillon, et faire du feu dedans pour se chauffer, ou bien donner un coup en robe à la nymphe.' Not perhaps so very different from some people's ideas on caravanning today.

The Colonel's first entry at 'Raits' was that he went shooting: 'killed two brace of ducks and a brace and a half of snipes; but cut one of the tendons of my heel with the hard seam in my fen boots and was obliged to hobble home before nine o'clock'. These were probably a type of leather 'Wellington' which, unless well greased must have been exceedingly uncomfortable. He later noted when out on the hill: 'though, from experience, I had ordered the strongest bear-soles to my shoes, my feet were severely cut and bruised and both my ankles mangled with the stones'. There is no doubt that it is still important today to wear suitable stout boots on the hills. Unsuitable footwear can very easily lead to a broken ankle.

Another interesting sartorial point he made was: 'Soon dressed, without the aid of a *friseur*, having effectually got quit of that unnecessary trouble by curtailing my hair.' Long hair was still generally the fashion then and after shaving presumably came a session of hair-curling. One can sympathize with Thornton's attitude with a certain amount of complacency today.[16]

While on the hills the Colonel often had to take shelter in bothies, as on the occasion when he described the smokey atmosphere and his 'wizened' hostess with gusto. A more detailed though less evocative footnote he included, almost verbatim from Pennant, is also of interest: 'Bothie, or sheelin, is a cottage made of turf; the dairy-house where the Highland shepherds, or grasiers, live with their herds and flocks and during the fine season, make butter and cheese, gather juniper berries, which, in parts of the Highlands, abound, and sell for a good price. Their whole furniture consists of a few horn spoons, their milking utensils, a couch, formed of sods, to lie on, and a rug to cover them. Their food, oat cakes, butter or cheese, and often the coagulated blood of their cattle, spread on their bannocks; their drink, milk, whey, and sometimes, by way of indulgence, whisky.'

On his first visit to a church in the Highlands he noted: 'I found a much thinner audience than I ever remembered, and, conversing upon this subject with the . . . gentlemen of the neighbourhood, they informed me that the spirit of emigration had seized the people of these parts, and that many handicraftsmen and others, whose services I much wanted, had actually left the country . . . this fully accounted for the thin congregation.' He also mentioned: 'Mr Anderson, though a Lowlander, by absolute perseverance, has taught himself the Erse language, in which he preaches a sermon, after delivering one in English. It appeared to me that the men come here to eat tobacco and the women to sleep . . . a tax on sleeping females at church would bring in a pretty revenue.'

Considering his descriptions of their wretched living conditions it is scarcely surprising that the Highlanders felt they could improve their lot elsewhere. With the opening up of the Highlands following the '45 and the breakdown of the old clan system the way for change was inexorably opened. It is difficult today to appreciate that, less than two hundred years ago, the Highlands were only just emerging from a tribal system and living conditions which had endured almost unchanged since pre-Roman days. With the enforced impact of the much more advanced civilization of the South, change was inevitable, just as with improved road communications it is inevitable today.

Thornton went into some detail on the subject of the 'Act of Parliament, restoring the estates forfeited in Scotland by the rebellion of 1745 to the respective heirs, [which] received the royal assent on the twentieth of August'. Thus one of his visits to Speyside may be placed accurately in the year 1784.

He was very critical of the Act, apparently accepting graft in Parliament as a commonplace: 'There was certainly a fair opening for opposing the bill in the House of Commons and at least a new modelling of it; which was prevented, I fear, more from private than public views. Considerable sums are appropriated by the Act, to the completing of sundry public works begun in Scotland, to be paid out of these restored estates; such as some public edifices at Edinburgh, etc., which could not be finished without such an aid; but the chief of these works, the finishing of the noble canal of Glasgow, for which a large sum of money is allotted, and in which some powerful members of the House of Commons are particularly interested, silenced any opposition. . . .'

'The present Act, though it carried with it, at first the appearance of great liberality, will not be attended with those advantages, at least to the present possessors of the restored estates, which might have been expected . . . owing to the following causes: . . . after the forfeiture, in order to serve their clans and disappoint Government, many false debts and pretended mortgages were added to the just demands on the estates, which the agents for the Government were obliged to pay off. As the interest on these sums has accumulated, this, together with the charges made by the agents for improvements . . . amounted in many cases to nearly the value of the estates, and, to such of the present proprietors as are not opulent, the acquisition is rather ideal than substantial. . . . .'

Owing to the passing of the Act, Thornton 'found a very polite invitation from Colonel M'Pherson and the clan, requesting me to dine with them the next day, which was set apart for general festivity and rejoicing. . . .' He accepted the invitation and described, with relish, the subsequent Ceilidh, or Highland party.

'At five o'clock dinner was announced and each gentleman with the utmost gallantry, handed in his tartan-drest partner. The table was covered with every luxury the vales of Badenoch, Spey and Lochaber could produce, and a very substantial entertainment it was; game of all kinds and venison in abundance, did honour to Mr M'Lean who supplied it.

'I had no conception of any room at Pitmain large enough to

dine one-tenth of the party, but found that the apartment we were in, though low, was about fifty feet long, and was only used, being a malt-kiln, on such occasions.

'When seated no company at St James's ever exhibited a greater variety of gaudy colours, the ladies being dressed all in their Highland pride, each following her own fancy, and wearing a shawl of tartan; this contrasted by the other parts of the dress, at candle light, presented a most glaring coup d'œil.

'The dinner being removed, was succeeded by a dessert of Highland fruits, when I may venture to say that "George the Third, and long may he reign", was drank with as much unfeigned loyalty as ever it was in London; several other toasts were likewise drank with three cheers, and re-echoed by the inferiors of the clan in the area around us.

'The ladies gave us several delightful Erse songs, nor were the bagpipes silent; they played many old Highland tunes. . . . After the ladies had retired, the wine went round plentifully . . . but, as we were in possession of the only room for dancing, we rose the earlier from the table, in compliance with the wishes of the ladies, who, in this country, are still more keen dancers than those of the southern parts of Britain.

'After tea . . . we returned; and . . . danced, with true Highland spirit, a great number of different reels, some of which were danced with the genuine Highland fling, a peculiar kind of cut.

'It is astonishing how true these ladies all dance to time, and not without grace; they would be thought good dancers in any assembly whatever.

'At ten o'clock the company repaired to the terrace adjoining the house, to behold . . . . bonfires . . . of . . . piles of wood, peat and dry heather on the tops of all the different hills and mountains, which, by means of signals, being all lighted at the same time, formed a . . . magnificent spectacle . . . while our eyes were gratified with this solemn view, our ears were no less delighted with the different bagpipes playing round us; when, after giving three cheers to the king and the same to Mr Pitt, etc., we returned to the ball-room.

'At one I withdrew, took some refreshment and then returned home, highly delighted. . . .'

I have given Thornton's description of a Highland Ceilidh at some length, because, bonfires on such a scale possibly excepted, it could be a perfectly good description of a modern Ceilidh. The Highlander still believes in getting down to it if he is going to have a party and a real honest-to-goodness Ceilidh is something to remember. It is also noteworthy that, along with the Welshman Pennant, Thornton was an eye-witness of tartans at a time when some people have claimed that their manufacture was a forgotten art.

We visited Pitmain, which now consists of a farmhouse tenanted by a Mr Charles Mcdonald. In the circumstances it was perhaps unfortunate that my farming friend was with me at the time as they were soon deep in technicalities about corn prices and farm implements. However, Mr Mcdonald did his best to help. The old road wound past his farmhouse and it is clear that the long low room to which Thornton referred is now his barn. Investigating this, we found it surprisingly roomy. It must have been quite a spectacle filled with a tartaned company.

'This must be it, all right. It's the largest barn for miles around,' Mr Mcdonald assured us proudly.

He went on to tell us that his landlord was an American, a Mr Kramer, who had been shooting with Prince Bernhard of the Netherlands, presumably over the same ground that Thornton had sported over and leased from the Duke of Gordon. From the amount of new building in progress it appears that Mr Kramer takes his duties as landlord seriously. In Thorton's time the only connection with America was that several of the local 'gentlemen had served in America, during the war [of Independence]' and Captain MacPherson of Indereschy had been badly wounded there.

While we were inspecting the old buildings at Pitmain, which were being in part rebuilt, I noticed the dogs pointing into some gorse a few yards away. On command they flushed a couple of strong, healthy rabbits.

'You've got them back here too,' I commented.

'Oh, yes,' he agreed. 'They're back all over the place.'

After thanking Mr Mcdonald for his help we went on to Raits, the other side of Kingussie. Just off the main road, now it is a pleasant old house. Inevitably when we asked someone living in the cottages behind it what the name of the place was we had some strange answers.

'What is this house called?' we asked.

'Oh, this is Balavie house.'

'But what was it called before that?'

'Oh, I dinna ken that. I'm just new here masel'.'

As a variant of the eternal 'just a stranger here myself', whom the traveller invariably encounters, it was, I suppose, only to be expected.

What appears to have happened is that a larger house, called Balavie house, was built behind Raits, but burnt down. Now Raits is known as old Balavie. By modern standards it is rather a pleasant size, although a trifle near the road. Thornton, however, was not pleased with it.

Although he actually arrived on July 10th it was not until July 12th that he chronicled: 'Arrived at the house of Raits to breakfast (having been out examining his pastures) find its outside appearance by no means equal to what it had been represented on paper, except in the prospect of sport and would willingly have made off on any terms, and lived in camp, had I not engaged it at the desire of my friends, whose wishes and whose health made it necessary for them to have one; but daily expecting them, I had no alternative, therefore took it with all its servants, gardens, grasses, conveniences and inconveniences. . . . What wines and other things they had in the house I took on their own terms; which I afterwards found, in future negotiations, it is not always prudent to do.'

Whether this was an oblique reference to his quarrel with the Duke of York is not certain. If not, on the principle of once bitten twice shy, it may have made him a little more careful in such deals when it came to buying Allerton Mauleverer from the Duke at a later date.

He had scarcely settled in at Raits when his first visitors arrived; Captain Waller and Mr Whitaker. I too had hoped to have a Mr

Whitaker with me, but unfortunately he was unable to come. The Colonel's early sporting experiences with them included fishing the Spey:

'I hooked a salmon, which gave me the first notice by leaping quite out of the water, and, assisted by the current, ran me off fifty yards of line with such velocity, that, in passing, it actually cut my thumb and carried away the handle of my wheel . . . his great effort was to run under a hollow bank, from which Captain Waller . . . took great pains to dislodge him; but in the attempt . . . broke my tackle short by the hooks. Readjusted it, lamenting.'

His boats had not yet arrived by road from Forres and he had borrowed one which was not particularly sound. Trying it out on Loch Insh he imagined himself in danger of drowning: 'Found when too late, that our boat, which was dangerous in a river became still more so in Loch Insh . . . and that if the wind grew still higher, which, was however scarcely possible, we must inevitably perish.'

On our first visit in July my scientist friend and I turned off the main road at Kingcraig to eat our picnic supper on the banks of Loch Insh. We were eating a roast leg of deep-frozen pheasant apiece and washing it down with a draught of beer when we noticed that a rise was beginning on the loch. As we watched with increasing interest it began to amount almost to a 'boil', with fish rising wherever one looked. My fisherman's instincts were strongly roused when, just at that moment, a local man passed.

'Who has the fishing on the loch?' I asked.

'It'll be the hotel.'

That was enough. We were packing the remains of the meal when there was the distant roar of an engine. A moment later a tractor came down the hill from the main road at about twenty miles an hour, swaying from side to side, with the figure 'in the saddle' swaying even more uncontrollably. As he reached the Rolls parked by the roadside I shut my eyes and waited for the crash of rending metal. Miraculously he made it, though we saw, by the wheel marks, that it could only have been by the proverbial coat of paint.

Slightly unnerved we turned back to the inn. Here my friend, no fisherman and faintly amused by my eagerness to get on to the loch, insisted on having a large dram to fortify him. Mr MacBain, who owns the Suie Hotel, was very helpful in the matter of flies, but by the time we had returned to the loch it was too late. The rise was over, and though we flogged the water for an hour and a half it was hopeless.

That night I sustained the most fiendish midge bite on my eye-lid. The midges apparently never bothered Thornton and normally they do not bother men, but this bite was a beauty. My eye swelled more than any black eye I ever sustained in the boxing ring. Apart from not being black it was a splendid sight. Those subject to that sort of thing are well advised to use some of the very effective modern insect repellents on the market.

The following morning Mr MacBain added insult to injury, after inspecting the only 'bite' we had had, by showing us three excellent trout caught by his son in the brief period of the rise we had seen. A three-and-a-half-pounder, a two-and-a-half-pounder and a one-and-a-half-pounder; as nicely graded a trio as anyone could wish for anywhere. There are still, undeniably, good trout and salmon to be caught in the Spey.

Chapter 7

A CAST BACK

Around her northern and her western shores,
Throng'd with the finny race, Loch Laggan roars;
The midland sea, where tide ne'er swell'd the waves,
In richest lawns the southern border laves.

T. THORNTON

Speyside

Since a number of different visits are undoubtedly condensed into the next three months of Thornton's 'Tour' all that can be done is to take the various expeditions he made and incorporate them into something like their natural sequence. Thus, almost at once, he backtracked and took a cross-country route to Aberarder on the banks of Loch Laggan, sending his boats up the Spey to meet him there. This expedition was not an unqualified success, as one boat was swamped on the way and some of his possessions, 'amongst the rest, my dressing case, a very neat uncommon one', were lost. As it was sunk in only five feet of water the boat was saved and the boatmen recovered most of the 'effects remaining in her, conceiving them to be of great value; which in fact they were, the fishing tackle alone being worth fifty pounds'. This would be about the value of two first-class rods and tackle today.

He was impressed by the beauty and wildness of the country and the number of fish in Loch Laggan. Although still a wild and beautiful piece of country the North British Aluminium Company have now reduced the loch to nothing more than a reservoir, and it was interesting to note the various levels showing on the banks. This must have affected the fishing very considerably.

Thornton 'got a view of the almost unpassable road over the Coriarich; also discerned, at a distance, Ben Nevis'. Since he later described seeing the Duke and Duchess of Gordon at Fort Augustus, 'who passed over the Corriarich', there seems to have been some uncertainty in his mind about this. In fact the Corrie-yarrick is, and always has been, passable, but is rocky and danger-ous. It was, only this past year, the scene of a fatal accident when six men set out to cross it and were caught in a blizzard and died. It cannot be too often stressed that anyone climbing or walking in the Scottish mountains should know their route, pay close attention to the weather and be suitably clad and equipped.

The Colonel next seems to have indulged in a type of advanced 'pony trekking' expedition. Scottish pony trekking was first popularized at Newtonmore, and to judge by some of the lame and bandaged ponies we saw it must sometimes be more in the nature of pony wrecking. But, in practice, the Highland garrons can stand almost any amount of weight and are an ideal means of con-veyance in the hills, being particularly sure-footed. As they are usually rather broad they are not very comfortable to ride; however, this should not be confused with riding. It is merely sitting on a horse.

On the Colonel's expedition they started at eight o'clock across the river Feshie and up Carn Ban. 'At twelve o'clock we got up to the first snow ... then depositing our champaign, lime, shrub, porter, etc., in one of the large snow drifts we agreed to dine there. In my way up, the pointers had found some game and I killed at two points an old moor-cock and a ptarmigant, which I ordered to be well picked and prepared for dinner.'

The portable cooker, 'the Censurer', although noted as missing at York, when setting out, now made its appearance. Together with the unexplained absence of Mr Parkhurst this points to another expedition and another year; possibly 1785.

Having found a viewpoint above Loch Eunach, Thornton apparently indulged in another of his notable errors of measure-ment. He enthused: 'Let the reader figure to himself a mountain at least eighteen thousand feet above him, and a steep precipice of thirteen thousand feet below.' Since Braeriach, the highest of this group, is only 4,248 feet this would appear to be an obvious mistake, but those, including Sir Herbert Maxwell, who accused him of 'monstrous exaggeration' should have noted that he prefaced his comment with 'Let the reader figure to himself . . .'. As Pennant gave the height of Ben Nevis as the highest mountain in Scotland, Thornton must have known quite well he was exaggerating. If challenged I suspect that he would have argued, with his tongue in his cheek, that he was only speaking figuratively.

He then shot some ptarmigan and waited for the exhausted Captain Waller to join him. He continued: 'A thought struck me: I placed a ptarmigant in such a position that it appeared to be alive, then mentioning to the captain that I had seen one, which he never had, immediately on discovering it, he fired and shot it; this revived him more than anything I could have given him. The having shot a ptarmigant was now the only topic of his conversation, and it would have been cruel to have undeceived him.'

Their dinner he noted consisted of: 'Two brace and a half of ptarmigants and a moor-cock, a quarter of a pound of butter, some slices of Yorkshire-smoked ham, and reindeer's tongue; with some sweet herbs, pepper, etc. . . . These with a due pro-portion of water, made us each a plate of very strong soup. . . . We drank, in a bumper of champaign (gentlemen and servants faring alike), success to the sports of the field, and, with the addi-tion of a tumbler of sherbert and cordial, were enabled to . . . pro-ceed.'

He noted: 'The heat on the top of this mountain was very great, at the bottom it was really an oven. . . . We did not get down till near eleven.' It must therefore have been after midnight when they returned to supper and 'weak, but warm lime punch' and 'well satisfied, to bed'.

His description of the heat is reminiscent of the weather during most of my visits. It was really too hot for shooting in August, and even September, on several occasions. The grouse seemed to have deserted their usual moors in many cases and were either to be found near water and shade in the low ground, or above the two-thousand-foot level along with the ptarmigan on the high tops where it was cooler.

In some respects Thornton's day above Loch Eunach was very like a day my East Anglian friend and I had on some moors about thirty miles away. We were in the company of a town clerk, the Bailie (i.e. municipal magistrate), Water Convener and a master baker. Mr friend, though a keen partridge shot, had never shot a grouse. At Carnwath, where we had already shot, by a quirk of fate he had only succeeded in shooting a partridge. On this occasion he was determined to shoot at least one grouse.

It so happened to begin with that, although we did not see many grouse, all that we was were pointed and flushed in front of me and I had the first three birds. My friend then had a chance but missed with both barrels and I regret to admit one bitch picked a grouse, which had refused to get up, as sometimes happens in hot weather, and handed it to me. Then the Water Convener, in front, drove a bird over us, which came like a bullet directly between my friend and myself. I knew I was on it as I fired and I heard his gun at the same instant. He, however, had obviously not heard my shot and he heaved an enormous sigh of satisfaction as the bird crumpled and fell behind us. In the circumstances I felt, like Thornton, that 'it would have been cruel to have undeceived him'.

Thereafter I had a long crossing shot at a hare, which I was sure I had hit hard. Setting a dog on to the scent, as it was off to the right of the line, I saw it come to a halt and remain standing on point at a hole. Going forward and thrusting my arm down I managed to extract the dead hare. Blue hares, like rabbits, and unlike the brown hare, will take shelter in holes. Thornton's description of them in a footnote, taken from Pennant, is intriguing: 'Cairvanes: Species of hare, never found, but on the summits of mountains; it seldom mixes with the common kind; it is less than them, its limbs more slender and shorter; its flesh more delicate; it is very agile and full of frolic when tamed; is fond of honey and other sweet things; prognosticates a storm by eating its own dung; in a wild state protects itself by taking shelter underneath large stones; during summer is grey: the leverets have a bluish appearance.'[17]

Apart from several hares and a woodcock shot by my friend, we had little else in the morning. Although slightly smaller than brown hares, it is true, there blue hares can weigh a great deal in a game bag after a short while on a hot day. By lunch-time we were extremely glad of a rest and a bottle of beer apiece.

In the afternoon we tramped miles over another moor in the blazing sun, the Water Convener having apparently given up. I was fortunate enough to be in shot of the only grouse we saw. Finally it became obvious that the grouse were not there and that we had all had enough, including, for once, the dogs. We returned to the cars where we found the blessed Water Convener waiting for us with a fresh supply of cool beer. No champagne Thornton drank ever tasted as good.

With very few differences this was much the same as the sport that Thornton enjoyed. Given reasonable conditions it should be better. It is only in fishing that we could not hope to achieve similar results today. For instance his record pike on Loch Alvie is unlikely to be repeated:

'I saw a very large fish come at me, and collecting my line, I felt I had him fairly hooked; but I feared he had run himself tight round some root, his weight seemed so dead: we rowed up, therefore, to the spot, when he soon convinced me he was at liberty by running me so far into the lake, that I had not one inch more of line to give him. The servants, foreseeing the consequences of my situation, rowed, with great expedition, towards the fish, which now rose, about seventy yards from us, an absolute wonder. I relied on my tackle, which I knew was in every respect excellent, as I had in consequence of the large pike killed the day before, put on hooks and gimp adjusted with great care; a precaution which would have been thought superfluous in London as it certainly was for most lakes, though here, barely equal to my fish. After playing him for some time I gave the rod to Captain Waller that he might have the honour of landing him; for I thought him quite exhausted, when, to our surprise, we were again constrained to follow the monster nearly across this great lake having the wind too much against us.

'Frequently he flew out of the water to such a height, that, though I knew the uncommon strength of my tackle, I dreaded losing such an extraordinary fish, and the anxiety of our little crew was equal to mine. After about an hour and a quarter's play however, we thought we might safely attempt to land him, which was done in the following manner: Newmarket, a lad so called from the place of his nativity, who had now come to assist, I ordered with another servant, to strip and wade in as far as possible, which they readily did. In the meantime I took the land-ing net, while Captain Waller judiciously ascending the hill drew him gently towards us.

'He approached the shore very quietly and we thought him quite safe when, seeing himself surrounded by his enemies, he, in an instant made a last desparate effort, shot into the deep again, and, in the exertion, threw one of the men on his back. His immense size was now very apparent; we proceeded with all due caution, and, being once more drawn towards land I tried to get his head in the net, upon effecting which, the servants were ordered to seize his tail and slide him on shore.

'I took all imaginable pains to accomplish this, but in vain, and began to think myself strangely awkward, when, at length, having got his snout in, I discovered that the hoop of the net, though adapted to very large pike would admit no more than that part. He was however completely spent and, in a few moments we landed him, a perfect monster! He was stabbed by my directions in the spinal marrow, with a large knife, which appeared to be the most humane means of killing him. . . . On opening his jaws to endeavour to take the hooks from him, which were fast in his gorge, so dreadful a forest of teeth, or tusks, I think I never beheld; if I had not had a double link of gimp, with two swivels, the depth between his stomach and mouth would have made the former quite useless. His measurement, accurately taken, was *five feet four inches*, from eye to fork.

'The weight of this fish, judging by the trones we had with us, which only weigh twenty-nine pounds, made us, according to our best opinions, estimate him at between forty seven and forty eight pounds.'

There is no reason to doubt this story, especially as his estimate of the weight tallies with that of subsequent pike of similar measurements. Although rare, pike of fifty pounds have been caught since and it is not surprising that Thornton should catch some outsize fish with his comparatively modern tackle in these nearly virgin waters.

He noted: 'We afterwards tried this loch several times, but could not get a rise, from which I inferred that there were few, if any large pike left in it. In fact, if we reflect on the quantity of food so large an animal must require every year, it cannot be expected that any piece of water can supply many such fish.' No one would be likely to dispute this observation. From every point of view it is desirable that such fish should be caught.

On our visit to Loch Alvie in August we did not fish. However, while at the Lynwilg Hotel, the attractively modernized fishing inn on the shores of the loch, near the spot where Thornton's wooden house must have stood, we were shown a six-pound pike that had been caught there on a spoon, just previously. There are still plenty of pike to be caught in the Highlands for those who like pike fishing, and the more that are caught the happier everyone should be. In practice pike, especially in open water, can be a more sporting fish than many fishermen who have never caught them might imagine, but there are obvious objections to allowing pike fishing in waters preserved for salmon and trout.

It was while 'taking refreshment', to use Thornton's euphemism, in the bar of the Lynwilg Hotel that we encountered an ex-Speaker of the House of Commons, the owner of a 1934 Lagonda, drawn up alongside our Rolls. As it happened I had once owned a Lagonda of the same year and type, except that mine had a special gear-box, which I never liked. This was a 'through-the-gate' box and, for once, I was able to talk knowledgeably of matters mechanical and expressed my admiration of it.

'D'you want to buy it?' he asked hopefully.

I explained hastily that I knew the snags, while appreciating the car, and that I was well satisfied with my own.

'Hmph. If you find a good vintage year stick to it,' he agreed.

With that we departed on our way to Loch An Eilan. Thornton described the road from Pitmain to 'Loch Neiland' as 'one of the very first rides in the world'. Unfortunately the railway line, running between the road and the Spey, now detracts considerably from what must once have been a delightful drive. Even so, once under the railway bridge at Aviemore and into Rothiemurchus, the road is still most attractive.[18]

The small Cockney evacuee's remark when he arrived at Rothiemurchus during the war and first saw the Cairngorms is extremely apt.

'Cor! Ain't those 'ills camouflaged luvvly!'

On our way up to the loch we passed two fluffy red squirrels, one with an almost albino tail. We also passed a small army of fluffy boy scouts about to encamp. Fortunately they can be relied on to leave no litter or unpleasant traces behind them, which is more than can be said today for too many campers without the necessary guidance and experience.

The last time I had seen Loch An Eilan was when, aged four, I paddled and, inevitably, fell in. Even then it had made a considerable impression on me, but I was surprised and pleased to find that, apart from seeming a little smaller, it was still much as I remembered it. With the Cairngorms in the background and the ruined castle on the island, where ospreys used to nest, although Thornton made no mention of them, it is still exceptionally beautiful.

The Colonel said of it: 'Loch Neiland is a most enchanting spot. . . . To the south are discerned some very lofty perpendicular mountains, rising directly out of an immense forest of the finest pines; and to add to the wildness of this romantic scene, innumerable trees of prodigious size, appear torn up by the roots in the strangest manner; this has been caused by the violence of the preceding winter's hurricane, from which my friend Mr G., the proprietor, assures me that he suffered a loss amounting nearly to one thousand pounds.'

This would seem to place this visit in the year 1783, as the 'hurricane' he referred to was probably that mentioned in the *Edinburgh Review* of March 1782. It was accompanied by heavy snow and must have had much the same effect as the violent gales of 1592, which did so much damage in the Highlands. Traces of this were still evident in the layers of well-grown trees which we saw in a number of places lying rotting on the hillsides, at all angles, their bark peeled off and the bare wood showing dead beneath. The damage then was reckoned in hundreds of thousands of pounds.

Thornton's 'friend Mr G.' was Mr Grant, the laird of Rothiemurchus. His descendant, Lieutenant-Colonel J. P. Grant, younger, of Rothiemurchus, is a busy Highland laird, a keen bird-watcher, naturalist and sportsman. When we visited him he was just off to the St Kilda's islands and was then going on to Fair Isle. Unfortunately he had no records of Thornton's day and at the time I was prepared to agree with his view that the Colonel was the biggest liar unhung.

Colonel Grant's house, Inverdruie, was built in 1750 and therefore is probably the house Thornton mentioned: 'Mr Grant of Rothiemurchus has built a very commodious house, not in the best situation, though his table etc., is the most enviable in the world, as is his estate. . . . As proof that his table is well served I will only mention that he has, added to every other luxury, what few possess, viz. roebucks, cairvanes, hare, black-game, dottrel, white-game, partridges, ducks and snipes; salmon, pike, trout, char, par, lampreys and eels, all of which are in abundance on his estate.'

Thornton seems to have overlooked red deer, and in addition to all these Colonel Grant could now add pheasants and capercailzies. At one time he might have added reindeer, as the experimental reindeer herd, which was introduced to the Cairngorms in 1952, was first established on his ground. Later the herd was moved to higher ground where conditions were found to be better for them.

Reindeer were originally indigenous to the Scottish mountains and the object of this experiment was to find out if they could be satisfactorily re-established, on a commercial basis, as an addition to the country's meat supplies. Whether today's altered circumstances warrant encouraging reindeer when we are trying at the same time to curb red deer numbers is a moot point, but it is an interesting fact that there is a flourishing herd of some twenty reindeer on the Cairngorms. It is not, however, an easy matter to see them. It means climbing above the two-thousand-foot level. The story goes that an English journalist insisted on going up to see them, though advised that it was an unsuitable day, and was lost with the herdsman, who knows the hills, for several hours in pouring rain. Only those who know the hills can appreciate how easily this can happen.

It is interesting to note that Thornton never mentioned capercailzies at all. Pennant mentioned them as 'that rare bird Capercalze, or Capercally, the Cock of the Wood'. He indicated that they were seen only near Inverness, Glen Moriston and possibly Castle Grant, in large pine woods. It seems to be generally agreed that by 1800 they were practically extinct.

The history of their reintroduction is an interesting one. As early as 1822 Sir Fowell Buxton, a Norfolk landowner, had tried unsuccessfully to establish in his local woods a pair of capercailzies sent from Sweden by a friend. Subsequently he decided to repeat the experiment in Scotland with the help of Lord Breadalbane on his estate at Taymouth. In April 1837 Sir Fowell's head keeper, an Irishman named Larry Banville, crossed over to Sweden and took charge of some thirteen capercailzies that had been collected for him. The next month was spent in trapping others and preparing coops for the return voyage. Banville appears to have been a man of resource, and in spite of considerable handicaps carried out his task and delivered the birds at Taymouth in July.

The next year, 1838, some sixteen more capercailzies were sent to Taymouth from Sweden, and by 1839 Mr Guthrie, Lord Breadalbane's head keeper, estimated their numbers at 'between sixty and seventy young ones'. It is significant that he mentioned two of the birds being shot 'in the north of Scotland' that same year. Whether these were the Swedish birds might conceivably be open to question. However, there is no doubt that thanks to the efforts of Sir Fowell Buxton and Lord Breadalbane and their respective head keepers capercailzies are once again well established in the Highlands. From my own experiences I would say that they are flourishing and that they and blackcock are increasing in numbers rapidly every year, especially in Forestry Commission ground, which is usually ideally suited to them.

They can provide good sport. Driven over a young plantation they appear to be flying deceptively slowly and it is easy to miss behind. Their size is only appreciated when the branches are heard cracking as they crash earthwards. Examined closely their powerful beaks are more reminiscent of a bird of prey than the turkey to which they are related. When it comes to eating them, once they are full grown, they are liable to taste strongly of turpentine from the pine needles on which they feed. The young, however, taste and look very like pheasants.

At Aviemore, Thornton noted: 'It hurts me to say, I found the inn I now put up at differing from those I had passed, it being but very indifferently kept, the rooms very dirty; whereas when I was here before, no inn could be in better order.'[19] This of course is one of the occupational hazards of travelling, even today. I visited a number of inns which varied between middling to good and frankly bad on the different occasions I stayed in them. The height of the tourist season, in some ways, is not a good time to judge, and, in others, the best. If they can stand up to the strain and still be efficient it means they are worth staying at, whereas if their efficiency breaks down it may mean there is a flaw in the management. Unfortunately owing to the Catering Wages Act the innkeepers are to a large extent at the mercy of their employees. With seasonal employees, standards may vary from year to year. Other inns run by a family or full-time employees may always be reliable.

Thornton mentioned an eagle's eyrie on Cnoc Fraing, one of the hills west of Aviemore, and added an interesting note: 'A Highlander here has taken a young eaglet . . . and by tethering it, and watching the old ones, which regularly come to feed it, and taking away such provisions as they bring, which consist of fauns of the roe, lambs, kids, hares, black-game, grouse or ptarmigants, wild ducks, etc., he amply supplies his family for some weeks; consequently it is a great acquisition to him.'

I gather that the eyrie is no longer there, but I heard a charming story of a photographer who was sent to the Highlands to get some nature photographs and instead found himself on his arrival involved in a Ceilidh. In the morning he belatedly remembered his mission and looked round frantically for inspiration. His bloodshot gaze fell on a stuffed eagle in a glass case, which had accidentally been smashed the night before. With the willing assistance of some newly acquired friends he soon had it out of its case and was posing it carefully on the rockery in the garden.

'Thish'll make a wonderful nachure photograph,' he prophesied happily as he clicked the shutter.

The delightful thing is that it did. Today postcards are to be seen on sale all over the world of a golden eagle in glorious Technicolor, poised on a 'rock', ready for flight, at a slightly suspicious angle to those who know, against a magnificent background of the Cairngorms.

Thornton next fished 'Loch Petulichge', by which he meant Loch Pityoulish, and caught another large pike. This one caused the rings of his rod to 'rattle' and he only landed it through the use of his 'multiplying wheel'. Greenhearts were liable to 'rattle' when strained, just as nowadays some types of nylon lines are liable to 'sing' when under strain.

He next tried to shoot a roebuck in Glenmore Forest and failed dismally. Today this is part of the National Forest Park, which has been created here. In it is the newly built training centre of the Scottish Council of Physical Recreation, Glenmore Lodge. This may be comfortable inside, but it is an ugly glass shoe-box piece of architecture, which clashes violently with its surroundings. The Council is primarily an educational body which aims to encourage outdoor sports and to provide an opportunity at Glenmore for those who might not otherwise be able to afford it, to learn to swim, sail, canoe, or climb, or simply walk and study nature reasonable cheaply.

Organized recreation of this nature is anathema to me, but I have to admit that for the schoolboy or young person who wants to learn rock climbing, or one of the other subjects offered, it is probably a good thing. I somehow expected that a body with the resounding title of the Scottish Council of Physical Recreation, which has expanded its functions considerably during the past few years, would be composed of red-cheeked male extroverts bounding with vitality. Instead it is organized in Edinburgh almost entirely by middle-aged, efficient and determined, but very charming, Scotswomen, than whom there is no more potent force that I know.

It is probably worth pointing out here the main difference between the Highlands at the time of Thornton's visits and today. Then the Highlands were slowly readjusting after rebellion and martial law. The military dictatorship was coming to an end. New roads had been built and emigration and depopulation were beginning.

Today the Highlands area is the cockpit of committees.[20] I have already mentioned, directly or indirectly, the National Trust for Scotland, the Scottish Tourist Board, the Scottish Council of Physical Recreation, the Highland Council of the Scottish Tourist Board, the Cairngorms Winter Sports Development Board, the Reindeer Council of the United Kingdom, the Forestry Commission and various Hydro-Electric Boards. These are but a few of the boards, councils and commissions, most of which have resounding titles and sizeable committees and all of which have a say, or want a say, in anything and everything to do with the Highlands. With the eternal tug of war which must result it is surprising that anything is ever achieved and it is certain that no action taken will please everyone and that inaction will displease everyone even more.

An interesting point about committees is that they have a quite remarkable breeding potential. Wherever there are two committees with a single point in common there appears, after a due period of verbal gestation, a sub-committee. Where there are several committees concentrated together there are inevitably a multiplicity of sub-committees. It is, I suppose, an extension of Parkinson's Law, but nowhere is it more obvious than in the Highlands today. However, for better or for worse, now that new roads are being built, change is inevitable. The trend is now likely to be towards increased industrialization and increasing population. Not even a special sub-committee of Highland Canutes could hold back the waves of Progress much longer.

On our journey in July we made a point of visiting the osprey's nest about which there was considerable publicity following the dastardly and futile attack of the previous year, when a notorious local eccentric rifled the nest, although there was a watch on it, and succeeded only in breaking the eggs. This year there were unprecedented precautions, including barbed wire round the trees and listening and recording apparatus loaned by the B.B.C. This time the ospreys hatched off successfully.

After a very good lunch at the inn at Boat of Garten, consisting of grapefruit, turkey and an excellent cheese accompanied by a pleasant hock, we enquired the way to the nest. We need scarcely have bothered. Cars were lined up nose to tail on the roads leading to the site and the scene was more reminiscent of a Bank Holiday crowd on Hampstead Heath than bird-watching in the Highlands. The track from the parking point to the hide and viewpoint was well trodden. At the hide was a caravan providing sleeping quarters for the watchers and, mounted on a tripod, a pair of powerful Japanese binoculars focused on the nest.

It was rather like queueing to see 'What the Butler Saw' on the pier at Brighton, and one of the watchers kept up a somewhat condescending patter of explanation, but the ospreys themselves were interesting. When we arrived the young fledglings were being fed on a fish just caught from the loch. Very soon they would be reaching the stage when they were ready to leave the nest, and it is to be hoped that this will mean, in due course, the return of the osprey to the Highlands in real earnest.

No sportsman would wish it otherwise, and I found it

disturbing to hear it suggested that the young birds might be in
danger from the 'guns' on the 'Twelfth'. It is really high time that
some of these bigoted bird-watchers realized that true sportsmen
are as interested in nature as they are and have no desire to shoot
everything that moves or has a hooked beak. This dissemination
of anti-sporting propaganda, spoken with the air of an oracle, is
an insidious and deplorable practice, most often indulged in by the
extremist crank type of 'feathered friends' friend'. The idea that
all men with guns are villains has no place in reality, and this
should be generally accepted today. Only the really ignorant
emotional romantic or the vicious-minded bigot with an axe to
grind could seriously suggest that the ospreys were in any danger
from a grouse-shooting party.

The huntsman with his pack of hounds also comes in for this
type of irresponsible criticism, but both he and the game preserver
with his gun deplore cruelty as much as the sloppy thinker
wallowing in misguided sentiment, and they also know more
accurately what they are talking about, often from a lifetime of
experience. The sensible modern ornithologist appreciates this
and does not subscribe to the theory that all men with guns are
equal. As with politicians and bird-watchers, some are more equal
than others.

Anyone shooting a bird on the protected list is breaking the
law, but apart from ignorant louts and very occasional mistakes,
it is not common. The game preserver who destroys the predators
of his game birds is also saving the lives of many others. The timely
death of a nest-robbing magpie or chick-killing carrion crow is
likely to result in the lives of many harmless and attractive smaller
birds being saved and possibly some rare specimens as well.
Sentimental woolly thinking has no place in Nature.

Literally hundreds of thousands of birds, protected, preserved
and common, are killed each year by cars, aircraft, poisonous
sprays or seed dressings and similar causes. It is against these that
the ornithologist and sportsman should combine. Their aims are
basically the same, and that fact should be plain to everyone today.

Regarding cruelty Thornton made a point with which every

sportsman would agree. 'To allow a wounded bird to draw out a miserable existence, when it can in any way be prevented, is surely brutal; and I trust that other gentlemen make it a constant rule never to allow, if possible, a wounded bird to live, Many an hour's sport have I given up for that purpose.'

His descriptions of sport are inclined to become a little tedious, being very much the same, alternating between fishing, shooting and hawking, However, he described many incidents which are of interest. One in particular he mentioned on a very cold day when they lit a fire to warm themselves. He went on: 'Having ordered the gun to be washed I dried it . . . by some inattention the barrel slipped through my fingers, and unluckily, falling upon a stone, the upper pipe was bent so flat, that I doubted if I should ever be able to get the rammer-rod to go down; which, however, with some difficulty and great care, I at length effected.'

Presumably he meant that the 'pipe' for the 'rammer-rod' was bent, not the barrel itself, otherwise he would certainly have been courting a burst barrel. In those days this was quite common in any case when one barrel of a double-barrelled gun was often inadvertently loaded twice. It is not, however, an accident he recorded at any time.

It so happened that while writing this book I was invited to work my dogs at one of the early shoots in August at an establishment which charges from two to four hundred pounds a week for 'driven grouse shooting' with a 'country house atmosphere'. This was a facet of 'sporting tourism' which had interested me since first hearing about it, and I was delighted to have the opportunity to see for myself what was involved. As it happened to be almost on Thornton's route with all expenses paid, I accepted with alacrity.[21]

It appeared that although the managers of these moors did not approve of shooting grouse over dogs, about which they knew nothing, a party of their guests, some charming Italians, had insisted that they preferred shooting over dogs to driven game. Introduced to them on the evening of my arrival, I was offered champagne, whisky or brandy. I chose whisky, and my glass was constantly replenished until nearly midnight. Thus, when I rose at four-thirty to reconnoitre the moor over which I was to work the dogs I was not feeling at my best.

In the darkness of my bedroom I pulled my gun through with a wad of tow, glanced through each barrel, and then drove out to the moor with the dogs. Almost immediately on opening the car door a hare got up from the heather in front and the youngster joyfully started a riot. I hastily slipped a couple of cartridges into the barrels and fired. With the first shot I missed the hare. On pulling the second trigger there was a resounding bang, but nothing else. Examining my gun I found that the second barrel had blown open, fortunately some inches above my hand.

Now those barrels were old and thin, admittedly; much thinner indeed than I had ever imagined. But the only real explanation of that burst was carelessness on my part. There must have been a small wad of tow left in the barrel. Had I not been in a hurry and had I observed the usual precaution of glancing down the barrels in broad daylight, before loading, it would never have happened, if my guess as to the cause is correct. Familiarity breeds contempt. I thought I had already glanced down the barrels when assembling the gun, but that is no excuse. Fortunately there was no damage, except to the gun, but that is the way serious accidents happen. However accustomed one may be to handling guns and to observing the usual safety precautions, it only needs a moment's mental aberration or a moment's carelessness and the harm is done. Let no one adopt a 'holier-than-thou' attitude. It cannot be too often repeated, even *ad nauseam*, that a loaded gun is a lethal weapon and should at all times be handled with the utmost care.

Like drink and driving, drink and shooting do not mix. The party the night before had contributed to my carelessness and I was not surprised that the Italians failed to shoot more than ten brace of driven birds. To be fair, the birds would not move in that exceptional weather, or else they simply were not there. On the moor reserved for dogging only four and a half brace were shot, which was just about all we saw on a very long walk. Very expensive birds at four hundred pounds a week.

I suppose everyone knows the old chestnut about the game-keeper who attributed his longevity to always falling flat at the cry of 'Cock'. I am inclined to attribute my survival that day to falling flat whenever my dogs came on point and I heard the safety catches click. However, I liked the Italians, who were good sportsmen, but the 'country house atmosphere', stage managed with girl undergraduates in caps and aprons, was unlike anything I have ever known.

Thornton occasionally seems to have been careless with his guns, too, as one incident shows: 'A bird I had shot apparently dead, after lying some time, rose, while I was reloading, and, before I perceived it, was flying in my face; I struck at it with my gun and in this operation the rammer-rod flew out.' Sometimes an apparently 'dead' bird, which must have been only stunned, will fly off apparently unharmed, either before, or after, being picked. It is one of those things which happens occasionally, but it is not advisable to use guns as clubs even in those circumstances.

His remarks on his dogs are interesting and to the point. After lending a pair to his friend Mr Drighorn, who was a good shot, he went out with them himself and noted: 'The pointers soon stood and I came forward, but could not get a shot, except at a great distance, so much had Mr Drighorn's mode of shooting spoiled the dogs I had lent him I therefore caution gentlemen always to keep their own dogs scrupulously to themselves and to have a set allotted to strangers; for many good sportsmen differ in their manner of treating their dogs; some care not how their dogs behave, providing they can get shots.

'I conceive the great pleasure and elegance of shooting depends on the good order in which the dogs are kept.

'I never saw two dogs more savage; and though they never committed a fault unpunished, still it was above two hours before I could make them attend; they then behaved better, and I shot incomparably.'

A contrast with the last sentence was provided at the Duke of Gordon's later on, when he noted: 'My dogs were hunted, and gave satisfaction; we had very good sport. . . . I shot very indifferently, nor do I, in general, shoot well in company.' This is a familiar excuse of those who are accustomed to shooting alone.

It certainly seems as if Thornton preferred his sport with an eye on his dogs. Of particular interest was an allusion to netting over setters for the benefit of Mr Garrard, who had never seen this. It is the only reference to this form of sport, which seems to have been going out of fashion even then. Nowadays it is generally forgotten that originally the setter was intended for netting. Once he had 'set', i.e. pointed the game, the setter was expected to crouch down to allow the net to be drawn over him. The same instinctive reaction can still be seen in some working setters today.

According to his book it was the end of September before Thornton left Speyside and set off for the Duke of Gordon's castle at Fochabers. So much had been condensed from various years, however, that by this time his records were hopelessly confused. It is impossible to say when he really visited Grantown, his first stop on the way, where he found the inn 'very neat and clean, and so cheap a bill I scarcely ever met with'.

Chapter 8

A CAST FORWARD

A rule of life it is perchance,
Always to look a shade askance,
At men of small significance,
Who're full of pomp and circumstance.

Grantown to Forres and back to Speyside

Near Grantown Thornton noted: 'I was astonished to note how very much all ranks of people were changed in their manners in the course of ten or twelve years. Luxury and effeminacy have proportionately found their way hither, and through the facility of intercourse with the South, by means of the high military roads, have almost totally destroyed the power of the chieftains.'

There can be little doubt that by building his military roads Wade was the English General who did most to alter the Highland way of life after the '45. By providing a ready means of communication between North and South he effected a more permanent change than any physical suppression could have achieved. Instead of draining the manpower from the Highlands the new roads being built today are more likely to reverse the process and attract fresh blood and new industries to the Highlands, but they also are certain to cause permanent changes.

Beyond Grantown most of the Colonel's description of the route was borrowed straight from Pennant, except for one very characteristic touch: 'The moors seem very even and well adapted for shooting, which may be followed more conveniently here, on horseback, than in any place in Scotland.'

He went on: 'As I approached Forres, the road improved and

was crowded with numbers of country people, both men and women who adopt the Lowland fashions, the men not retaining the least mark of Highland dress, which is entirely exploded, except the bonnet, and even that has here a different shape, not near so smart as the Highland; and in their persons they want that lively gait peculiar to the Highlander; nor are the women, in my opinion, better featured.'

He made another mild slip in plagiarizing Pennant: 'Near Forres, on the roadside is a vast column, three feet ten inches broad, height twenty three feet. . . . This is called King Sueno's stone.' Thornton must certainly have been in Forres, and, when there, must just as certainly have seen the stone, but he had obviously forgotten that it lies on the other side of Forres to the Grantown road. Once again he was simply using Pennant as a handy means of reference to save himself bother when his memory failed him. He wrote at times like a man out hunting; determined to get there no matter how.

A more genuine entry was: 'On my entrance into Forres found there was a fair, which accounted for the crowd I had met on the road; and to their credit be it related, I did not see one person intoxicated.'

He stayed at the Falcon and in the company of his wine merchant 'Bailie Forsyth' passed a pleasant evening.

The stranger driving today from Newtonmore to Grantown, up the Spey valley, would observe the characteristics of this part of the countryside. It is formed, in effect, by a series of fertile basins in the hills joined together by short stretches of wilder moorland. The Spey itself, in a similar way, flows into quite considerable lochs, like Loch Insh, and then runs in narrower, faster rapids. After Dulnain Bridge it is not far to Grantown, and from there to Forres the road passes through wilder country once more, with rolling moorland stretching on either side, very gradually becoming agricultural again as the coastal belt is reached.

On the subject of Forres Thornton did not have much to say: 'The town is very moderate; it is seated under some little hills, which are prettily divided; there is not anything in particular worth seeing.' I myself found Forres a charming little town, well worth visiting.

It is, of course, noted for the famous 'blasted heath' near by, where Macbeth was reputed to have encountered the three witches. It is impossible to forget this association. Pennant mentioned it at length and Thornton copied him faithfully. It seemed, therefore, only fitting that the owner of the garage where we left the Rolls for the night should have been named Duncan. Although obviously a man who had started with horses he was duly appreciative of the car. Asked about King Sueno's stone he proved a mine of local information.

'Aye. You should see that', he ended. 'And the Witches' Stone too. Just down the road oppostie the police station.'

After giving the dogs a run in the pleasant little park, where there were flocks of oyster-catchers proclaiming the closeness of the sea, we went in search of these stones. Opposite the police station and sticking out of the ground beside the pavement we found the Witches' Stone, a large split boulder with an inscription on a plaque above it, reading matter-of-factly:

'Witches Stone. From Cluny Hill witches were rolled in stout barrels through which spikes were driven. Where the barrels stopped they were burned with their mangled remains. This stone marks the site of one such burning.'

Looking at it with interest we noticed the faded remains of some flowers, or weeds, placed carelessly on top of it like some childish bouquet flung down and discarded. And yet was it? Closer inspection revealed henbane and coltsfoot amongst others. Could it be that witchcraft still flourishes beneath the respectable façade of modern Forres? Outside the police station too! Was some outwardly respectable citizen still practising half-forgotten rites, or was it merely that someone was suitably remembering the anniversary of their less reputable ancestor's decease?

We went on to investigate the Sueno stone. A sandstone column carved with figures of men and beasts, it is supposed to commemorate the victory of Sweyn over Malcolm II. Though interesting enough, it did not hold such spectacular possibilities as a revival of witchcraft. Yet it would not be difficult to imagine weird figures dancing in the darkness round this queerly carved stone. The choice of this part of the world for the meeting of the three witches was not by any means accidental. There is still a certain atmosphere which is not entirely dispelled by the air of utter respectability which Forres now wears. Surely it is almost too good to be true, just a little too douce, solid and respectable? Surely there is a little original devil still lurking somewhere in the background?

We went on to take a look at Culbin Sands, the famous moving sands which have buried the ancient town and harbour of Findhorn and which, within living memory, have covered the house and estate of Culbin. At times these sands have been known to recede and the house has been completely exposed to view. However, as it was raining we did not get much of a view of them, but it was easy to appreciate how Forres must once have been a useful port. Now it is quite hard to visualize it as a coastal town at all. It gives more the impression of an inland market town, largely agricultural, without any connection with the sea.

From there we went towards Elgin, following Thornton's route closely. He observed: 'The land, in general, seemed to be in a high state of cultivation and lets at from three pounds ten shillings to four pounds an acre . . . it is a light sandy soil.' This is a description which has not altered in any respect, which, all things considered, is in itself remarkable. The rents of the land then seem to have been high compared with the general rise in financial values today. The land is still intensively cultivated and looked very similar in many respects to the land of East Lothian further south in a similar border belt.

Thornton next reached Elgin, which he treated unkindly. He dogmatized: 'All these towns, Inverness, Nairn, Forres, and Elgin, have a very dismal appearance, being built of dark stone; nor can they claim the merit of being clean, and, Elgin, in filthiness, exceeds them all.' He then included a large extract from Pennant on the merits of the cathedral ruins.

We did not stay long in Elgin, but we found it clean and trim and neat. It has a comfortable, prosperous and rather lazy, retired air. We had a good tea of buttered scones and toast, which some-how fitted in well with the faintly cathedral atmosphere that still hangs over the town. For anyone wanting to retire I can think of few better places than these towns which Thornton mentioned in such disparaging terms.

He then continued: A few miles up from Elgin . . . stands the abbey of Pluscardin, renowned . . . for its fruit trees. . . . They are all planted on circular causeways of flat stones. The bed of stones prevents the roots from striking downwards, giving them a hori-zontal direction. It is in a similar, though inverse ratio, that . . . fruit bearing trees, are greatly improved by . . . leading them by espaliers along the ground.'

It is of interest today to note that this abbey, having been in private hands, is once more the property of the Roman Catholic Church and is being rebuilt by an Order of Cistercian monks. Ac-cording to Mr Shaw, Minister of Elgin, quoted by Pennant, the last lot of monks there 'becoming vicious were expelled and other monks brought from Dunfermline'. There can be no doubt that Roman Catholicism has revived all over the country now in a way which would scarcely have been credited in Thornton's time, when 'Propery' was still suspect.

In this area the Colonel also noted that he 'was particularly happy in meeting with Lord Mountboddo, a gentleman of very excellent and uncommon abilities. No man surely was ever so enthusiastic an admirer of the ancients, whose manners he adopts in many pointed particulars. Whether it arises from this circumstance, or from natural good stamina. I know not, but I scarcely ever saw a man of his lordship's age, upwards of eighty, able to undergo the fatigue he sustained . . . several days together'.

From Elgin we turned aside to visit Mr Brander-Dunbar, a well-known local laird and possibly some distant relation of mine. We arrived outside his ivy-covered mansion and parked the car beside a heap of cannon balls surmounted carelessly by two small copper cannons and a rusty Lewis gun. At the door we were met by several of the old type of curly-coated retrievers, of which he breeds one of the few working strains left.

A short sturdy figure, with cropped hair, in a saffron kilt, the laird greeted us with Highland hospitality and led us into his house, where the walls display the results of a long life devoted to sport all over the world. They are literally covered with the heads of every imaginable type of shootable animal known to man. Nor was it difficult to get him to talk enthusiastically of them, once we had displayed our interest.

'Go up the stairs and have a look at the rhino's head on the landing,' he said. 'My first shot ricocheted off his horn—you can see the mark—and, if I hadn't dodged aside, he'd have had me. When he turned round to have another go I got him with the other barrel.'

He illustrated his movements with a nimble sidestep and pointed to the stairs. Sure enough, in the place of honour, at the head of the stairs was a baleful rhinoceros head of enormous proportions with a bullet mark showing clearly where it had glanced off the horn.

'Still go out wildfowling. Not bad for an old man of ninety, eh?' he declared enthusiastically. 'You'll have a wee something. Not teetotallers, I hope?'

Without waiting for a reply he poured out a generous tot apiece.

'You know I was the original of Buchan's John Macnab, I suppose,' he went on. 'Come and have a look at this.'

He led us into his inner sanctum, a glorious book-lined untidy room with comfortable arm-chairs round a littered desk and a memorable fug of leather, tobacco, tweed and dogs. On the wall was a good stag's head and under it a framed cheque for twenty pounds made out to 'B. Dunbar, Poacher'. He had made a bet with his neighbour and friend that he could shoot a stag on his ground undetected and on this incident John Buchan founded his book *John Macnab*.

Having won the bet and shot his stag he explained with gusto: 'I cut off the head and the testicles and sent them through the post with a label on them. He had to pay the postage.'

It is impossible to remain impervious to such a robust personality, or not to admire the remarkable agility and liveliness of this elderly laird. To look at him it is difficult to believe that he is within twenty years of eighty, let alone approaching ninety. For sheer virility and vitality he would be outstanding in company of half his age and as a raconteur and lively host it would be hard to find his equal anywhere.

It so happened that my companion, the East Anglian farmer, had been a Lieutenant-Commander in the Fleet Air Arm during the war and at this point he insisted on visiting the Fleet Air Arm Station at nearby Lossiemouth, where the C.O. was an old friend of his. Knowing something of naval hospitality it occurred to me that this might mean a somewhat protracted halt in our journey. Possibly it was just as well that the C.O. had left that morning to go down for the day to the Farnborough Air Display. Few things could better illustrate the changed travelling conditions since Thornton's day. Instead of taking several weeks to make the journey it is now possible to think in terms of covering over a thousand miles in a quick flight there and back, leaving after breakfast to have lunch, visit an air display and return in time for dinner.

In the course of my travels I made several visits to this part of the world, and on one of them we went along the coast through Buckie, Portessie and Portnockie. These small coastal villages merit Thornton's description of Inverness, Nairn and Forres. They are dirty, unattractive and smelly. In spite of new coats of paint on the buildings the nature of the inhabitants appears to have been affected by the appearance of their surroundings, or vice versa.

It is an interesting feature of travel in a vintage car of unusual design and colour that people in well-developed, healthy and prosperous areas tend to smile and even wave or cheer, as the car passes. In underdeveloped areas, on the other hand, they tend to scowl and mutter and even jeer. It seemed to us to be a sound index of the general living standards of the local inhabitants, and here, it is worth noting, they scowled and jeered.

We arrived at last at Cullen, a much pleasanter village, which was our objective. Here we visited the Countess of Seafield's factor,

Mr Ritchie. Unfortunately we were too late to see over Seafield House, another 'stately home', which is, I understand, well worth visiting. However, it was a bright sunny day and we did not regret the detour, although we made a point of taking the inland road back to Fochabers.

Here Colonel Thornton stayed with the Duke of Gordon, and described Gordon Castle at some length as one of the most magnificent buildings in Britain. He found life there the 'ne plus ultra of my wishes'. His only complaint was, 'it is astonishing how plain the country women are here; I did not discover one that was tolerable, except a very pretty girl we met on our return from the moors. . . I was much at a loss to account for this scanty distribution of beauty'.

Enquiring in Fochabers itself we learned that it was not too late to visit the Castle and that all we had to do was drive in through the gates. As the gates were shut, although we saw someone walk through, we enquired again, out of politeness, at the gatehouse. Rather to my surprise the girl who answered the door said firmly that it was absolutely forbidden to go through. I found this difficult to believe and enquired from whom I could get permission to enter. At this point her mother appeared and also maintained that it was absolutely forbidden. As, however, they would not give me the factor's name or telephone number, or the telephone number of Major-General Gordon Lennox, who now owns the Castle, it was soon obvious they were merely being obstructive.

'They're living in the house. You'd not like people driving up to look at your house when you're living in it?' the old woman argued.

'In the circumstances all I want is the telephone number and I will enquire for myself.' I replied. 'As you won't help me I will find out elsewhere and ask permission.'

'It's absolutely forbidden,' she shouted after me, but by this time I was bored with useless argument.

We retired to the nearest telephone and found that only the housekeeper was in the house. She seemed extremely surprised at anyone asking permission and informed us that we could certainly look over it. With this we returned and opening the gate drove down to the house without further parley at the gatehouse.

Amongst Thornton's descriptions were the phrases: 'This splendid residence, not yet quite completed . . . will be the most princely residence, when the whole of the extensive improvements are completed. . . . The whole front has an extent of more than five hundred and fifty feet.' It must clearly then have been a magnificent building in the making.

It is now the most appalling scene of desolation and modern ruin I think I have ever seen. Inevitably we were reminded of Shelley's *Ozymandias:*

'Look on my works, ye Mighty, and despair . . .'

All that remains of the 'whole front' is the semi-derelict stable block, the central tower surrounded by half-demolished ruins, and one remaining wing which has been converted into a house feasible to live in by modern standards. The tower, for some reason, has been scheduled as an ancient monument. Round it, in rooms open to the sky, gilded and fluted pillars remain as evidence of short-lived splendour. Grass grows waist high on once immaculate lawns and terraces, watched over by mouldering lions and dilapidated statues. Admittedly the work of demolition and clearing up is not yet finished, but it is a deadening spectacle.[22]

Returning to the gate we found it padlocked and the elderly termagant vindictive:

'My husband's away with the key to fetch the polis,' she said triumphantly.

I was not going to waste further time in ridiculous argument and I had not been in tanks during the war for nothing.

'Tell the police we will be delighted to see them at the inn,' I retorted, and got back into the car.

Swinging the wheel round I drove the old Rolls through a large hole I had seen in the wall about a hundred yards farther down. We then retired to the inn near by, where we had a dram to take the taste away. Needless to add, no police arrived.

Thornton had a similiar spot of difficulty at one point in his

Inverary Castle and Town, circa 1784, by Garrard

The Entrance into Kelso, circa 1784, by Garrard

Kelso. The Price of Progress, same viewpoint, 1959

Landing the Great Pike in Loch Petullich

journey, which he solved in his own way: 'Arriving at the gate . . .
we requested to be admitted; the gardener, who had attended us,
at first pretended to make some difficulty; he said he had positive
orders not to show the cascade without leave from his master, the
obtaining of which would have lost some time and much impeded
our schemes. . . . I adopted the usual recipe, and found means to
convince him of the impossibility of such an order. . . .'

While at the inn at Fochabers we decided to investigate the
landlord's shooting, which he offers to his guests. Meeting the
gamekeeper, Charlie Smith, by appointment, we went round with
him. It is an interesting shoot, being partly moorland, partly low
ground and with a lot of young plantations. We went round the
edges of the plantations and then back across part of the low
ground. Working three dogs together we had several excellent
points and when we came to a large field of roots the dogs were all
pointing and backing at practically every step. We flushed a
number of well-grown pheasants and also what looked like a
number of young capercailzies. When young they look very like
pheasants except for the squarer tail and clumsier flight.

Apparently a visitor from the South last year had three capercailzies in one day and departed highly satisfied.

'It's just as well you're not shooting with those dogs, though,
sir,' said Charlie Smith, 'or there soon wouldn't be enough game
left to last the season.'

It must be one of the problems of letting people come to shoot
in this way that one does not know the standards of the man shooting. He may be safe. He may be unsafe. He may be a brilliant shot,
or he may not. It must be a tricky task to make such a shoot,
where the standards and numbers of the guns are constantly
fluctuating, a sound and paying proposition. It seems to me that
it is done here, at Fochabers, as well as anywhere I know.

While I was there in August we saw some of the few salmon
caught. Four, including a grilse of eight pounds, were caught
near the mouth of the Spey. It is unfortunate that since a single
channel has been excavated at the mouth of the Spey the netting
has been very much too effective. The fishing has apparently

suffered throughout the length of the Spey as a consequence, apart from the effect of the abnormal drought.

It is regrettably easy nowadays with the power take-off on a modern tractor and very strong nylon nets to take more fish than by the old methods, when every spate meant stopping netting, or losing the nets. Now that improved methods of netting have become so efficient it is surely time for a revision of the netting time limits or at least for a more rigid enforcement of the present laws, which are frequently ignored or not properly enforced. Without greater control of river and estuary netting the Spey and many other rivers in Scotland are likely to be very adversely affected. In this connection it is interesting to note that on a commercial map of Scotland, dated 1760, there was a note to the effect that the Spey fisheries were 'farmed to London Fishmongers, who refuse to supply the inhabitants at any price'.

Fochabers itself is a pleasant enough, plain, small town. Its only real claim to distinction is that it was the first place in Great Britain to be lit entirely by electric light. It was at the inn there, on an earlier visit, that I fell into conversation, quite by chance, with an elderly sportsman in a well-worn Lovat tweed suit and matching deerstalker. The talk turned to the grouse prospects.

'The trouble is that I'm getting past a day on the moor,' he said regretfully. 'But if you'd like to shoot my moor any time, you're welcome to do so for the rent of a brace of grouse a day.'

I looked at him searchingly.

'I may take you up on that,' I warned him.

'I'll be pleased if you do,' he assured me.

'Right. You've got a deal,' I replied.

And that was how I came to have the shooting on a grouse moor not far from where Thornton shot.

On his way back from Fochabers to Raits, Thornton was nearly stranded at a very poor inn at Ballindalloch. 'It is really a perfect burlesque of the name;—a house with rooms, indeed, but no windows. I fancy the people, from their extreme poverty, had taken them out, as I observed many other more creditable persons had done, to save Mr Pitt's additional duty; which proves the folly of a heavy tax; for when severely felt, it will always defeat itself and be evaded.'

He pressed on and lost his way: 'I saw a young girl attempting to ford the Spey under the directions of another. Not seeing me, she made no ceremony, but came forward, till at last it proved so deep, had she got a glimpse of my carriage, which I had stopped (only to give my horses their wind) after a severe pull, I am apt to think she would have blushed for her situation. As I had not met above one or two persons for miles, the animation these females had given to the scenery, I felt with uncommon emotion.' He felt compelled, apparently, to add in explanatory brackets his 'only' reason for stopping. It is, however, another indication of the differences between travel then and now. Even with a very old Rolls it is not necessary to stop on hills to give it a rest. As a result one does not see so much of the countryside, but one covers more ground.

So it was that, having been flogging the waters of the Avon from four-thirty one morning until breakfast-time to no avail, I came to be working my dogs on a moor within ten miles of Ballindalloch. An acquaintance of mine, a surgeon from Ireland, and Mr MacNiven, landlord of the Richmond Arms at Tomintoul, were shooting over them and we were driving to Mr James Birnie of Dufftown, of the Lovat tweed suit and deerstalker, our host. On reaching the edge of the moor the dogs almost at once came on point, one in front of each gun. On command the dog in front of Mr MacNiven flushed a covey of grouse, from which he skilfully selected a right and left. At the shots the dog in front of the surgeon blotted her copybook by retrieving a young capercailzie which was over slow in rising from the heather. Unfortunately it had a leg broken and had to be added to the bag.

After that, without further mistakes, we had a very pleasant morning, though, as the sun mounted in the sky, it became hotter and hotter. The birds, unluckily for the surgeon, all broke in front of Mr MacNiven, who took his right and left with most admirable regularity. Finally we arrived across the moor where our host, Mr Birnie, was waiting for us. Not being used to pointer work he thought the dogs were ranging too wide, until a few moments later they came on point again. Unfortunately the sun and the wind were in our eyes and when the covey was flushed nothing was shot. However, he was more than satisfied thereafter and we had some excellent sport before adjourning for lunch.

Over our picnic lunch and beer the subject of poachers arose, and with a reminiscent twinkle in his eye our host told us of the day a kilted party had trespassed over his boundary from his neighbour's ground. When he rang up to complain that evening it was only to discover that his neighbour had been on the point of complaining to him under the impression it was his party.

'Yes. We were caught that time,' he admitted, with a smile. 'But there was another party I heard banging away on the moor one day. I saw their cars parked down here and I didn't feel like chasing away up after them, so I just sat down and smoked a pipe and waited for them. When they did finally come down I asked to see their bag and they had fourteen brace.'

'Had they, indeed?' said the surgeon. 'And what did you do then?'

'Oh. I took the grouse and gave them a brace for their pains and told them not to come back.'

One simply has to appreciate the touch about giving them a brace for their pains. I am happy to say that his rent was well and truly paid that day, and I think he had good sport himself, though the heat, as throughout most of the summer, was almost unbearable on the moors.

From there we followed Thornton back to Grantown and Raits where he made his preparations for leaving. It is noteworthy that he twice sent his servants home, and it was here that he finally parted from Mr Parkhurst, who seemed to have recovered from his mysterious illness and accompanied him on a few days' shooting and fishing around Dulnan and Glenmore.

Before leaving Speyside he recorded that he intended to send one of his dogs to Gordon Castle as a present. 'Wishing to have one day with Dargo before I sent him to Castle Gordon, I went out with him, and no dog ever behaved better; Pluto was still more fortunate, making five points in fifty-one more than he; though considering Dargo as an excellent dog, and Pluto to be merely a whelp, I had the greater hopes of the former. The birds were uncommonly wild, and except in deep ling, would not lie; I shot at great distances. Returns: shot twenty-nine moor-game; three snipes.' This is better than most of his days, but it indicates the sort of sport they had then. Considering that he would seem to have expected one misfire in at least three shots he must have been doing well. For instance the next day he chronicled: 'At eight good shots my gun mist fire, though I put in five different flints.'

Another interesting sidelight he cast on shooting in those days was on the effect of rain: 'I again wished to shoot, as it was then fair for a short time, but my rammer-rod was so swelled that it was impossible. However I then bethought me of using the cleaning rod, which answered the purpose.'

Before following Thornton to Moy Hall, which was his next stop, it is worth noting that he was given a goshawk, if not two, which had been bred in an eyrie in Rothiemurchus forest. He noted: 'In Rothiemurchos Forest are also some eyries of goshawks, some of which we saw. This hawk is very rare.' In fact it has not bred in Scotland for over a hundred years now, although imported birds are still frequently used by falconers.

I had hoped to arrange some hawking expeditions, but unfortunately, not having any hawks of my own, I found it too difficult to make arrangements for times and places which would fit in with my various journeys. I have therefore left most of Thornton's many hawking exploits unmentioned as I could draw no first-hand comparisons. I must, however, quote one entry:

'This day I had dedicated to public hawking, the amusement being little known here; about twenty-five people met on the field, more I believe to visit my kitchen, as I have since had reason to believe, than to see the hawks. We had some uncommonly good flights in front of the encampment, so that those sitting there might see the sport perfectly.'

These sporting exhibitions, in which he seemed to have taken particular pleasure, have no real parallel today apart from the

Game Fair. I took time off from my researches on Thornton to visit the Fair in the South, and again it was noticeable that the tremendous heat of the summer had in many ways had an adverse effect. The hawks in the enclosure devoted to falconry looked decidedly jaded, as did the game in their pens and the unfortunate dogs in their kennels. The crowds, on the other hand, certainly streamed to it, and since the basic idea is to publicize field sports, as well as to provide a centre for sportsmen, it could only be regarded as a considerable success.

On his road to Moy Thornton noted: 'Pass through the forest of Dulnon, near the new bridge (the former having been swept away, and the arch being stopt by a float of firs, improperly made, soon blew up the whole).' The practice then appears to have been to float timber down the Spey in the form of rafts whenever there was a suitable spate. I can imagine some objections being raised today, if anyone were to try this, but in those days it was the only feasible method of transport, as in Canada and elsewhere now.

Finally Thornton arrived at Moy, and here we have another perfect cross-check on his movements. Sir Aeneas Mackintosh of Mackintosh of Moy, who had been a captain in Fraser's Highlanders during the American War of Independence, had recently returned to his estate, and, for the first few weeks of his return in 1784, kept a diary, which has since been published. In it he mentioned Thornton's visit.

It should be borne in mind that, apart from the dates, Sir Aeneas Mackintosh's notes are not necessarily more accurate than Thornton's. In some respects, after comparing the two very carefully, I consider Thornton was the most honest. But compared with each other, representing diametrically opposed views of the same events, they make rather amusing reading.

Sir Aeneas noted, on September 21st, in Inverness: 'Met some English gentlemen who had come to shoot in and see the country. Anecdote. Being strangers they thought nothing could be got the other side of Edinburgh. They bought no less than 13 stone of powder and shot and sent it North, the carriage of which cost them £4, when they could have got it in Inverness.'

He went on: "22nd September: Return to Moy about half past seven in the evening. Colonel Thornton, an English Squire from Yorkshire, arrives in company with Mr Garrett, a landscape painter, after I had given over all hopes of seeing him, though they had promised being with me this night on the 15 at Aviemore.'

Thornton noted: 'Oct. 4th. Got to Moy about eight o'clock, and found the laird politely ready to receive us.'

Thornton continued: 'Oct 5th. Day continued showery until eleven, when I sailed out, accompanied by the laird, who, though no sportsman, was polite enough to show me the likeliest ground for black-game, by which act of civility he was more than once in danger of a fall; for, being mounted on an English gelding, not at all accustomed to wild moory ground, he found it no easy matter to follow my horses, real Highlanders, perpetually trained to the business.

'We found plenty of black-game and some moor-game, both of which, owing to the rain, were exceedingly wild. The black-game would not allow me to come near them, except in birch-cover, so thick that it was almost impossible to get a shot. With great labour however, I killed five, but lost one, which I saw fall near a stream, and suppose it must have floated down.

'Returns: black-game, five.'

Sir Aeneas noted, contrastingly: '23rd Sept. The Colonel goes a-shooting. Out of compliment I attend him on horseback through a rough moor to the West of the house covered with birch wood and shrubs. See from a dozen to fifteen black-game, of which he kills one, but by four, being tired and my leg very uneasy, return and obliged to wait dinner till seven in the evening.'

The next day Thornton went out to shoot a roebuck. It is clear from all his remarks on the subject of deer that he had no conception of deer-stalking in the modern manner. He chronicled: 'October 5th. Morning delightful. The laird's family do not rise with the lark, but take a comfortable nap; I therefore amused myself by ordering the nets to be cast into the lake to try for some char, and we caught a few very fine. . . . I now adjusted my bullet-gun, by which time the company came downstairs; and at twelve I went out, intending to try for a roebuck. . . . Saw one and got a glimpse of another at which I shot, and seeing one bound from the place feared he was only slightly wounded, for I was certain I had not missed him. . . . Found him dead, being shot through the heart. . . . Returned to the mansion, where the laird added much to the satisfaction my success had given me by the pleasure it seemed to afford him.'

Sir Aeneas on the other hand recorded: '24th Sept. The Colonel having applied for leave to shoot a roebuck, send my servant to attend him, and go myself to visit my farms in the neighbourhood, which I frequently do. Return by four when I understand that Thornton had killed a doe giving suck. I in consequence entertain him very coolly and form in my mind that it was the first and last he should kill any time he should be at my house. My observations on the subject to be enlarged.'

His remarks do not ring altogether true, however, for he continued the next day. 'Sept. 25th. From irregular hours and my chagrin at Thornton's behaviour obliged to lie in bed longer than usual. Thornton goes to Inverness and carries the doe with him. Yorkshire huntsmen, observations thereon. The Colonel makes present of the deer at Inverness instead of leaving her with me.' His diary shows he was used to irregular hours and seldom rose early. His 'chagrin' seems chiefly due to not receiving the roe deer himself.

Thornton continued: 'October 6th . . . being Saturday.' By reference to the perpetual calendar this would have placed the visit in 1787, but Sir Aeneas Mackintosh's September 25th was a Saturday in 1784. Therefore this record can undoubtedly be taken to relate to September 1784. Owing to Thornton having combined a number of visits his dates no longer bear any relation to reality.

Before leaving Moy the Colonel referred to meeting his 'old acquaintance the Reverend Mr Gordon. This gentleman has a very mechanical turn of mind and has made himself a very good electrifying machine. He is a young man remarkably modest in his deportment and in every sense keeps up the character and decency consistent with his profession; but, being fond of fishing his parishioners find fault with him; however he has the resolution and good sense not to give up so innocent an amusement on account of their bigotry and folly'.

Today, any clergyman whose parishioners objected to his fishing would certainly consider himself hard done by and would probably take the first opportunity of moving to another parish. With the name of Gordon in this part of the world it is probable that Thornton's acquaintance was some relation of the Duke of Gordon and as such his living would in any case have been a sinecure. As with the Church of England, the livings were then frequently the property of the local landlord to dispose of as he pleased.

When we visited Moy at the kind invitation of Mrs Mackintosh we learned something of the history of the estate since Thornton's visit. There remains only one rather crude drawing of the house Thornton described as 'a very comfortable habitation'. It appears to have been a four-square box of a building. It was burnt down prior to the end of the century and Sir Aeneas Mackintosh then erected, some distance behind the site of the old one, a new building, which can only be described as 'Scottish Baronial' at its worst. It bristles with turrets and Gothic arches.

The subsequent history of this building is a sorry one. The level of the loch was lowered artificially to 'improve the view'. This had the effect of drying out the foundations and parts of the house sank, causing great cracks in the structure. Following this, in due course, dry rot set in, and now the turreted pile remains standing deserted and the present Mackintosh of Mackintosh has a new and pleasant small house almost on the site of the original one.

We investigated Sir Aeneas Mackintosh's edifice. Through the large front doors standing open on the hallway the distinctive smell of dry rot permeating the building came out to us. Inside on the right, with the floorboards torn up, there is a large room where, over the mantelpiece, in the place of honour, must have reposed the two swords referred to by Pennant: 'The sword of James V, given by that monarch to the Captain of the Clan Chattan. That of the gallant Viscount Dundee is also kept there.' Such enormous double-handed exhibits are awkward things to display on the walls of a modern room and they are now relegated to a glass case above the umbrella stand in the hall of the new house.

Although a sad spectacle, as any such recent ruin is liable to be, this was not somehow quite the same depressing sight as Gordon Castle. This, one felt, would have happened anyway in the nature of things and was not in any way hastened by the times we live in. Nor does one feel that a great deal has been lost with its decay.

Shortly before our visit, apparently, Mr G. Friend of the physiology department of Edinburgh University had been netting Loch Moy to obtain specimens of char. He told me that they had found it surprisingly difficult at first. However. with practice they had improved and their results latterly had been very successful. Starting with only one or two char to a cast they had ended with over twenty a time; more than enough for their laboratory work. Judging by his comments Thornton did not do so well.

On leaving Moy Thornton referred to the ride to Inverness as 'being over the most dreary, barren country ever beheld'. This is certainly not so today. The road runs through some extremely attractive countryside, and coming down the steep slopes above Inverness especially there are some wonderful views right across the Firth to the Black Isle on the other side with the blue hills shimmering in the distance beyond.

Chapter 9

SOHOWE

Many's the lad fought on that day,
Well the Claymore could wield,
When the night came silently lay,
Dead on Culloden's Field.

SKYE BOAT SONG

Inverness to Fort William

A large part of Thornton's description of Inverness and its environs is taken directly from Pennant, but there is one notable omission. He made no mention of Culloden Moor, the graveyard of the old clan system, where the final curtain fell on the '45 and the scene was set for a new age in the Highlands. It may be that he never went there, or it may be that his memory failed him and that, for once, he did not feel justified in copying from Pennant. The latter's brief account of the battle and the 'Pretender's' alleged cowardice is so blatantly biased that the Colonel, with his Highland sympathies, probably baulked at including it. I was delighted to see in the margin of the copy of Pennant's *Tour* in the National Library of Scotland the annotation in faded ink opposite his comments: 'A lye!' Today Culloden Moor is one of the National Trust for Scotland properties.

From this direction the entry into Inverness itself is marred by a remarkable assortment of what can only be described as hovels. This gipsy encampment is something of an eyesore and it is scarcely an introduction to the county town that Inverness can wish to boast of to strangers. Not much better than the bothies Thornton described and sheltered by the railway embankment, they give a clear illustration of the meaning of the Americanism 'the wrong side of the tracks'. However, it may be that Inverness cherishes the right of the individual to choose the way he should live more than it desires to alter the lives of all to a drab uniformity and, if that is the case, perhaps Inverness has a point.[23]

One of the Colonel's comments, which had the genuine Thornton ring to it, is worth noting: 'The tradesmen, who are reputable and substantial, are very polite, and desirous to render every service in their power to strangers.' One can see them rubbing their hands at the advent of the rich English Colonel with his orders for reindeer tongues, Yorkshire hams and other delicacies: not to mention his almost insatiable demand for wines and porter. It is clear from Sir Aeneas Mackintosh's notes that they were used to importing anything that was required from the South and that, even then, the capital of the Highlands was a thriving commercial centre.

Today Inverness still conveys an impression of busy hurlyburly. It strikes one at once as a merchant town that has consistently over the years made a living out of buying and selling, packing and dispatching, importing and exporting. Yet withal it has a Highland leisureliness and something of the withdrawn and retired look of Elgin, although that is clearly a cathedral town, whereas there is a bracing air about Inverness which is not easily associated with the cloister.

This is still the 'Gateway to the Highlands' and therefore it should have an air about it that is difficult to define. Where else could you find a town where, if you are lucky, you can catch a salmon almost in the main street. Junction of both land and sea routes, at the head of the beautiful Caledonian Canal, there is no doubt that Inverness is different, even though at the first casual glance it might be just another busy market town.

Thornton repeated, from Pennant, the old story about the speech of the people of Inverness. 'The people of Inverness speak both Erse and English, the latter with remarkable purity; partly because they learn it, not from vulgar conversation, but from book, as we do Greek and Latin; partly, it is said, because English garrisons, from the time of the civil wars, having, in a great measure, given the tone, in respect to diction and pronunciation, to the neighbourhood of this natural barrier between the northernmost and the middle division of Scotland.'

It has never been my experience that soldiers were particularly skilled as elocution masters, and in those days, when they were inclined to be recruited from the rabble who were unemployable in any other capacity, I cannot believe they were liable to pass on any 'purity of diction'. However, where Gaelic is still the basic tongue and English is acquired there is admittedly an absence of accent, beyond the natural lilt of the Gael. This is no longer apparent in Inverness, where the influence of the B.B.C. and the influx of tourists has now reduced the standard of speech to the common low.

Thornton also noted from Pennant: 'The principal business carried on by the town's people is the spinning of thread, making linen and woollen cloth for their own consumption and cording and sacking for exportation. Several large buildings have been erected for those purposes and much business is carried on in private houses. The rest of their exports are chiefly salmon (those of the Ness, being esteemed of more exquisite flavour than any other). . . . The linen manufacture, however, is the most considerable and saves the place above three thousand pounds a year which used to go to Holland for that article.'

The centre of the jute industry is now Dundee, but it is interesting to note that Holland had lost a trade with this part of the world. It may be that the Dutch who emigrated to this coast in some numbers during the days of religious persecution in Holland a century earlier brought this industry with them. There is still a noticeable difference between the inhabitants of some of the coastal towns between Inverness and Aberdeen and those of the surrounding countryside which is also reflected in the prejudices of some older Scots. It is noteworthy that Thornton saw a considerable difference between the inhabitants of these towns and the 'Highlanders'.

After dining off Sir Aeneas Mackintosh's roe deer in Inverness,

Thornton set off the following morning along the side of Loch Ness for Fort Augustus. Although he dated it October 7th it was probably only towards the end of September, but he noted the corn was only half cut and 'I am told the grain raised here scarcely suffices for the inhabitants'. He went on: 'The scarcity of corn is well illustrated by a circumstance . . . which is not a little curious. It is common . . . to start a number of domestic fowls like partridges. These creatures, which travel many a mile . . . and like the cattle of the country do not find sustenance within a narrow compass, being equally lean and vigorous, will spring into the air and fly over an incredible space, cackling like a parcel of wild geese.'

I doubt if this is common today, but on some hill crofts it might still be the case. I do remember thirty years ago being impressed by the powerful flying abilities of some of the hens I met in the Highlands, but I was not then old enough to judge accurately whether this was an isolated phenomenon or a common one. As a sidelight on the condition of the cattle it is an interesting entry.

Thornton mentioned also: 'Fifty thousand head of black cattle, it is computed, are driven annually from the northern counties of Inverness, Ross, etc., into England.' Pennant mentioned that from Lochaber alone three thousand head were sent out annually, but that with the addition of part of Inverness-shire ten thousand, so that Thornton's figures may not be so far out. Even if one accepts twenty-five thousand head as a more accurate assessment it is still a considerable figure.

It is worth just pausing for a moment to consider the picture this provides of a cattle-producing Highlands. The early Highland chieftains were judged by the number of fighting men they could produce to follow them. After the '45 it came to be the number of cattle they could produce and then the cattle were slowly replaced by sheep. Finally the sheep gave way to the sporting deer forests of the Victorian era.

Today we have the anachronism that the Highlands are supporting a deer population, which, though smaller than before the war, is computed variously at from 120,000 to 200,000 head. Yet venison is not popular in this country, and to obtain a reasonable price it has to be exported to the Continent, where it is canned, and even, on occasions, returns in that form to this country. Around 14,000 head are shot on average each year, and, if one accepts an overall average of three per rifle, then these deer are being supported merely for the benefit of some 4,600 people.

This, of course, is putting the matter far too baldly and it is not nearly as simple as that. There is, however, no doubt that the situation at the moment has got completely out of hand. At present there are too many deer and, due to lack of proper control during the war years, too many poor deer, which are merely a liability. Deer poaching of the most brutal and appalling kind has been carried on for a number of years. It was, however, this last factor which may indirectly have led to some solution of the problem. Due in part at least to the public outcry against this, the Deer (Scotland) Act was passed.

By this, at long last, a close season has been decreed and the police now have greater powers to deal with poachers. A Deer Commission has also been constituted with powers to order the reduction, or extermination, of deer in an area where they have caused damage to agriculture or forestry. This is a start.[24]

With considerable areas afforested and others taken over by hydro-electric schemes, apart from the expansion of agriculture, the total acreage suitable for deer has decreased considerably since before the war. Hardly anyone nowadays feeds the deer in winter, but it is still reckoned that it requires about twenty-five head of deer to produce a shootable stag each year. It is therefore arguable that deer are an expensive method of producing a meat which the public has not been educated to want, that is only available fresh from September to October 10th, and that cattle ranching on the scale started by Lord Lovat is a more suitable method of using the land today.

It must be remembered, however, that not all the land is suitable for afforestation or cattle. Much is really only suitable for deer, which are indigenous to the country and have always been there in some numbers. Deer-stalking is a tourist attraction and is one that could be considerably more publicized. I am sure that many people would like to shoot a stag if they knew how to set about doing so. Kept within reasonable bounds the red deer of Scotland can still be a considerable asset.

Another point, which Thornton mentioned outside Inverness, is of interest in view of the often repeated assertion of the time that there were no trees in Scotland: 'The large plantations of firs, intermixed with oaks, render the scene here truly magnificent; and on approaching Loch Ness, a wonderful piece of water, the road runs winding along the shore.' The mention of 'firs intermixed with oaks' is interesting. In recent years it has been Forestry Commission policy to concentrate purely on quick-growing conifers. There was a good deal of opposition to this undue concentration on soft woods and it was finally proved that mixed woodlands stand up to winds and weather better than plantations of one type.

It was on this road on one occasion that I saw, by the light of the headlights, what may have been an ordinary tabby bounding across the road; but from its suspiciously bushy tail I took it to be a wildcat. These are now back in quite considerable numbers in places in the Highlands, as the Forestry Commission consider that they do more good than harm in killing rabbits and similar pests in plantations and therefore do not attempt to check them. In practice the Forestry Commission has areas too large to hope to control them properly, and foxes and other vermin abound in most of their woods.

Up to the first world was the wildcat and the marten were becoming almost extinct, having been largely killed off by game-keepers. Since then they have gradually returned, and, though martens are still extremely rare, there are frequent reports of wild-cats. The true wildcat is probably a rarity, but there is little doubt that tame house cats gone wild have interbred with the old wildcat with the typical bushy tail and their progeny are not uncommon: larger and a good deal leaner than a house cat, they are extremely fierce.

Thornton had an interesting note at one point on the subject of wildcats: 'The dogs ... got upon something, I could not tell what, which they footed a considerable way, and by the bristles rising on their backs, I plainly perceived it was not game, but vermine. Conceived it to be a wild cat, or martin, which in these moors abound, and should have been particularly pleased to get a shot at it, but it escaped me. The wild cats here are very large, nearly the bulk of a middling sized fox, remarkably fierce, and very destructive to game and lambs. Their brush is nearly as thick as that of the fox.' It is a thing that not everyone appreciates, but a pointer will in fact point on foxes, deer and cats.

Nowadays another predator that may be found occasionally is the wild mink which has escaped. Like the coypu, which is now found in considerable numbers in the South, these have not yet penetrated to the Highlands. They are, however, occasionally reported in the Lowlands.

The most famous denizen of this part of the world, of course, is the noted Loch Ness Monster. It is easy to laugh at this and set the whole thing down to imagination. Unfortunately certain notoriety-hunters in the thirties made it the subjects of their hoaxes and the whole matter at one time became a Press joke, from which, in some people's minds, it has never recovered. Why, it might be argued, if there is something there has it not been photographed more effectively than has so far been the case? Surely by now more concrete evidence of its existence could have been produced, at least one good photograph.

However, I am prepared to wager that if any sceptic were prepared to live for twelve months in one of isolated crofts or cottages on the side of the loch he would no longer scoff. It is easy to be mistaken, agreed. We saw a boat tossing on the waves, appearing one moment, disappearing the next, and for a moment it might have been anything. But Loch Ness is a loch in which there might well be anything.

The weight of evidence about the 'monster' is too great to dismiss it as mere mass hallucination. Too often it has been seen by acknowledged sceptics and others who by no stretch of the imagination could be accused of lying. It has even, and not many people appreciate this, been the subject of an organized watch by a series of watchers posted at suitable vantage points round the loch. It was seen and noted by every watcher.

It is obvious enough that if there is anything there it is extremely shy and elusive as well as rare, but it should be easy enough to obtain a good photograph of it, if suitable measures are taken. It would involve a certain amount of preparation and considerable expense, but it could be done. The system of watchers stationed at key points in contact with each other by short-wave radio sets would be the first step. A yacht moored in the middle of the loch or off a suitable point would be the control centre. In a convenient field a small plane of the Piper Cub type would be standing ready. At the first report of a sighting the pilot could take off and planing over the spot could obtain a close-up picture. For what it is worth, that is the answer to obtaining a worth-while photograph of whatever there may be in the loch. After that, it would be up to the scientists to argue about what it is. I am not prepared to give any views on that, but as regards photographing it, if there is anything there I am sure it could be done as suggested.

Thornton next mentioned the waterfall at 'Fiers', meaning Foyers. He described an anecdote about a previous visit when he had crossed the falls on 'a rough unpolished fir-tree laid across' followed by 'a favourite pointer'. The dog refused to return and 'I very cautiously began to recross, taking Ponto in my arms . . . about half way over, the dog, through fear, sprang from me. I luckily fell flat on the fir, and throwing my arms and legs across, continued passively in this situation for some minutes, till . . . I recovered my alarm, and crawled very slowly. . . . It seems that on my falling, he (the dog) at one bound from the fir had made an immense leap and got safe; but he was so terrified, that he avoided us, and we found him waiting for us with the horses.' ·

Having dramatized his own escape, Thornton had the grace to add: 'A more foolish attempt was never made. I apprehended, at the time, that some person would perish there.' He then mentioned: 'a gardener . . . being with some friends at a burial, when, agreeable to the custom of the Highlands, they generally drink freely . . . left the company, taking his dog with him, tied by his garter; some little time after the dog returned, and making a piteous moaning, too plainly indicated what the *circle* suspected that he had fallen into the dreadful chasm . . . thirteen months elapsed before his remains were discovered.'

In a footnote he added: 'The custom of inviting the friends and neighbours of the deceased to make merry at funerals is not confined to the Highlands, but prevails . . . in some parts of the North of England. The company usually sit round the corpse in a circle. . . .'

While as far as I know this is no longer the case, a funeral in the Highlands is still usually an occasion for some heavy drinking and the burial is generally only attended by men.

We visited the Falls of Foyers, but owing to the unprecedented drought there was barely a trickle coming over them. A burst water main or even a bath unplugged would have provided a more spectacular flow of water. Matters were so bad that when we visited the Flichity Inn in the hills near by on the same day we found it closed because they had no water left at all. A shooting party staying with them had used the last of their supplies.

The inn at Foyers is a pleasant and attractive one, with a fine view of the loch and good fishing facilities. Farther on the inn at Whitebridge is also an excellent centre for fishing. Thornton missed a splendid opportunity for sport when he passed by here without fishing. All he seems to have done was to ask a Highlander who could not speak English 'What fish were taken in the two lakes we saw?' only to learn 'that they were full of black and white fish'.

From the point of view of beauty this road on the south side of the loch is much preferable to the newer road on the north, but it is mostly single track with passing-places and is not for those in a hurry. The entrance downhill into Fort Augustus is much more impressive than the approach by the other road which winds round the end of the loch and arrives on the same level. Viewed from above, Fort Augustus can be seen lying at the foot of Loch Ness, the monastery, which now incorporates some of the old fort in its buildings, standing out conspicuously with the Abbot's yacht at anchor near the small pier in front of it. Apart from the monastery and a few hotels and Forestry Commission cottages there is little more to Fort Augustus today.

On his arrival Thornton met the Duke and Duchess of Gordon and the Duke informed him that the Government had abandoned Fort William. He commented: 'These Forts are numerous and useless and I trust this economical plan will be followed up with respect to many others.'

He noted: 'The mountains extending from Fort Augustus have a manifest advantage in point of profit over those of Badenoch being covered with a fine verdure and a numerous breed of cattle far superior to any I have seen in Scotland; but in point of beauty and pleasure, the Badenoch country far exceeds these hills, which are spongy and the climate rainy.'

On my first expedition round this part of the route, although not actually raining here, the mist was such that I could barely see the hills or more than a few hundred yards on either side of the road. In the sunlight, however, it is, in spite of Thornton's comments, a beautiful countryside; very different from Badenoch, admittedly, but still very beautiful.

Leaving there, the Colonel noted: 'Loch Oich is a very delightful finely-broken piece of water.' He also noted the 'ruins of the castle, burnt in the year 1745'. Going down the side road, which leads to the ruins and to the Glengarry Castle Hotel, we noticed, quite by accident, what I think is one of the most impressive village war memorials I have seen. The Scots have a genius for commemorating their slain in stone, as anyone must agree who has seen the memorial chapel in Edinburgh Castle with the solid chunk of native granite bursting through the marble in front of the altar. Here, at the union of the two side roads, a massive rough-hewn boulder of granite projecting from the embankment is inscribed with a plain plaque and a roll of honour. Its stark simplicity gives it an arresting impression of dignity.

Captain Hunt, the proprietor of the inn at Invergarry a little farther on, makes a feature of offering stalking to his guests. The fishing, which he has in Glengarry, has undoubtedly been affected by the hydro-electric scheme there, but in this instance it may be argued that in some ways the fishing has been improved since the river is now no longer dependent on the weather, as the level of the water is controlled artificially. We are then getting into the tricky questions of stale water and artificial spates, but there are grounds for argument either way, Certainly the salmon fishing may not be as good as when the Duke of Portland had it before the war. The beauty of the river, too, in many ways has been lost, but there are still salmon to be caught, and while I was there on one occasion considerable execution was being done amongst the trout in Loch Quoich.

I have a friend who has fished these waters both before the war and since the hydro-electric scheme, and, of course, in the manner of all who look back on past days, he is not prepared to admit that the fishing is as good today, yet the fact remains that he still goes there and still catches fish. I would certainly advocate that no one be put off by reports that the fishing here has been affected in the same way as the fishing on the Garry in Perthshire. It has not. This is one hydro-electric scheme which has not had the dire results prophesied by the Jonahs.

On one of my journeys round this part my friend and I were stranded at this point with darkness upon us and every inn full. We finally found a Forestry Commission croft with a bed and breakfast sign and spent the night there. It turned out that our landlady had been a nurse evacuated from Eastbourne during the war, who had married a forestry worker and remained North ever since. We spent a very comfortable night. Apart from a slightly understandable objection to 'people who hang up their things to dry in my bathroom', she apparently enjoyed taking guests and found it a paying proposition, although we were given comfortable beds, clean sheets and an admirable breakfast for a matter of twelve and sixpence apiece.

Farther along the road, above Spean Bridge on a splendid vantage point overlooking the countryside, is the Commando Memorial. It consists of three larger than life-size figures in Commando garbo, with an inscription:

To the Officers and Men of the Commando who died in the 39–45 War.

This was their training ground.

United we conquer.

I am perhaps biased in that the only ex-Commando I know well is a particularly small man, though broad in proportion. Admittedly the first time I saw this group in swirling mist and darkness it loomed impressively above me, but perhaps the setting is too magnificent. In daylight, somehow, it is just another memorial, rather well placed. Seen in a mist or in the gathering twilight, it is, like the Commandos themselves, at its best.

Passing on from there over Spean Bridge, which Thornton mistakenly noted as being over the Brander, not the Spean, we turned up Glen Roy towards the parallel lines, or roads. Thornton recorded: 'We took a view of the parallel lines ... passing by some very picturesque finely winding glens, ornamented with an infinite variety of different kinds of wood, with many waterfalls; and a quantity of deep dark lins, i.e. deep basons excavated by falling water. So called in Scotland.' Like many another short entry of his this turned out to be well worth pursuing.

The approach to the parallel lines, or roads, along a single-track road, is still as he described it, probably unchanged since his day. It is extremely beautiful. Finally one arrives at a modern tarmac car park thoughtfully provided by the Scottish Tourist Board. From here there is an excellent view of the parallel lines, which are a perfect example of the effect of glacier movement in the Ice Age, when this was the basin of a vast lake. They were originally thought to be man-made roads.

It is interesting to note that Pennant and Sir Aeneas Mackintosh both quoted the theories that they were built either by the Romans in a bid to conquer this part of Scotland, or else by some powerful early chieftains to provide suitable roads for hunting game. Sir Aeneas added cannily: 'But what conjecture is just, I cannot pretend to say.'

While we were sitting here enjoying the view in the sunlight a figure on a bicycle came towards us; a weatherbeaten clear-eyed man of the hills. He was wearing an old pair of plus-fours of faded tweed and a tattered blue denim jacket with a telescope in a leather case slung round his shoulders. Dismounting from his bicycle, he sat down near by and we started a conversation with him.

'No sign of any grouse,' we commented, by way of an opener.

'No. There are no grouse left hereabouts,' he agreed. 'There are ptarmigans on the hills there, but a long way up'.

'How do you get the sheep in?' we asked.

'Well, there will be a dozen or more of us, maybe. Each with our dogs. Then one or two will be acting as stops and the rest will drive the hillside down to them with the dogs and in that way we get them in before the weather breaks.'

'You've a croft up here then?'

'Aye. But how long that will be, goodness knows. The Forestry Commission is wanting to take our good grazing land for trees, instead of planting on the high lands where it might be some use to us as shelter belts and where the grazing is not so good. Then, when we've no land worth grazing we'll have to sell our sheep and take jobs with them looking after their plantings. It's the great land we live in. They'll be buying our crofts from us and then selling them back as long as we agree to work for them so many days in the year. But what's the use of a croft without the land to go with it?'

'What about the Crofters Commission?' we asked.

'Ah, yes. The Crofters Commission is supposed to be protecting our interests, but they've never even discussed the matter with us. First of all the Nature Conservancy people said the parallel roads were too valuable a geological formation to have trees planted on them, so now the Forestry Commission wants the low ground and the Crofters Commission is doing nothing to stop them. They promised us a land fit for heroes after the first war. Well, I've one son in the R.A.F. and he's not wanting to come back. The other is out now and back with me working the croft, but the way it is there's no future in it.'

This was a fresh angle on the familiar tug of war between committees which bedevils most issues in the Highlands. In the circumstances it was not surprising that he was bitter about the Forestry Commission. We had not noted any great love for it even amongst its workers. We steered the conversation round to the animals of the countryside.

'I'm over seventy, mind you, and I've only three times seen an eagle take a lamb. Once before the first war, then once shortly after and the last seven years back. . . . The first time I'd ever seen a badger was just the other year. I'd never heard of them in these parts before.'

We parted from Mr Angus Campbell with regret. He is a clear-sighted, clear-headed product of his native hills and it would be a tragedy if the march of progress ousted him and his kind; the sort of man whose sons make Air Marshals, Archbishops and sometimes even Prime Ministers.

It was up Glen Roy that we heard of a forty-two pound salmon sniggled by a poacher in the upper reaches in 1947; the biggest fish heard of in those parts for many years. It was here also that we heard the story of the poacher who regularly sold his salmon at the inn. One year the inn took the fishing and shortly afterwards he appeared as usual.

'Would ye be wanting a fush?' he asked.

'Oh, yes, I think so,' agreed the landlord. 'Where did you get it?'

'Just down the water. . . . Och, dammit. I'd clean forgotten you'd taken it yourself.'

Out of sheer amusement the landlord gave him two shillings a pound for it, but the same man told us that in an effort to curb the poaching he had offered the locals free fishing. None of them would take advantage of the offer. They preferred the illegality of sniggling their fish and in the end the innkeeper had to give it up as not worth the candle. As, however, he was offering a market to the poachers in the first place I have no great sympathy with him.

It is unfortunately the case that by Scots Law it is legal to fish for brown trout anywhere in Scotland, and the result is that, on many of the large lochs, bus parties arrive at the week-ends and spin or fish with worm at their pleasure. Unless an interdict is obtained, which is a lengthy and expensive business, nothing can legally be done to stop them. This is just one of the anachronisms of the law as it stands at present. Any poacher who cares to do so may freely fish any water, where he is not actually trespassing, under the guise of lawful fishing for brown trout. It is time this loophole was stopped before more waters are grossly over-fished by these week-end bus parties, who descend like locusts on the countryside, to take full advantage also of Scotland's absurd licensing laws, whereby inns are allowed to sell 'alcoholic refresh-ment' on the Sabbath to 'travellers only'.[25]

After crossing Spean Bridge the next impressive feature of the countryside is the 'Great Glen Ranch' running alongside the road for some miles almost into Fort William and suitably posted with large signs proclaiming what it is. This venture in ranching cattle on a considerable scale in the Highlands, which has met with the success it deserved, was started after the war by Mr Hobbs, of Inverlochy, and Lord Lovat. The buildings, all distempered a particular shade of yellow, not unpleasant although slightly bilious, make it easy to identify the property. The cattle are to be seen grazing in herds, by the roadside or in the distance. Loading ramps built at intervals and neatly hung gates proclaim the efficiency with which this concern is run.

Colonel Thornton appears to have foreseen the possibilities of some such scheme: 'Everything for the comfort of life may be had in the Highlands at least nine months in the year, superior, if not to all, to most other countries. Nature has given to the face of the country a large proportion of barren heath, but in the valleys every luxury of animal food and that of the most excellent kind, abounds during the winter months. Indeed, the mountain cattle are too fat in summer; and, with a little attention and some expence, might, no doubt, be enjoyed during the whole winter, as they suffer less from the snows than might be imagined. The tops of their lofty mountains are certainly buried, as it were, in eternal snows; but their altitude does not affect the valleys; and here,

being protected by immense mountains, clothed with impene-
trable forests, they are warmer than in most situations.'

According to Pennant an early example of the 'protection racket'
now prevalent in America used to flourish in this part of the
country and appears to have been organized on an exactly similar
basis. It may even have been one of the origins of the word 'black-
mail'. He chronicled: 'A contribution, called the *Black-meal*, was
raised by several of the plundering chieftains. . . . Whoever paid it
had their cattle ensured, but those who dared to refuse it were sure
to suffer.' Any such approach to Mr Hobbs, with his colourful
background of rum-running during prohibition days, or for that
matter to Lord Lovat, would not, one feels, have been likely to
succeed.

On the other side of the road on the way to Fort William can be
seen the three great pipes carrying the water supply of the North
British Aluminium Company from Loch Laggan down to their
factory on the outskirts of the town. Apparently this was the one
site in Great Britain where they could obtain a suitable volume of
water for their needs. My scientific friend who was with me on one
of the journeys I made round this district extolled the whole thing
as the outstanding engineering feat it no doubt is. To me, purely as
an observer of the results, it seems they have made a mess of the
countryside. Yet, oddly enough, those three vast pipes winding
along the hillside and turning abruptly above Fort William to
sweep down to the factory are not without their own peculiar form
of beauty. Basically, however, they are a man-made excrescence
and the countryside would be better without them, for their
beauty, such as it is, depends on the nature of the ground in the
first place. Were it not for the hill they would simply be three
crawling monster drainpipes.

Above Fort William looms Ben Nevis, reaching ruggedly to the
clouds. The point about the Highlands which is often overlooked
is not so much the fact that the mountains are large. They are, of
course, far smaller than the Swiss Alps, for instance, but there
comes a stage when any mountain is large enough to impress,
especially if one starts to climb it. The whole scale of the Highlands

is sufficient to be impressive in itself, but it is the infinitely varying effects of colour which are really most appealing; the deepness of the blues in the West, the variations of the purples and the saffrons in the East, the ever-changing kaleidoscope of colour, not only throughout the seasons, but from hour to hour. That is the secret of their attraction both to the stranger viewing them for the first time and to the native and the reason why it is impossible ever to tire of them.

Thornton noted: 'About a mile from Fort William is Inverlochy, an old castle with large round towers.' A new castle has been built near the ruins of the old one and is now the home of Mr Hobbs. The headquarters of his ranching enterprise are close by and the North British Aluminium Company buildings and factory are situated almost immediately beyond. Above it all broods Ben Nevis, magnificent and untouched.

Thornton went on to mention particularly the salmon fisheries here: 'Two hundred barrels, containing from twenty-five to twenty-seven fish have been taken in one year, which is reckoned very successful fishing. These barrels have occasionally sold as high as seven pounds. . . . This fishery is farmed for a rent of one hundred and fifty pounds per annum, including land to the value of fifty pounds per annum more. The fishery, there is every reason to suppose, would be very profitable, if means were taken to fish the river properly, which does not at present appear to be the case.'

Thornton's conclusions on this point are not likely to be disputed. By simple arithmetic it would seem that the fisheries should have made something like a clear hundred per cent profit each year. They are now, I believe, in the hands of the go-ahead Mr Hobbs and are no doubt still proving profitable. Certainly salmon fishers farther up the river have complained that it is no longer worth fishing the river owing to the netting which is practised farther down and to the water abstraction of the North British Aluminium Company.

It is interesting that in his diary of 1784 Sir Aeneas Mackintosh noted the presence in Fort William of a Dr Anderson, who was prospecting the ground for the Caledonian Canal and who had estimated its cost at about £60,000. Today the ideal way to see the stretch of country between Inverness and Fort William is to travel in a yacht down the canal. It is surely one of the most lovely inland voyages one can make, with long stretches of open water and glorious scenery on either hand.

Fort William itself lies in a hollow below Ben Nevis. Having told us earlier that it had been abandoned by the Government, Thornton forgot himself again and quoted Pennant to the effect that 'there are now two companies of infantry in it; the hills near it command the whole fort, and part of the wall having lately fallen down, has left the north side quite open'. It certainly sounds as if it was high time that it was abandoned, as Pennant's account, which was written in 1779, reads as if it was in a parlous state then, yet it was garrisoned until 1784. Another example of Governmental delay, which is no new thing.

Fort William has been reoccupied again today by an army of tourists. It is now one of the places that live off the memory of the '45 and 'Bonnie Charlie' and assists in perpetuating a legend. The museum is full of Jacobite relics; some of them, such as the 'Hidden Portrait', which merely resembles random splodges of paint until looked at through the viewer, are very striking. I was amused by Pennant's note of an earlier history. It was near Fort William that Sir Ewen Cameron of Lochiel had a desperate struggle with Cromwell's soldiers at the time of the Civil War in 1654. According to Pennant, Lochiel was wrestling for his life in hand-to-hand combat with a much larger English officer when 'jumping at his extended throat, he bit it with his teeth right through, and kept such a hold of his grip, that he brought away his mouthful; this, he said, was the *sweetest bite he ever had in his life time*'. Possibly strong meat for tourists.

When we entered the town, on each occasion, there were cars parked several deep outside every hotel and the streets were packed with people. It was impossible to get a meal or to find a room vacant. The seething masses and the heat of the summer in this popular stopping place, a hundred and fifty miles from

Glasgow, were such that we continued our journey. On the road towards Glasgow we were interested to see that the bed and breakfast signs everwhere displayed, as usual, were subject to a variation. They read: 'Supper, bed and breakfast.' Proof, if any were needed, that this is just a suitable easy day's drive from Glasgow and the West.

It is worth noting here that most inns miss a golden opportunity by not taking sufficient care to produce a really good packed lunch. Well produced, this is a most desirable thing to have. Unfortunately it is also very rare, and even if one's stay at an inn has been very pleasant the memory can be marred after one is miles away from the place, when some inadequate and unimaginative sandwiches are disinterred from their wrappings. Packed lunches are almost invariably eaten in the open and are an integral part of the memory of a pleasant holiday and as such are good, or bad, advertisement. Inns everywhere would do well to remember this.

Chapter 10

A GALLOP

Although my lands are fair and wide,
Its there nae langer I maun bide;
Yet my last hoof and horn and hide,
I'll gie to Bonny Charlie.

OLD JACOBITE SONG

Fort William to Inverary

As I have indicated, unlike Thornton, we did not spend a night in
the neighbourhood of Fort William. On each of my visits it was
too crowded. It is obviously a popular holiday resort and it appears
to have most of those factors for which people visit the Highlands,
namely beautiful scenery, romantic associations, sporting facilities
and comfortable hotels. It is a good centre for those who want
to visit the Islands and there is both sea and freshwater fishing
available as well as deer-stalking. This is one of the North British
Aluminium Company's 'by-products' and is surely one of the
oddest sidelines of any industrial company in the country,
making it positively worth being a director for that alone. One
wonders whether shareholders qualify for a reduction in stalking
rates, or whether they can expect a haunch of venison in lieu of
dividends.

One point Thornton noted about the woods near Fort William:
'Roes breed here in great numbers; being better preserved by the
gentleman; and the profitable fishery employing the inhabitants
their attention is taken off from poaching, which practice has nearly
destroyed the breed of that elegant animal in the vale of Badenoch.'
Roebuck are still to be found in plenty on this west coast.

The road beyond Fort William towards Glasgow, bordering on

Loch Linnhe, is beautiful, but not particularly good. The pot-holes in places would have been enough to break Thornton's carriage springs yet again, for in the area beyond Aviemore this seems to have happened to him a number of times. However, here in the West new roads are also planned, although they are not yet as far advanced as in the East of Scotland.

There is another gap in Thornton's description of his journey here, which, once again, was clearly written in part from his diary and in part from memory, aided by Pennant. He neatly glossed over the hiatus by noting: 'Having received very in-distinct and contrary accounts of my intended route, I stopt at . . . Airds.' There is no mention of the journey between Fort William and Airds, or of the ferry at Ballachulish, which he must have crossed.

This ferry is unusual in that the boats are small and have a turntable on them so that, when the pier is reached, the cars may drive on to the turntable. It is then turned manually and the ferry chugs over to the other side, where the turntable is revolved once more and the cars disembark. On one occasion here we met a consider-able queue of cars. The funeral of the Roman Catholic Bishop of the Highlands and Islands was in progress and no less than three ferry boats were rushing to and fro in the strong current like moorhens on a pond. Having embarked at North Ballachulish one is then landed at South Ballachulish and follows the coastal road to Airds. Although beautiful, with charming views across Loch Linnhe, it could do with resurfacing.

Airds itself is pleasantly placed on a point overlooking a bay in the centre of which are the ruins of Eilean Stalker castle on an island. It is an attractive ruin and in the evening light the blues and greens here merge into wonderful, almost unbelievable, shades so that it is easy, looking across the Firth of Lorne towards the islands, to understand the attraction of the west coast. There is a romantic, almost magical, quality in the air which makes the venture of the '45 entirely understandable.

Checking on Thornton carefully, we climbed up the hill behind Airds and found that the view more than justified the slight effort involved. His description we had to admit was entirely accurate. He mentioned a view of 'Loch Kneil', which Sir Herbert Maxwell, in a footnote, incorrectly interpreted as 'Lochiel'. In fact it was intended for Loch Nell, which can be seen from here, as well as Dunstaffnage, as Thornton recorded. Looking over the sea and Loch Linnhe the view on a clear day is magnificent, and in the soft light of the evening the painter who tried to emulate the colours would be called a stark, raving, mad impressionist. It would be impossible to capture accurately the changing tints of violet glow in paint or print.

It was in the car park of the inn at Airds that the Rolls suffered the only dent of our journeys due to the incompetence of another driver manoeuvring into the space beside us. It was only a very minor affair, and it was fortunate for the other driver that he got into position when he did, as almost immediately afterwards what we took to be a Forestry Commission lorry came hurtling down the hill in the twilight, swaying from side to side of the narrow road at over forty miles an hour, with only one side-light dimlo showing and no rear lights. Had I been able to take the number of the reckless or drunken fool driving it I would have done so. It was the second time that I had seen really reckless and dangerous driving as opposed to the merely inefficient, or purely foolish, which is all too common amongst inexpert drivers on roads crowded with holiday traffic.

A little beyond Airds, where the road winds round Loch Creran, is Druimavuic House. Here we stopped and asked the owner, Mr Davenport, about the sporting facilities he offers. He lets a small lodge built in the Swiss chalet style, capable of sleeping six, complete with furniture, linen and the services of a house-keeper, by the week or month. He provides roe and red deer-stalking in season, as well as some rough shooting, and a boat and ghillie are available for those wishing to fish.[26]

He showed us some of his collection of roe heads and his game books for the past few years. He certainly has roe and red deer, as the heads prove. He agreed that as yet he has not much in the way of rough shooting, though there must be some sport for

Inch Murrin

Kelso Abbey, today

those who enjoy walking out with dog and gun. Whether he has much in the way of fishing is questionable. It may merely be that his guests have not been good fishermen. It is mostly a question of sea trout and some brown trout in the burns as well.

We asked him if he found it difficult at times not knowing the standards of his guns beforehand.

'Yes, I know what you mean,' he admitted. 'We had one Italian Count who got into the Land-Rover with one up the spout and his safety catch off. We have to be careful of that sort of thing. That's why I always insist on a ghillie accompanying my guests.'

It occurred to us that possibly he might be needing a new ghillie in the near future, but no doubt the latter has learned to look after himself. Certainly it is an attractive place. The wooded mountains rising steeply above Loch Creran are strikingly reminiscent of parts of the Rhineland and the house itself is pleasantly situated at the edge of the loch. At high tide sometimes the road is under water here and a detour has to be made through the drive leading to the house. Even if the sporting facilities were non-existent it would still be a charming place for a holiday in fine weather.

We spent another night near here, on one occasion, in a Forestry Commission house and again found it eminently satisfactory. These new Forestry Commission houses are quite well built and comfortable. Once again, however, we found that there seemed to be a certain dissatisfaction at the low rates of pay of forestry workers. In this instance the wife's complaint was that having been brought to this area where the main work of planting was now over her husband was taken off by lorry to another plantation forty miles away and only returned to her at week-ends. This, she felt, obscurely, was a breach of their original contract of employment. As she was discussing all this over an excellent breakfast which she had produced I did not feel bound to do anything but agree with her, although the facts of the case were by no means clear.

Having fared well here we went on by a side road towards Bonawe Quarry and so round the edge of Loch Etive towards Connel Ferry. On the way along this most attractive detour we overtook a pedestrian on the single-track road. Armed with an extremely ancient-looking rusty hammer-gun slung over his back by a piece of string he looked an interesting character.

'What are you after?' we asked him.

'Foxes,' he answered promptly. 'I'm the local fox-hunter.'

We would have liked a longer conversation with him, but at that moment Her Majesty's mail van on its morning rounds came up behind us and in order to avoid holding up the early delivery we were forced to go on once again.

Thornton at one point also had an encounter with 'fox-hunters', whom he described with relish: 'English sportsmen must not conceive that these men are mounted, even on Highland *shelties*, or that they are furnished with caps, whips, horns and thirty couple of hounds. They are merely on foot, dressed in Scotch bonnets, with *brogues* by way of shoes, the rest as they can. They carry an awkward gun, loaded with swan-shot, having a brace of half-starved mongrel grey hounds, four or five couple of still worse fed hounds, called here *slow-hounds*, in opposition to the *grey-hound*, and a couple or more of lame, but savage, bandy-legged terriers. . . .'

Continuing on the extremely pleasant road running alongside Loch Etive, we next turned inland to join the main road to the Connel Ferry again. The road here went through a small crofting community sheltered in a glen below the hills. The peats were being dug and many could be seen piled against the winter. With the hills rising sharply behind them this seemed a most attractive fertile glen.

After rejoining the main road we soon reached the so-called Connel Ferry. In practice this is nothing more than the bridge floored with wood over which the railway runs and a single-track system of traffic controlled by lights which are operated by a toll collector at each end. It is most exorbitantly expensive, being virtually the same as the Forth Ferry. Presumably this is to defray the cost of the men employed, but this is surely a case where British Railways could introduce some form of automatic control and remove this imposition altogether.[27]

The tidal falls below the bridge are worth watching at the turn of the tide. One of the few of their kind in this country, they build up into quite spectacular proportions. At the time of the spring tides they must be impressive to watch. Thornton mentioned them, quoting Pennant, in somewhat exaggerated terms: 'The ferry, called Conhuil, or the Raging Flood…astonishes and deafens all around it.'

According to Thornton's account he seems to have been waiting on the north side of the ferry while at the same time visiting Dunstaffnage Castle on the south side. In practice he undoubtedly took a good deal of his description of Dunstaffnage from Pennant and there is no certainty that he visited it himself at all. He made no direct reference to doing so, and the subject is neatly avoided in a way that is highly suspicious.

We arrived at Dunstaffnage at about ten o'clock in the morning. Although signposted on the Oban road not far from Connel Ferry, we were dubious of the turning because it seemed merely to be leading into a newly built village. Hesitantly we turned down the side road past the group of white-painted council houses towards what appeared to be the remains of a wartime camp. Some very dilapidated prefabs, still inhabited but falling to pieces, stood on the left of a track full of potholes. On the right were the remains of rusty Nissen huts and sheds. Ahead of us, on a small, tree-covered mound, was obviously the castle. We drove towards it and drew up beside a stalwart figure in a kilt.

'Can I help you?' he asked.

As it happened, we were lucky. He introduced himself as Michael Campbell, 21st hereditary Captain of Dunstaffnage, and showed us over the castle. While doing so he related a rather amusing story of history repeating itself. Apparently the previous Captain of Dunstaffnage was a prisoner of war during the first world war. While returning to Scotland by train he fell into conversation with a fellow traveller. On learning his destination his acquaintance became confidential.

'If you're going up there you should get hold of the factor. He rents the shooting and fishing, you know. Deuced cheaply too. I've had some good days there.'

'Oh! Is that so?' replied the Captain of Dunstaffnage. 'I must certainly look into that.'

On his return he found that as well as renting the shootings and fishing the factor had been neglecting his job and the castle had been allowed to fall into disrepair. The small inhabitable house within the castle walls had been allowed to fall down. This is a great pity, as it must have been of considerable architectural interest. Now all that remains of it are the foundations and the chimney-piece.

The sequel to the story is that during the last war the present Captain of Dunstaffnage was also a prisoner of war. It would be pleasant to add that it was only on the train up to Scotland that he learned that Dunstaffnage Castle had been taken over as a naval base, but it was certainly only on his return to this country that he was told of it. It is in fact only recently that he has been able to start setting it to rights once again after this second period of neglect.

It is a great pity that the castle has been so neglected. It has certain unique features and is of interest still, as much for its attractive position as its historical value. To quote Thornton (or Pennant abridged): 'It is built upon a rock, called St. Stephen's Mount, on the south side of Loch Etive, the sides of which have been pared away to render it precipitous and make it conformable to the shape of the castle. . . . The entrance towards the sea is at present by a staircase, in ancient times, probably by a drawbridge, which fell from a little gateway.'

Inside it is quite small, with a square well taking up a fairly large space in the courtyard. There are some rooms still inhabitable, and in order to retain his title as 'Captain of Dunstaffnage' Mr Campbell has to sleep there once a year. At one time the Duke of Argyll challenged the right of the Captains of Dunstaffnage to retain the key of the castle and claimed an ancient right of over-lordship, but, when taken to law, the case was finally judged in favour of the Captain. In full dress, therefore, the Captain carries a gold key on a chain, symbolic of his title.

These Dunstaffnage Campbells always seem to have been some-what prone to flout the authority of their clan chief, the Duke of

Argyll. Apparently in the confused inter-clan warfare of the seventeenth century the Dunstaffnage Campbells were on good terms with the MacDonalds, one of whom, Colla MacDonald, was imprisoned there. Hearing that he was not being chained as ordered, the Duke sent a messenger to check the facts. Fortunately a Dunstaffnage Campbell got there first, and Colla MacDonald hastily ran and chained himself up 'in durance vile'. Subsequently he was hanged, by order, and his last request was that he should be buried near the Captain's tomb to allow for 'a subterranean exchange of snuff mulls'. Later on, in 1692, the Dunstaffnage Campbells were reputed to have hidden the heir of Glencoe after the massacre.

Amongst other details Mr Campbell told us that his family possessed what was always supposed to be the original treasure chest of the Tobermory galleon. As he pointed out, there was another similar one in Inverary Castle. In the circumstances of the day, when possession of a large quantity of gold was liable to invite a cut throat, it would have been surprising if anyone had admitted to looting a sunken galleon and finding treasure. This may explain why continued searches at Tobermory have come to nothing.

We spent an interesting morning looking round the castle. There is a collection of antique weapons, including a couple of crossbows, which I believe are extremely rare in Scotland, and, to quote Thornton again, 'a sculpture, which is of ivory, curiously carved ... supposed to have been cut in commemoration of the coronation chair, long preserved in Dunstaffnage'. This odd little curio, a reputed replica of the ancient throne of Scotland, subsequently removed to Scone, is somewhat blackened, having nearly been burned in a fire which destroyed the Captain's house on the mainland.

Investigating the ruined chapel near by, which Thornton also mentioned, we noted the numbers of 'Bardwell' graves there. This is an old family name, and it seems that the present Captain of Dunstaffnage was born a Bardwell, in East Anglia. On inheriting the title he had to change his name to Campbell by deed poll. There is thus the anachronism of one born, to all intents and purposes, an Englishman in East Anglia inheriting an ancient Scots title and wearing the Campbell tartan. Yet it may be said he wears the kilt well and naturally. I have seen many worn with less éclat and many figures less suited to it.

When we were about to leave we were amused to see a small seedy-looking individual sidle up to the Captain of Dunstaffnage. 'You the boss 'ere?' he asked with cocksparrow jauntiness. 'Nice spot you've got. Wonder if you'd let us shove up our chairoplane outfit here for a week?'

It was good to hear the blunt refusal that ensued. It is unfortunately too common nowadays for proprietors of ancient houses, stately homes, or ruins to include every form of attraction from juke-boxes to ice-cream vans and roundabouts to menageries. It is a deplorable trait, although if the view is held that they are in the entertainment business and that no holds are barred in attracting crowds then I suppose it is understandable enough.

We had intended to spend that afternoon trying for the *Salmo ferox* for which Loch Awe is noted. However, having seen the dogs which we had exercised in the castle grounds, Mr Campbell very kindly offered us the opportunity of trying for a snipe or ptarmigan on the part of Ben Cruachan he owns. Apart from the fact that it was an unlikely day even for Ferox, being boiling hot, we decided that this was too good an offer to miss. After getting precise instructions as to where his boundaries lay we went on our way.[28]

Passing the Connel tide race again and a tiny modern Roman Catholic church, we went on to the pleasant inn at Taynuilt, where we duly 'took some refreshment'. Thornton's description of an incident here is rather interesting, as it seems he was not above a little poaching now and then, although admittedly shooting in those days appears to have been regarded as more or less free, as in many parts of the United States today, unless preserved.

He wrote: 'Following now the course of Loch Etive, we passed some delightful scenes. . . . I heard a shot, and immediately saw a covey of partridges fly over my head; I jumped off my horse, and having my gun slung in the German fashion, fired, but at a great distance; however, having marked them, I killed a brace, and then proceeded up Glen Brander, through which the river Brander runs, or rather flies. I thought the Spey and the Leven rapid; but they are by no means to be compared with this river, which in size, and rapidity, far surpasses anything I have ever seen, not excepting even the Rhine.' This, of course, is a considerable exaggeration even when it is in spate.

The beauty of this part is now somewhat ruined by the convergence of power and telegraph lines and road and railway on the Pass of Brander, which looms up in front of the traveller, gloomy and forbidding even in the sunlight. This is soon to be the scene of yet another hydro-electric scheme, and already the road is being raised several feet in preparation for a higher water-level. It is feared that this may adversely affect the fishing both in the Pass of Brander and in Loch Awe.[29]

Parking our car by the railway halt half-way along the pass we started up Ben Cruachan with our dogs in search of snipe and ptarmigan. Almost at once we had a shot at some rabbits which the dogs pointed, but we saw no snipe. Instead a pair of what at first we took to be buzzards rose above us at the sound of the shot. It was not until we appreciated their enormous wing span that we realized that we were only a hundred yards or so from a pair of golden eagles. They were a fine sight, but they may have been responsible for the total absence of other bird life. Certainly we saw nothing.

In the boiling hot weather we toiled up the first steep thousand feet. After that the climb became easier. Finally we reached ptarmigan level around the two-thousand-foot mark, but we saw none. although it was likely enough ground for them. The eagles by this time had dwindled to dots in the sky and finally vanished from sight, but still we saw nothing moving.

It was at this late stage that I suddenly realized that my friend, the East Anglian farmer, was one of those peculiar people who do not see a mountain as just another hill, but who regard it in some obscure way as a personal challenge. I pointed out that the aim was to shoot ptarmigan, not to climb mountains, but he remained obdurate, set on reaching the top.

'You wait for me, if you like,' he said cheerfully but obstinately.

I saw it was useless to explain to him that on mountains in Scotland, however calm the day, it is unwise to separate. He was set on going to the top, and reason was not likely to sway him in that mood. I knew him too well. I also knew that if we separated and either of us slipped and broke a leg, as could happen easily enough, it was infinitely desirable that the other should be present. I therefore set the best pace I could for the highest point, as being the quickest way of settling the matter.

Far be it from me to deny that the view from about three thousand feet was very fine indeed. It was possible to look down on all the neighbouring mountains and to see right over to Mull and almost the full length of Loch Awe itself. It was like looking down at an aerial relief map with the glittering waters spread out below us shining like silver in the sun. I was sufficiently small-minded to point out to my friend that the view there was not a great deal better than five hundred feet lower down and nor was it any better at the top (3,389 feet). However, he seemed satisfied, as if some inner compulsion was purged. We had made the journey up and down inside four hours, having admittedly seen a magnificent view in the process, so that, although we saw no ptarmigans, I suppose we had accomplished something.

By the time we had reached the bottom we were certainly in need of a bath. Hot and sticky, we drove carefully along the winding pass road as, on a previous occasion, I had seen a large lorry upside down through the fence there. We went on round the end of Loch Awe to the inn at Ardbrecknish, where I had often stayed, and after a bath, we crowned a pleasant day with an extremely good dinner and an excellent bottle of Pouilly Fuisse.

There is a small lochan near there which is full of trout that bite freely and where some amusing sport can be had if the weather on the main loch is unsuitable. Mostly they are just tiddlers, but there are occasional sizeable ones. This is the nearest I know to anything resembling a matter Thornton mentioned: 'Though scarcely a laird's estate is to be found where there is not plenty of fish. I scarcely ever saw any freshwater ones at their tables. If they would make reservoirs, and fill them as we have done our fish trunk, they might have a regular supply.' He appears to have taken this 'fish trunk' with him, and presumably it was literally a trunk with perforated sides kept in the water. As he could not possibly have eaten the enormous quantities he caught this must have been a necessity.

I was still regretting at dinner not having made my intended attack on the Ferox, but my friend, not being a fisherman, did not know what he had missed. The theory is that these are in fact large cannibal trout, which have gradually, with increased size, taken to living in deeper water. Thus, in water where char live and abound in shoals, as they do at a depth of about thirty feet, these cannibals have gradually come to live on a diet of char. The way to catch them, therefore, is to troll a large minnow very deep. Normally this is simply a question of rowing with two trolling rods in the stern of the boat. However, I had a different plan. Trolling I felt was too dull.

It had been my intention to try spinning with a large minnow and a two-ounce lead, using the very stout spinning rod I had bought earlier for this purpose. This I felt would add a certain amount of interest to the game, and I was certain I would stand a good chance of catching one of these monster trout, which run from about ten pounds upwards, and for which several lochs, like Loch Rannoch and others, as well as Loch Awe, are noted. But this will now have to wait for another year.

The probability is that Thornton caught a number of Ferox and he himself at one point noted four different kinds of trout: 'The fourth kind, called the duermain, I did not catch. They are said to be very large, exceeding twenty pounds. . . . The description I had of the duermain is that of a trout, whose head in size bears no proportion to his body, being infinitely larger, of a blackish colour and a monstrous size; and which I conceived to be the bull-trout. *Vide* British Zoology.'

This is in fact quite close to a description of a Ferox, which frequently is an ugly brute, with a typical 'killer's head'. The four types of trout he mentions are in reality all the same; the differences in flesh and colouring are merely due to differences in bottom and feeding, as Sir Herbert Maxwell pointed out correctly. It is surprising how one trout in one part of a large loch may have pink flesh and in another white flesh and their markings also may be entirely different.

Thornton went to the inn at Dalmally, where he too had an excellent meal: 'Having heard the sound of music and understanding it was a dancing-master's ball, in consequence of the harvest home, I made the landlord introduce us to him. So goodly a scene and so motley a set, exceeded anything I had before met with. They were dancing a country dance when we entered.

'The company consisted of about fourteen couples, who all danced the true Glen Orgue (Orchy) kick. I have observed that every district of the Highlands has some peculiar cut; and they all shuffle in such a manner as to make the noise of their feet keep exact time. Though this is not the fashionable style of dancing, yet, with such dancers, it had not a bad effect. . . .

'The scholars having done sat down, when from the closeness of the room, and the great pains they had taken to warm themselves, though, no doubt, greatly fatigued before with the hard labour of the day, we were very desirous of retiring as expeditiously as possible, requesting their acceptance of some whiskey-punch to drink their landlord's health, but were not permitted, till we had seen a specimen of the master's talents, who was requested to dance a horn-pipe.

'After having made several apologies for his want of pumps . . . he ordered his fiddler to play his favourite tune, and from the shelf tumbled down a pair of Highland brogues. . . . The eyes of the scholars were all upon him, and at every extraordinary exertion they showed signs of their perfect approbation by loud plaudits. . . . From the causes already mentioned, which by no means subsided, but rather increased, we were heartily glad when he had finished. But it gave me great pleasure to see those poor people so innocently amused, and to observe with what spirit they danced. . . . How much more rational is this conduct than that of our labourers in England, who in their way, would be intoxicated and riotous.'

Apparently the smell of sweaty bodies was too much for him, but according to the niceties of the day he did not say so in so many words. Yet in many respects his descriptions is intriguing. It is questionable whether the performance he described had anything in common with the sort of country dancing that is passed off now as old-style country dancing. It is also interesting to note that a fiddle was the source of music, rather than the pipes which are often used today.

The next day Thornton set Mr Garrard to making a sketch of the ruins of Kilchurn Castle which still stand on the island at the Glenorchy end of Loch Awe and which, from the picture, appear little altered since then. This ancient stronghold of the Mac-Gregors belonged at that time to the Breadalbane family, whose subsidiary title is Glenorchy accordingly. As Thornton recorded from Pennant, the castle was garrisoned in the '45 by Lord Breadalbane 'for the service of the Government in order to prevent the rebels making use of that great pass across the kingdom, but it is now fast falling to decay, having lately been struck by lightning.'

Considering its position on an island it could not have been a great deal of help in preventing the use of the Pass of Brander, and it is not surprising it was struck by lightning. I have been in Loch Awe in all sorts of weather, having even caught fish there in the middle of a snowstorm, when, with the rise in water temperature, fish will often take, oddly enough, but only once was I caught in a thunderstorm, and that I did not enjoy at all. One is most uneasily conscious in a boat on a large loch in those circumstances of one's nakedness and insignificance in the face of Nature. When lightning starts flickering along the surface one remembers that one's rod is a perfect conductor. If sensible one then turns for the shore at full speed.

Thornton chronicled here: 'Had then an extraordinary point at six old black-cocks together. . . . I fired and though I thought I saw my bird spring, it did not fall, I therefor hope I was mistaken.'

As regards his shooting Thornton does seem to have acted up to his own maxim that wounded game should always be followed up and dispatched if possible.

He noted: 'Labour in this country is from tenpence to one shilling a day.' Compared with 'wages at sixpence a day' in the Taymouth area this is quite a considerable difference. If he is accurate it is interesting to note the widely different wages ratios in areas not much more than fifty miles apart.

He also noted: 'In a neighbouring mountain, called Ben Chruachan, is a lead mine, which they have just begun to work and met with very good success. The miners of Ben Chruachan have taxed themselves in a moiety of their wages, for the purchase of books, and the gradual establishment of a library, for their amusement in this sequestered situation. This fact is strongly descriptive of the speculative and literary turn of the Scots.' Quite when these literary miners ceased working I am not sure, but the mine is now disused.

The road from Dalmally in Inverary is a pleasant one. Half-way along it in a commanding position on a knoll above the road there is a cairn. We stopped the car and climbed up to examine it. The inscription is quite simple.

Neil Munro

1863–1930

This impressive eighteen-foot cairn in memory of the Scots author stands overlooking the countryside where he was born, which he described so well in so many of his books and in his poetry and which he loved. To some the name Neil Munro may not mean much, but the visitor to Scotland would do well to read him in order more fully to understand Scotland and the Scots. It might be a mistake to recommend those inimitable stories about Parahandy, the skipper of the *Vital Spark*, but no one with a grain of humour could fail to enjoy them. In them, as in much of his writing, is epitomized his love for the west coast of Scotland. His work is his best monument.

From this point the road winds slowly downwards towards his birthplace, Inverary.

Chapter 11

VIEW HOLLOA

Rous'd from my dreams, all bent on game,
I rise and wander o'er the heath'ry plain;
Led by my dogs from point to point I run,
Mark the stretch'd line, and raise my Spanish gun.

T. THORNTON

Inverary to Hamilton, via Glasgow

Arriving at Inverary we enquired at the Argyll Arms, the inn
there, if they had a room available for the night. We were told
there was one with a dripping tap. Tired after our day's exertions
we did not feel that a dripping tap was likely to bother us. Nor did
it. We slept extremely well, waking early to find that the boots was
not astir. We rang without effect. We rang again. Finally we got
our morning tea. Eventually, however, we had to chase the boots
in person to get our shoes cleaned, and I was appalled later to see
this dilatory young man actually following some foreigners downstairs while they carried their own bags. This is not the sort of
service calculated to make tourists wish to return.

The castle at Inverary and the seafront itself, judging by the
picture Garrard painted, remain much as they were at the time of
Thornton's visit. He recorded: 'The town of Inverary . . . is hardly
worth noting, being a small, inconsiderable fishing place, and
chiefly dependant upon the castle, from which it is removed about
half a mile. It is situated on a point of land that runs into the loch
and consists of about two hundred houses, many of which, though
small, are neatly built. The people are chiefly employed in fishing,
which sometimes employs near one thousand people. Although
the herring be a whimsical as well as a migrating animal, I must

here contradict the report of the herrings, having, in great measure, forsaken Loch Fine. . . .'

Somewhat irrationally, possibly merely as padding, Thornton also quoted, without acknowledgement, Pennant's description of five years earlier to the effect that Inverary Castle 'bids fair, in a short time, to be very magnificent, and is only disgraced by the view of the old town, composed of the most wretched hovels'. Presumably by Thornton's visit the conditions had been improved. Today Inverary is a neat, if small, fishing village with a population of five hundred and twenty-nine.

As another 'stately home' worth a visit, Inverary Castle now qualifies for its 'half a crown.' Apart from the addition of inverted cones on each of the turrets, the exterior does not seem to have altered greatly since Thornton's day to judge by Garrard's picture and the accompanying photograph, which were both taken from the hill dominating the whole castle and park. The interior should certainly not be missed by those who enjoy examining antiques or armouries of weapons.

Thornton's opinion of it was as follows: 'The range of offices underground are not only extensive, but surrounded by a most spacious area. . . . But it struck me that if the architect had built the house on any other plan than that of sinking the whole of the offices, the edifice, on the same scale, would have been more roomy, better calculated to correspond with the surrounding objects, and affording a neatness and salubrity which areas cannot have.

'However, from these offices, placed as they are, the chimneys run up through the house, acting as flues; by which means it is really made the warmest residence imaginable; so much has good sense been exercised in making the *useful* the first object, the *beautiful* the second, which has not been always attended to in houses of such consequence.'

Quoting Pennant again, actually with acknowledegment on this occasion, Thornton gave an amusing anecdote about the execution of the Earl of Argyll, who supported the Monmouth rebellion in 1685.

'On the day of execution he ate his dinner and took his after-noon's nap with his usual composure. . . . Just before he left the prison his wife, a frugal lady, asked him for the gold buttons he wore in his sleeves, less the the executioner should get them.

' "*Is this a time for such a request?*" says the brave earl.

'He ascended the scaffold and then took them out, and ordered them to be delivered to the countess.'

I like the touch about his wife, 'a frugal lady'. The poor woman was probably dithering and wondering what to say next, like someone waiting on a platform for a train to leave. I also like the touch of asperity with which the Earl replied to this exceedingly tactless remark. The italics are Pennant's, but I suspect that Thornton appreciated it too.

He noted: 'In the park there is very singular curiosity. A lake called Loch Dow, at the influx of the tide, abounds with both sea and fresh-water fish; and I am well informed that salmon, pike, herrings, trout and whitings have been taken together in the same haul of the net.' In practice, apart from the pike, this is possible in estuary fishing in a number of places round the coast. It is, how-ever, sufficiently unusual to be worth noting from a sporting viewpoint as providing a good deal of variety and interest. Fishing with a spoon bait one could never be certain what was likely to be hooked next. Especially on this west coast the sea fishing can provide a great deal of sport and variety.

At this point Thornton added in a footnote, with the occasional quite infuriating inaccuracy typical of him, that at Inverary Castle a Lord Stonefield, 'favoured me with an accurate account of the wonderful phenomenon lately felt on Loch Awe . . .'. Actually, he meant Loch Tay, as he then included a lengthy description, which he appears to have copied from the *Gentleman's Magazine* of 1784.

'On Sunday, September 12th, 1784, between the hours of eight and nine in the morning, the water at the east end of Loch Tay ebbed about three hundred feet, and left the channel, or bed of the loch quite dry at that part where the water is usually three feet in depth, and being gathered together in the form of a wave, rolled on about three hundred feet farther to the westward until it met a similar wave rolling in a contrary direction; when these clashed together they rose to a perpendicular height of four feet and upwards. . . . Then this wave, so formed, took a a lateral direction southward towards the shore, gaining upon the land four feet beyond the high-water mark of the loch. . . . It continued to ebb and flow for about an hour and a half. . . . It is to be observed that during this phenomenon there was an absolute calm. Upon the two following days, at an hour a little later, there was the same appearance, but not in any respect to the same degree.'

Pennant gave an account of a similar, though much more violent, wave formed on Loch Ness on November 1st, 1755, at the time of the great earthquake at Lisbon. This wave was reputed to have gone thirty feet up the banks at one point. It was, however, noted that 'no agitation was felt on land'. It is surprising that there have been no reports of similar happenings during some of the earthquakes in this century.

It was at Inverary that there occurred the most obvious hiatus in the whole journey. Thornton chronicled: 'October 11th. Sunday, cold and very rainy. In consequence of the weather and the hooping-cough reigning in the vicinity of the castle we did not go to church.' By reference to the perpetual calendar this would make it the year 1789, but he then went on for the second time to include duplicate dates. He had two October 12ths in succession. He also sent home his party of servants 'hawks, guns and baggage wagons', but he had already done this once on October 4th, sending 'the falconer' and 'the others' back to Boroughbridge from Raits before leaving Speyside. The only conclusion is that certainly two, if not three, or more, years and expeditions are included and that he has so muddled his tracks that it is impossible to disentangle them.

On the first October 12th he recorded: 'Day fine. Lord Lorn, a very keen shot, politely attended me to the moors . . . being desirous to see my pointers out. We had several points; but the birds made to the full as good use of their optics as we did and took care not to be led into any danger from our fire. We killed three

brace of a kind of water-fowl called *muratts*.' According to Sir
Herbert Maxwell these were 'razorbills'.

He continued: 'After dinner we proceeded on our journey to
Sir James Colhoune's.' Then, describing his route over the 'Rest
and Be Thankful': 'We soon entered Glen Crow, where nature
seems to have used her utmost efforts in collecting as much rock
and as little verdure as possible. Saw very large herds of oxen and
flocks of sheep, absolutely hanging, as it were, down the mountains, and at one time were hemmed in by a large drove, some of
them going to Falkirk Fair; which, from the conversation I had
with one of the drovers, I found consisted of about five thousand;
the great prices they bore at the last market having induced the
Highlanders to send every beast that could be spared, or that was
in any way marketable. Thus, stops by the cattle of the hills and
the road, which was mending, made it a very long drive to reach
Tarbat.' This at least is one road hazard that is rare today.

The new road over the 'Rest and Be Thankful' is a fine one
with the Cobbler raising its craggy peak on the left. The old road
on the right is still the scene of hill climb rallies of enthusiasts.
Travelling this way by night it is as well to be careful of the sheep,
which, on this unfenced stretch, as in some others, seem to be
attracted by the heat-retaining qualities of the tarmac and deliber-
ately choose to sleep on it. Nor are they in any hurry to get out of
the way for cars.

On one of my journeys over this part I saw no less than three
buzzards quite close to the road, and up on the slopes of the
Cobbler a group of red deer. Glen Croe, as Thornton suggested,
is quite a wild spot and very beautiful in a wild way. Coming down
to Arrochar along the shores of Loch Long one dawn we were
mildly surprised to see a submarine gliding slowly along from the
naval base there.

From Arrochar it is a short distance back to Tarbet and the
shores of Loch Lomond again. Here Thornton once again visited
his friend Sir James Colquhoun at Luss. He described the house as
'modern and well built and in one of the finest situations imaginable'. Its position is still delightful, for it is beautifully placed on

the shores of the loch surrounded by trees and wooded grounds. It has, however, been rebuilt since Thornton's day and is now far too large by ordinary standards. Sir Ivar Colquhoun, the present owner, has divided it up into separate parts and only lives in part himself.

Thornton did not stay with Sir James Colquhoun, but 'sent forward my servant in a gig with a card to Mr and Mrs Ruits, saying that I intended myself the honour of passing the evening with them at Ruits'.

His next entry is dated again 'October 12th. Day heavenly. Mr Ruits has built a couple of well imagined wings to his house at Bel Retiro. . . . Passed by the monument erected to his own memory by Dr Smollett.

'O vanitatus vanitatum, est omnia vanitas!'

Subsequently, as I understand it, the family owning Bel Retiro and the Smolletts at Cameron House were united by marriage. Today Major Patrick Telfer-Smollett, M.C., late H.L.I., lives at Cameron House on the banks of Loch Lomond, and Bel Retiro, some distance back from Loch Lomond itself, is now a Youth Hostel. While corresponding with him on the subject of old game records he had very kindly invited me to shoot and subsequently extended the invitation to my East Anglian friend as well.

Arriving at Cameron House, after fortifying ourselves with coffee at the Duck Bay Road House at the gates, we realized that, like the house at Luss, it has been greatly altered since Thornton's time. It too has been greatly enlarged and there is room to hold a ball for two or three hundred people, as we found Major Telfer-Smollett had been proving the previous evening. In fact he and his brother, who soon joined us, were looking surprisingly fresh considering they had been dancing until four in the morning.

We drove to the home farm, where we left the cars and set off over the same moors on which Thornton must have shot. The dogs worked well, finding several coveys of partridges, but the shooting was of a particularly poor standard. Because of the heat I had very foolishly discarded my usual shooting coat as too heavy and was wearing a lighter jacket which had not been broken in to shooting and was just a shade too tight. My friend was not shooting well either. Major Telfer-Smollett and his brother, of course, also had a good excuse for missing. Added to which the kilt, which our host was wearing, although all right on the open moors, proved something of a handicap when barbed-wire fences had to be negotiated. Although the dogs worked well and made a number of good points we only succeeded in shooting one bird before lunch.

After lunch we fortunately managed to improve slightly as we learned that we were shooting our host's dinner. We just managed to achieve the required number, thanks chiefly to some good dog-work. Then, owing to the tremendous heat of the day, we were all glad to finish comparatively early.

I was particularly impressed by the views from these moors down over Dumbarton Rock and the Clyde in one direction and right over Loch Lomond in the other. Unfortunately the new buildings which are creeping up the valley beneath are also all too obvious. From the numbers of people exercising their dogs it was scarcely surprising that our host complained of poachers.

On our return to the cars we thanked him and said goodbye. At the same time I noticed a man hanging around with the look of a liar about to deny something, but it was not until we turned to put our guns away that I realized that my three rods had been stolen from the back of my car. My Hardy's Traveller's Rod, which I had had since the war and, worse still, the irreplaceable presentation rod I had inherited from my uncle and the new spinning rod, which I had hardly used, had all gone. This was the only occasion during the whole of my journeying that I had not left a dog in the car, as I had imagined them safe in the farmyard. It was possible to have very strong suspicions, but the difference between suspicions and proof is unfortunately considerable.

I reported the matter to the police without much hope of them succeeding in finding them and also told my host over the telephone. His reaction was one that almost made up to me for the loss.

'How rude!' he exclaimed, in shocked tones.

However, he was more than practical when it came to approaching the police, and as he is a Deputy Lieutenant of the County it was, I am sure, not through any lack of effort on his part or theirs that my rods were not traced and recovered. Unfortunately this is no longer true country. It is a built-up area and thieves are everywhere, unlike the Highlands proper. I had, the rough consolation, I suppose, that for once I had outdone Thornton. He only had one rod stolen, near Aviemore, as he noted at some length:

'Gave my rod and tackle to a man, who promised to meet me without fail with them. . . . I sent for him. In answer he said that Jonas had taken it by mistake with the waggon. . . . I found from Jonas that this was a falsehood. . . . Sent to a justice of the peace, but did not succeed. . . . The fellow having the insolence to deny positively that he ever received it. . . . The value of the rod . . . a most exquisite piece of workmanship might be about six guineas; but, here, where no such thing can be procured, it was *invaluable*.' He may not have been worrying about their value, but, at the present prices of rods, I was, apart from the fact that one had very considerable sentimental value and the other many pleasant memories associated with it. There is a lot in favour of insurance, but these cannot be replaced.

On returning to Dumbarton, Thornton appears to have taken the Erskine Ferry over the Clyde.[30] He then met his friend Captain Fleming, whom he had entertained at Raits and 'returned with him to Barochan; I shot thither. Partridges were not plenty but I was fortunate, killing four brace'. Barochan Castle is a mile or so inland from the ferry and no doubt the land was then unenclosed, for here, on the very outskirts of Glasgow today, he seems to have shot wherever he wished.

The next day he noted: 'A friend of Captain Fleming's a keen sportsman, wished much to see my dogs hunt, whose mode of education he was unacquainted with. We soon found some game, but in many fields the corn was not completely cut, and the birds sheltering themselves in it, we did not follow them, but the gentleman was much pleased with my pointers. I regretted much that the season was now so far advanced as to oblige me to curtail my visits . . . that I might be at home to hunt at Thornville.'

This is very probably another piece inserted from a previous visit, as it is unlikely in the first place that the corn would not have been cut by October and in the second place he has already noted that his dogs had been sent home. Nor did he show any signs of curtailing his visits after this. The whole of the rest of the journey bears signs of having been pieced together from a number of visits.

He went on: 'Taking my pointers . . . with me, I shot towards Glasgow, and had tolerable sport. . . . Returns, nine partridges.' The next day was foggy and he once again headed for Glasgow 'shooting as I passed. The day was so close, that the dogs could scarcely breathe, but they were more than fortunate; I got some shots and arrive at Glasgow long before dinner; Returns; seven partridges'.

He then returned to his old university: 'I paid my compliments to the professors, and took a walk about the college, indulging in the recollection of the many pleasant days I had passed there, free from care and anxiety.' He also had a reunion with some old university friends and sat up late drinking with them.

His description of the foggy day when the pointers could scarcely breathe is not unlike typical Clydeside weather at times today, but there the resemblance ends. It would be impossible to attempt to 'shoot towards Glasgow' from Barochan today. Glasgow Green, where he noted 'the soil is very rich and affords excellent pasturage for large herds of cows', now consists mostly of gravelled football pitches and concrete playgrounds with a number of thin, undersized, sickly trees giving a slight semblance of a park to the remaining grass.

The barrack-like tenement buildings which sprouted during the nineteenth century and are now the slums of Glasgow have provided the environment from which the modern Glaswegian has emerged. Yet, though Glasgow Green today may be the meeting place of 'Teddy boys' and the scene of gang fights on occasion, rather than the place where 'the gentlemen resort to follow their favourite amusement, the game of golf', there is surprisingly little crime in

Glasgow considering the size of the city. What there is tends to be highlighted by the Press, but, on the whole, the average Glaswegian is a law-abiding citizen.

The modern Glasgow, which is emerging slowly from the enormous building projects round the city, somehow has a more transatlantic air than before, but then Glasgow has always been the jumping-off point for Scots embarking for the New World. Now the process has to a certain extent been reversed and Glasgow is probably the first part of Scotland the Western visitor sees. It is probably here that his business is transacted, and Glaswegians, quick to adapt to change and admiring hustle and efficiency, now have a definitely North American air about them. During the build-up of its commercial strength in the past century and a half Glasgow has slowly, but steadily, divorced itself from the rest of Scotland and stands now as something different; neither better, nor worse, but quite separate, distinct and different.

October 15th, Thornton chronicled, 'was fixed to decide a match; my famous No. 2 against Mr Baird's famous gun that, some years since, challenged all England. Lord Eglinton, who was the challenger, was accepted for two hundred guineas by Lord Thanet, who was beat easy. I knew my piece to be an uncommon one, and thought myself confident; but as the guns were shot by gentlemen unacquainted with their loading, I lost my first match, though mine proved in the issue, very superior, by doing double the execution of the gun in question, when receiving her proper loading'.

This seems to have been a rather peculiar sort of competition in our eyes today, as the issue appears to have depended not so much on the grouping as on the penetrating powers of the guns. The interesting point is the relationship between charge and performance, which is often forgotten or not fully appreciated today. Sizeable sums appear to have been wagered on the results, and it is noticeable that Colonel Thornton did not lose. He continued: 'This bet being decided, I made a fresh one, my gun laying in, with the same shot, forty two grains, Mr Baird's nineteen. Another bet, for a rump and a dozen, was made (to be final, which proved so) with larger shot. No. 2, or Destruction, the name which the party christened my gun, drove into a quarter sheet of gilt paper, and through sixteen sheets, twenty seven grains; Mr Baird's fourteen. Thus the victory was gained by No. 2 challenging any gun . . . but all good for nothing.'

It is fairly obvious that this piece was inserted because Thornton could not resist boasting about his 'famous' gun and his victory in this match, as he went on: 'Dined with a very large party at Mr Marshall's and passed the evening. Here we more than tasted a hogshead of wine, given to me by the Duke of Hamilton, in return for fox-hounds sent him; it proved excellent.'

There is a double discrepancy here, as he then went on to dine with the Duke of Hamilton and mentioned: 'this country not being well adapted to fox-hunting, he has given up his hounds.' However, this is verging on purely carping criticism and it may be that Thornton had so muddled himslef about dates that this match he referred to took place before the Duke of Hamilton gave up fox-hunting. The fact remains that he certainly slipped in an extra day here, as the next date he gave was October 16th, by which time he was actually staying at Hamilton House.

He commented on the approach to the house: 'The approach to Hamilton House is through a beautiful lawn, of above three miles, with a road, not only spacious but truly noble. It winds through the park, which is one of the finest I know.' Today the bare, sad, remains of this once fine drive are still just visible as two single lines of trees nearly a hundred yards apart. Of all that has happened since Thornton's time to the various houses he visited, the changes here are perhaps the most dramatic and the most complete, epitomizing the struggle between the old age and the new.

Hamilton House, as he saw it, was not to survive long unchanged. In common with many others about that time the tenth Duke of Hamilton decided to rebuild his house, but unlike most he had the means and the mentality to build on a princely scale. The palace that he built after the Napoleonic wars must have been a vastly more magnificent affair than the old house which Thornton saw. Splendidly and defiantly Georgian, with twenty-five-foot Corinthian pillars, each hewn from a single stone, framing an enormous portico, it was without exaggeration a larger edition of Buckingham Palace, with a sweep of stabling including an indoor riding school. Yet today it has vanished as completely as if it had never been. All that can be seen is the slightly raised level of a grass field marking the remains of the foundations.

The sole surviving fragment of this magnificence that was Hamilton Palace is the enormous mausoleum also created by the tenth Duke to receive his body encased in the black basalt sarcophagus of an Egyptian princess, for which, even then, he paid £10,000. Approached now by a gravelled drive, not without potholes, with signs saying 'No buses beyond this point', this extraordinary edifice squats like some architect's massive nightmare, a ponderous phallic symbol of death.

Inside it is even more fantastic than outside. Although intended as a place of worship, the chapel was found to have such a tremendous echo that it could not be used as such. When the original solid bronze carved doors, weighing one and a half tons and costing £30,000, were in place, merely closing them caused an echo which lasted for twenty-five seconds. With the present doors it lasts only fifteen seconds, but anyone attempting to sing is liable to deafen himself.

There are four main alcoves inside, each of which has a whispering corner, functioning in the same manner as the famous 'whispering gallery' in St Paul's Cathedral. Each has two cherubim's heads carved out of one piece of solid stone above it. The floor is made of inlaid pieces of costly marble. Each stone of the walls was dovetailed into the next by the estate masons. The cost of the whole building was £100,000. It is thought that it was intended to have the twelve apostles in the twelve niches that remain empty below the vast dome. Nobody knows what the Duke's plans were, because he died three years before it was finished.

At a conservative estimate, however, it would seem that the Duke spent at least £140,000 on preparing a magnificent resting place for himself, quite apart from the countless thousands he spent on his palace.

Opposite the entrance doors today can still be seen the large black marble block on which the body of the tenth Duke lay in his black Egyptian sarcophagus. Around the floor beside the walls uncoils a marble design representing the stairs to Heaven. But the body of the Duke is no longer there. In spite of all his expenditure of money and in spite of all his planning he made one fatal error. He neglected to check the ground on which he was building. The whole area is honeycombed with mine shafts and the ground beneath both the palace and the mausoleum has sunk. The palace itself had to be pulled down and there is now a crack in the wall of the mausoleum which runs right up one wall 120 feet to the dome and across the floor and up the other wall. One feels that the whole thing could easily crack in two like a rotten coconut.

When the estate was sold in 1923 the mausoleum was brought by Hamilton Town Council for a token price. The body of the tenth Duke, still in his now priceless sarcophagus, and the bodies of fifteen other Hamiltons were taken from it and buried in a common grave beside Hamilton town cemetery. The palace, which had barely stood for a hundred years, was sold to a contractor and torn slowly stone from stone before the last war. It is difficult not to feel sententious at this total obliteration of one man's mighty plans within a century. The lesson, if lesson there is, apart from the obvious moral, is to choose a good surveyor before you start to build.

Thornton would have appreciated this magnificence which he never saw. In common with his times he loved the splendour of which the tenth Duke was clearly a past master. In 1784, which was probably the time of Thornton's visit, however, the tenth Duke had not succeeded to the title and it must have been the ninth Duke whom he met.

The Colonel's first note was: 'I found his Grace agreed with me in opinion that, after moor shooting, partridge has not the same charms. After dinner his pointers were brought in . . . one is a cross from a fox-hound, full of bone and strength, and appeared a most excellent moor-dog, but does not excel for partridge; the other, Pero, is not much better. No man can have any species of dog clever, without some pains, and in general they neglect them in Scotland.'

Having effectively damned the Duke's dogs Thornton then added insult to injury on the subject of pheasants. 'Pheasants are scarce, but we saw some. That they will ever increase in any quantity, may be desirable, but it is not reasonable to expect. It has astonished me frequently in life to observe men of good sense fighting against the nature of the soil, climate, etc., in many particulars beside the introduction of game. The soils of this country, or a situation in any part of Scotland, by no means agrees with pheasants. Game they have sufficient, if they would be satisfied with what nature has ordained. As to pheasants I have known Hamilton since a boy and with all the care and anxiety which has been taken, they have not increased one in five. This ought to discourage the keenest breeder.'

A day's shooting he had here was recorded as follows: 'October 17th. Day foggy and close. Having made some trifling bet with Her Grace that the Duke or myself brought in a woodcock, we tried for several hours, some having been seen the day before, but without success. The Duke shot a few partridges; I unfortunately at my second shot, found my hammer broke, which put an end to my sport. The gun lent to me was a sorry one, very innocent indeed; at a greater range than thirty yards I found it in vain to shoot.

'The gamekeeper, on beating the centre of the last wood, as we were returning home, flushed a cock, which, without waiting to give his Grace or me a shot, he killed. I think I have observed before—if I did not I take the liberty of doing it now—that the sporting servants all over Scotland are too much on a footing with their masters; it is the custom of the country. To allow a servant to sport with the master, on any pretence, except where the master is a miserable performer, which can alone make it admissible, amounts not only to the appearance, but in fact is poaching. Had my gamekeeper, in the above instance, shot the first woodcock seen, when beating for his Grace and me at Thornville, he would never have shot at another as my servant.

'Returns; the Duke of Hamilton, five partridges, one hare. Colonel Thornton, three partridges, two hares; gamekeeper, one woodcock.'

The incident of the gamekeeper wiping his eye on the woodcock certainly seems to have angered the Colonel considerably. He had already added a footnote while fishing Bardowie Loch during his first visit to Glasgow which read less irately: 'The Scotch gentlemen, I found, give the people that attend them on sporting parties more liberty than we do in the south, which, except among such as have a great share of good sense, is a misfortune. To a stranger, in particular, it seems bordering on insolence, which is by no means intended.'

Today the grounds, which were once so beautiful, still remain attractive. In spite of the smoking chimneys and the neon lights winking in the gathering dusk over the mound that marks the spot where the palace once stood, there is a haunting atmosphere of past splendour still in the air. The duck wheel overhead in the dusk and flight down to the nearby ponds. The pheasants which Thornton said would never survive still raise their hoarse 'Cock-up, cock-up' to the skies as they clatter up to roost in the trees. It is perhaps better to remember it in the fading twilight, as I last saw it with the silhouette of that astonishing building, which is all that remains of the past grandeur, standing clear against the evening sky. Compared with this, as a lesson in man's futility and the impermanence of mere bricks and mortar, both Moy Hall and Gordon Castle pale into insignificance.

Chapter 12

IN FULL CRY AGAIN

Three crests against the saffron sky,
Beyond the purple plain,
The well remembered melody,
Of Tweed once more again.
ANDREW LANG: 1888

Hamilton, via Edinburgh and Kelso to Wigton

From Hamilton Thornton passed on through 'Lanerk'. 'The road from hence to Edinburgh ... for want of guide posts, is rather difficult to find, and by no means answered the description given of it, being very stony and hilly; and not near so good as the Kirk of Shotts road; nor are the inns better, if I may be allowed to judge by their external appearance, for I proceeded directly for Edinburgh.' Remembering his description of the inn at Kirk of Shotts this is damning indeed.

It seems likely that he took the road through West Calder. Had he taken the route I followed, via West Linton between the Moorfoot and Pentland Hills, he would at least have been impressed by the beautiful countryside. When the natural contours of beauty are there they do not alter much in two hundred years.

He mentioned one feature of travel which is not likely to occur today: 'As I passed, we saw a tribe of gentry, whom I took to be smugglers, and, being in good spirits, I gave them to understand that some custom-house officers were behind in search of them. They thanked me for my hint, and availed themselves of it, by leaving the road instantly, which confirmed my suspicions, and I thought they unloaded their goods on the moors; but the day turning foggy, we soon lost sight of them.'

'We got to Edinburgh about six in the evening, and sat down to a comfortable dinner. . . . One of Dun's, for he superintends two or three, which I had formerly been in, being occupied, I was obliged to go to another, also a very good one; and considering the elegance of the lodgings, and the great rent he stands at, the charge was not exorbitant; to live well and cheap is impossible in any country I have ever yet been in.' It is one of the basic facts of travelling through the ages that if you want luxury you must be prepared to pay for it.

He noted when in Edinburgh that he 'sent to the ingenious Mr M'Lean in order to bespeak two fishing rods better calculated than any of my former for Highland sports; as containing, in two rods, joints to add and diminish, and different tops, so as to form a rod for any purpose whatever, to be packed in a case so light, but so strong, that no accident could possibly happen to them, even should a carriage go over it.' It sounds as if Thornton had even then thought up, with the aid of the 'ingenious Mr M'Lean' something on the lines of Hardy's Traveller's rod, which I have always found very useful.

Apparently bears on chains were still very common sights in the streets and at fairs in those days. On this subject he brought in a lengthy but interesting anecdote, introduced as a 'singular circumstance that happened in my neighbourhood. A man who gained a livelihood by tormenting this animal, in making him dance, etc., etc., travelling in Yorkshire, the bear, tired, poor devil, or possibly obstinate, as I understand they sometimes are to a degree, would not cross a bank. The bear-leader made use of every effort his senses could suggest, and the day being uncommonly warm, he soon became very irascible; fearing he would not be in time for the village feast, which was his market, he prevailed on a peasant, who was harrowing in the next field to assist him, which he did most willingly; but, after many fruitless attempts of both, Bruin still remained victor.

'The same causes that originally acted on the bear-leader in a

similar degree acted on the passions of the rustic; at last he bethought himself of taking his two horses and harness from the
harrow, and fastening them abreast to the bear's chain, who was
sullenly fixed on the opposite side.

'At a sharp exertion, occasioned by the whips well applied, this
additional force to the nearly-exhausted bear brought him preci-
pitately over the bank, and he demonstrated his disgust at such
unusual treatment by a dreadful roar, which so intimidated the
horses, that on the first sight and hoarse notes of their opponent,
they flew over hedge and ditch and ran directly through the
village; the bear, sometimes thrown by the velocity on their backs,
and tossed about, caught hold of them where he could with
his claws and feet. The country people assembled, unable to account for the phenomenon advancing, were full as much alarmed
as either horses or bear; they cleared the way; the apple stalls,
gingerbread shops, etc., were thrown into confusion, and, no-one
volunteering the stopping such a party they ran, till almost exhausted and mad, they reached their stable which they forced
open, and the end of the catastrophe was, that the bear languished
and soon died, and the horses, though they recovered after some
time, would never admit any kind of harness nor even almost any
living thing to come near them, and were thereby rendered useless
for ever.'

Thornton's conclusions about this are worth recording: 'Accidents of a more fatal nature have happened, and are liable to
happen, every day in great cities, especially in the streets of London,
from suffering the owners of bears, camels, and other strange
animals to parade them; for horses are very apt to take fright
when they come suddenly upon them; and in summer time, or in
frosty weather, when the pavement is glassy, the horseman, or the
driver of a carriage, may be thrown, and killed on the spot. . . .
Surely it would become the humanity, as it is the duty, of all
magistrates, to suppress this pernicious practice, by which foreigners chiefly, and other idle vagrants, gain a livelihood, who might be
otherways usefully employed for the benefit of the community.'

It is difficult today to remember that it is only within the past thirty years that the horse has really disappeared as part of the normal means of transport of the country. It is no more than sixty years ago that cars were regarded with considerable wonder and distrust by many people who had been used to horses all their lives. Flying machines were still only theoretically able to leave the ground and only eccentrics ever thought they would. Thornton's views might have found an understanding echo of agreement then. Today it is rare for a motorist to slow down when he sees a rider on horseback and that is usually solely from lack of understanding that the horse may be frightened. In many parts of the countryside it is the horse itself that is regarded as a 'strange animal' today.

While in Edinburgh on October 19th, according to his dates, Thornton claimed: 'I claimed on my friend Sir J. G., who did me the favour to introduce me to the Highland Society, then assembled, and finally determining the merits of the different candidates for the bagpipe. They politely ordered the fortunate candidate, M'Gregor, to play the *Glassfiel*, which he did in masterly style. The room was much too small for any instrument; judge then what it must have been for the great Highland pipes, adapted to the very large halls of ancient castles, where the chief summoned all his untamed clan, or played at a very considerable distance from the auditors, as I have heard it with best effect in the adjacent parts of a castle, and announcing dinner; but even with this manifest inconvenience I thought it not unpleasant.

Seizing this opportunity to indulge in some musical criticism Thornton continued: 'The present style of music is a constant critical attention to labour, art and trick; the anxiety and *terror* that the performer seems to labour under, destroys that exquisite satisfaction that I admire in more simple compositions. Another inconveniency arises, which is, that the present masters are so totally absorbed that there is no end to their concertos, which alone makes them disgusting to nine tenths of their audience.'

Once again the *Edinburgh Weekly Review* provides a very satisfactory cross-check on Thornton. The issue for October 1794 had an entry: 'October 9th. The annual competition for prizes given by the Highland Society of London to the best performer on the ancient martial Highland great pipe was held in the Assembly-Room, where a numerous company of ladies and gentlemen attended. There were sixteen competitors and the first prize was won by John MacGregor of Fortingal. . . .'

Apart from the date check the Colonel gave the impression that he had been invited to a private meeting rather than to what seems to have been a public function. It is of course possible that it was by invitation only. The point that particularly interested me was that it was the 'Highland Society of London' which had instituted the competition. Apparently even then, before Sir Walter Scott's romances, there must have been considerable interest in London about the Highlands.

As regards Thornton's view that the pipes are best heard in the open no one is likely to disagree with him. It is essentially an instrument which is at its best outdoors. There is in them then something which cannot be appreciated by those without some Highland blood in their veins but which can raise the spirits of every Scot and send an atavistic thrill coursing down his spine.

Today the pipes and Highland dancing have been commercialized to a quite extraordinary extent, not only in Scotland but abroad. I met a man in a Highland inn who informed me that he had been a pipe major in the Edinburgh Police bands; a full sergeant in line for promotion and a pension. He claimed that he had given it all up simply to make a tour of the 'Highland Games' where he could be sure of earning on average between twenty and fifty pounds a week. He also said he had had several good offers to go over to the United States to act as instructor to various pipe bands there. In spite of this he maintained that he preferred to stay in this country.

The bemedalled kilted girls who, like this piper, tour the various 'Highland Games' and dance before the judges on a raised platform are simply an anachronsim. Although their performances are sometimes quite remarkable they are not in the very least 'Highland'. They are in reality the opposite, since a girl in a kilt is, or should be, anathema to a true 'Highlander'. In spite of this the fact that it is a 'spectacle' for a television audience is enough to ensure that it will continue to flourish. Whether it bears any relationship to the original is presumably a matter of complete indifference to the organizers.

Tartans and massed pipe bands are of course inevitably a part of the spectacle during every Edinburgh Festival, but this annual festival has done a lot for Edinburgh. It has been an immense stride away from the old parochialism and narrow-mindedness into which Edinburgh had slowly sunk since the time of Thornton when it was one of the chief centres of learning in Europe. There is now a broader cultural awareness in Edinburgh and a more cosmopolitan atmosphere, which has only appeared in the last decade or so.

On leaving Edinburgh Thornton noted: 'The grass lands in the vicinity of Edinburgh have decreased in value within these ten years. The duke [of Hamilton] lately assured me that land for which he had received three guineas an acre, within seven miles of Edinburgh, now produced only two. Lord Haddington afterwards mentioned a similar circumstance; this decrease arising, not from the poverty of the country, but from there being many more inclosures, consequently the demand has proportionately diminished.'

This is an interesting sidelight on one of the indirect effects of the enclosures. It is also an interesting note on land values. From my own personal experience of land values within twenty miles of Edinburgh today, I can quote instances of seventeen and even twenty pounds an acre offered for grazing. There was one delightful story of an old hill farmer who came down to the market after the war and hearing land being bid for at around this figure promptly put in his bid and secured it at twenty pounds per acre. He was then seen going round the land with some satisfaction under the impression he had bought it, not rented it. In the circumstances not altogether an unreasonable mistake.

After the war the general effect of high prices for sheep and wool was to raise the price of lowland grazings to an unprecedented level, especially in some of the rich land near Edinburgh. The operation of the law of supply and demand is inexorable, and the supply of land being limited but the demand considerable the price rose accordingly. With the price of sheep it has now dropped to more reasonable levels.[31]

At Blackshiels Thornton caught up with some English travellers who had been in the Highlands. Probably they were the same party Sir Aeneas Mackintosh referred to scathingly as having taken powder and shot, at great expense, to Inverness. Thornton had made arrangements to meet them for dinner at Blackshiels the previous evening, but: 'A party of gentlemen honoured me with their company and the evening coming quick upon us, I was prevented supping with the English travellers at Black Shiels . . . but I sent my carriage with an apology by the servants.' This is one instance where a telephone would have been appreciated.

One point Thornton seems to have failed to realize is that within a very few miles of Blackshiels he could have had quite as good sport as in the Highlands; although this may well be truer now than then. There are certainly roe deer today in plenty in some of the wooded pasturelands of East Lothian and there are some fine grouse moors in the Lammermuirs and beyond Soutra, where I have often shot. Incidentally a head keeper friend of mine in that direction has twice since the war caught a golden eagle in a cage trap set for crows.

In late October I had one of the best day's rough shooting of the year within five miles of Blackshiels. I was lucky that the birds, mainly pheasants, mostly broke my way. They flew well and high and provided good sport. There were also woodcock, pigeons, snipe and ground game as well as some partridges, and wild geese were flying in cackling skeins across the sky, adding a distinctive flavour to the day.

It was on that occasion that I shot a half-grown roe deer with a shotgun. Put like that, it sounds a more murderous crime than Thornton's sucking doe, but in fact this roe had been badly savaged by the forester's dogs and was unable to jump a three-foot wire fence. As I was within ten yards' range I killed it cleanly with a shot behind the ears. It was perhaps the only circumstance in which shooting a roe with a shotgun is justifiable. They should always be stalked and shot with a rifle, but in this instance I knew that if I did not act the forester certainly would, and possibly less effectively.

Thornton next included a reference to Melrose Abbey, which he claimed to have visited on his way to Kelso. This looks very much like another insertion, as he paraphrased Pennant in his description of it. However, he may have gone that way and, as he suggested, crossed the Tweed there and so made his way to Kelso.

Melrose Abbey is still a beautiful ruin and the road through Maxwell, past Rutherford and down to Kelso bridge, with Floors on the right, is an attractive one. The stretch of water from here down to Kelso includes some of the pleasantest beats on the river. They are not perhaps very good before the end of March, when there are still liable to be too many kelts and when it is usually too early for fly, but they can be very fine from April to May. In October too, at the time of Thornton's visit, the river should have been in good fishing trim. The Tweed in those days, however, undoubtedly suffered from over-netting, when every stretch had its nets across the river and the likelihood is that the fishing is now much better than then.

Thornton's description of the country round Kelso is taken largely from Pennant, but some parts bear repetition: 'It is customary for the gentlemen who live near the Tweed to entertain their neighbours with a *fête champêtre*, which they call giving "a kettle of fish". Tents, or marquees, are pitched near the flowery banks of the river, on some grassy plain; a fire is kindled and live salmon thrown into boiling kettles. The fish thus prepared, is very firm, and accounted a most delicious food.'

On this occasion he arrived at the time of the Kelso races. His description of this is entirely his own and highly entertaining: 'Arrive at the inn. A charming scene of confusion; cooks, waiters, servants, and ladies running against each other. . . . The company is composed of the gentlemen of the turf on both sides of the Tweed, with their families and friends, and also the members of the Calendonian Hunt, with some few of the English borderers.

Dinner was just ready, and we scarcely had time to pull off our boots, which is indispensably necessary, ladies dining at the ordinary; this ceremony, however inconvenient, as from experience we found it in our situation, must be complied with, though the ladies in habits, in which case, in my opinion, boots are in character.'

His description continued: 'In the morning the fox-hounds and beagles hunt alternately; there is also a concert and races; the first . . . was but thinly attended, and, at the latter there was no sport. Dinner is on the table at four o'clock, and, fortunately, in one point of view, there is only one large room, which is really a very excellent one. From this circumstance, the company are obliged, contrary to the inclinations of many, to rise sooner than they would wish, which keeps up great decency during the evening. After the ladies have retired, some of the gentlemen form separate parties, others jointly with the ladies, to pass the evening; so that they are seldom in bed till four or five in the morning, which makes some confusion.

'The stewards, through whose means *only* any strangers can be introduced to the balls, *should not dance*, at least, as little as possible . . . otherwise gentlemen who are strangers feel themselves more uncomfortable here than in any other place in Europe; and this was the case with our English travellers, who finding themselves very much neglected . . . went off next morning reprobating the meeting.'

The next day Thornton recorded: 'Day charming, but too clear for sport. Scent is not easily accounted for, at least my ideas of it cannot be given in a few lines. . . . Sir Alexander Don offered me his hunters to see the harriers out . . . but I rather preferred attending his Grace of Buccleugh and Lord Haddington to see Fleurs, the seat of the Duke of Roxburgh, which is a pleasant walk from the town. . . . The approach to the house is not finished; when complete it will be very handsome. The house itself is an old one modernized, and more has been made of it than any I have seen altered. The rooms are numerous, but, in general, rather small; there is a neatness to a degree, free from gaudiness and show, which is very pleasing. The offices, with the kitchen, etc., are not to be excelled for comfort, probably in the whole island. . . .'

Thornton's description of many of the houses he visited tends at times to sound like a modern estate agent at work. Floors has been added to considerably since that date, and today is, like so many other large houses, open to the public for most of the year.[32] In common with most it is well worth a visit by anyone interested in architecture, antiques, or social history. Like all such houses it is a museum of a way of life that has now passed beyond recall, but which is still recent enough to be within living memory. More than almost any other single thing these houses demonstrate the speed with which changes have occurred over the past few decades.

After visiting the house Thornton continued: 'Having passed a very agreeable forenoon, we returned, prepared for dinner and the races; when I was requested by my friends, Messrs Hamilton and Baird, to see their fox-hounds in kennel; a very neat, small hound they were, and held in high estimation. Was happy to find that some draughts of the Conqueror's blood did not disgrace their ancestor.' (The Conqueror was the ancestor of Colonel Thornton's pack.)

'This day's race afforded no sport, and none being expected no attention was paid to it.'

From Thornton's descriptions the Kelso Races seem to have been mainly an excuse for a social gathering rather than a serious meeting. His account of the party that followed could only be equalled by one of the local hunt balls today, to which it bears some resemblance.

'In the evening the gentlemen of the Caledonian Hunt took the lead, and gave a very handsome ball, when the company dressed more than at any other. Having become better acquainted with the ladies, I gave myself little concern about the master of ceremonies and consequently asked such partners as I wished to dance with. I observed that the ladies, as well as the gentlemen, were uncommon good dancers. . . .

'After the ladies retired, which they did not do till four o'clock, the gentlemen, in general formed a party to drink their healths; the consequences of which I was not unacquainted with, and therefore the party to which I belonged, chiefly English withdrew; and got to bed as fast as possible.'

The next morning Thornton continued: 'Cloudy and likely to rain ... got up by eight and proceeded; and found, from the stupidity of the waiters, ringing of bells, etc., that the party which had sat down when the ball broke up was still drinking and meant to sit till the hounds went out.'

He noted that this was a particularly expensive meeting and mentioned an Englishman 'being obliged to pay ten guineas for his room, though he was only there five nights; nor were our expences proportionately less'. Considering that this might be considered expensive for a room alone today, although normal enough for room and board, it must have been quite exorbitant then. Obviously the law of supply and demand must have operated in the innkeeper's favour in a small town like Kelso, where the accommodation was severely limited.

Thornton's strongest criticism was about the organization of the ball: 'Great regulations might be made about dancing, which would tend to make the assembly more acceptable to strangers; indeed, throughout Scotland there is a strange custom, which is very disgusting to an Englishman. Though a lady is engaged as a partner for the evening, she conceives herself entitled to jump up and dance a reel with any indifferent person, without saying a syllable to her partner. Many disagreeable situations I have seen gentlemen thrown into, from not knowing this custom, which, though established, I cannot think very well bred.'

Dancing in Scotland today can still be totally different from dancing in England, although how much longer the difference will remain clear no one can tell. At the majority of popular affairs today there is little difference between them and their counterparts in the South except that there are a considerable number of reels. There are, however, occasions still when the dancing consists only of reels, but there is probably less abandon about them than in Thornton's time. The popular way to dance a reel today seems to be with an expression of deep thought fixed on a point a million miles away.

The Colonel breakfasted at Hawick, which he did not otherwise mention, and pressed on to Langholm. He 'had several smart sleet showers, which powered the tops of the mountains, but dissolved in the vale, and made me wish myself by our fireside for the winter'. This does not sound like our hardy sportsman speaking, but one can appreciate his feelings. From all his descriptions it seems they were undoubtedly then enduring a cycle of much harder winters than we have had in the past few decades.

He rode alongside the river 'Tivot' and particularly commented on the comfortable appearance of the farmhouses, 'testifying the generosity of the noble landlord, his Grace of Buccleugh, whose estate runs for about seventeen miles on each side of the road'.

While I was driving down this road to a field trial in July with a Border farmer friend of mine we noticed the Teviot was very badly polluted below Hawick. The foam was rising a foot or more above the surface at one place below a weir. It is remarkable that any fish could survive in such disgraceful conditions, although my friend assured me that it had been going on for years. It is certainly time it was stopped. When we halted for a meal at the pleasant little inn at Teviothead the landlord told us that poaching had nearly ruined his fishing on the higher stretches of the river there.

A statement my friend made about the farming in this area interested me particularly. He was talking about the bracken which could be seen encroaching in places very badly on good grazing land.

'You know we had an area like that where we were grazing sheep and it was getting worse all the time until a few years back.' he said.

'What did you do about it?' I asked.

'We started grazing a small herd of black cattle, just beasts for fattening, on it and the results were really quite surprising.'

'But they don't eat it, surely?' I protested.

'I'm not sure they don't eat a bit of it,' he replied seriously. 'But the main thing they do is that they trample it down. They keep moving from place to place and they don't stick to the one path and it really is astonishing what a difference they made. Inside a couple of years the bracken was receding quite fast. Now we've more or less got it under control.'

'In other words you've gone back to the methods your grandfathers used.' I suggested.

'That's right, exactly,' he agreed. 'They didn't have any problem with bracken, because they knew what they were doing. Too often today we rely on science for new ideas and forget that our ancestors had a perfectly good answer.'

I am not trying to suggest in any way that either he or I thought modern farming methods were wrong, or that all old ideas were right. However, there seemed to be no doubt that in this instance at least he had a good solution to a problem that has been puzzling a number of people for quite a while.

Thornton mentioned one point about this part of the countryside which I had never realized. Apparently since the union of 1707 the population had rapidly decreased. He instanced the population of Jedburgh, which had been 9,000 and was not a third of that. The reason he quoted for this, from Pennant, was that the chief trade of the borders had been smuggling. There had been the double smuggling of Scots articles into England and English articles into Scotland. Presumably once the smugglers found they had lost their trade they moved on to occupations elsewhere.

On entering Langholm, Thornton met an old acquaintance of his, Lieutenant Sykes, 'of the Third King's Own . . . who had so handsomely sold me my incomparable black mare'. This was the same Sykes mentioned in the Edinburgh Review as 'Captain Sykes' at the time of the Leith riots. Presumably a journalistic error. In order to appreciate the unconscious irony of Thornton's phrasing it is worth going back to the circumstances in which he described how he acquired the mare. He was on the road to Glasgow at the outset of his 'Tour'. 'Conversing with Mr Garrard on the merits of his hackney, he informed me that he had rode one so superior as to admit of no comparison, and that it was the property of Mr S.

of the Third Dragoons, who was disposed to part with it. Knowing the use such a trotter would be of to an artist detained frequently by following his profession I instantly despatched a messenger and purchased it.'

In those days apparently Langholm was the centre of the sheep trade and he noted: 'It is said from twenty to thirty six thousand lambs are sold in the several fairs that were held at Langholm in the year.' Nowadays Langholm no longer has any sheep fairs and it has a quiet, slightly withdrawn air, as if the hustle and bustle of modern life had passed it by. It is a sleepy, rather charming small town.

Thornton next passed through Canonbie over the Esk, 'which is full of salmon . . . and came into England'. He noted: 'Crossed the new bridge. . . . Some years since as I was passing over the old bridge, I saw several people very oddly employed; giving my horse to my servant, I went to see what they were about, and found they were hunting salmon; which was done in the following manner; the river was uncommonly low, the salmon in consequence flew to the deeps, and sheltered themselves under the great stones, from whence they were dislodged by men, who having driven them about, they made a run across a shallow for another deep, and people were placed there with large Newfoundland dogs, who with great facility took them; I saw at least a dozen which were taken in this way.'

It is not always easy to understand exactly what Thornton meant, and in this instance he could have meant that the dogs took the salmon, or that the men and dogs between them took the salmon. It may be that he intended the reader to accept the latter view, unless he was credulous enough to imagine that the dogs retrieved the salmon unaided. I can believe that a large dog might manage to hold a salmon in shallow water for a moment, sufficiently for a man to net or gaff it, but that is as far as I am prepared to go. I was unable to find anyone who had ever heard of this method of catching salmon, and the whole story has a somewhat 'fishy' flavour.

It was in this area on one occasion that I stopped at what had

clearly been an old fishing inn. In some way there was an inde-
scribable air, almost of dereliction, about it, which I could not
understand. It seemed to be well enough run, and after inspecting
it and finding it at least reasonably clean we decided to try it. It
was only on perusing the wine list that we found that the inn was
State-owned. Heaven forbid that the State should take over any
more. The soulless air was most adequately explained.[33]

Yet it is only fair to add that we had quite a good meal. I have
certainly had worse under private enterprise. There were five
courses well enough produced. It would be carping to complain
that the white wine we ordered was lukewarm. It was a very hot
day, and although we asked them to put it in the refrigerator it
appeared that the machine was beaten by the temperature. The
bill, though, was very reasonable.

It was not merely that the soul was missing but the individual
touch was lacking too. No one really seemed to care, and that is
probably the basic fault of nationalization. Mother State is left to
hold the baby and no one really cares what happens to it. It is a
form of escapism which inevitably means that one day the baby
grows up to be a monster and equally inevitably dominates those
who previously ignored it.

Thornton next noted: 'Passed through Longtown, the inn a
neat one, but went on, hoping to have some company to dine with
me at Carlisle. . . . .' He found his company at the Bush Inn. 'The
claret we found excellent, but the stock small.'

The next day he examined the castle: 'Though very well when
viewed at a distance, I found, on examination the rudest heap of
stones ever piled together by the industry of man. There are four
old invalids, who take care of the ammunition kept in it, of which
there is a considerable quantity, and five hundred stand of arms.
On the walls are thirty guns, from six to twenty pounders and
among these the guns with which the town was reduced in the
year 1745 by the Duke of Cumberland.'

He noted: 'Near the cathedral there is a very modern church,
which looks on the outside more like a ball-room than a place of
worship.' We searched around and found the place he described,

which seems to have served its purpose well enough for at least a century and a half. It now looks more like a seedy pool-hall than a ball-room, but he certainly had a point.

His final comment was: 'The ditch around the castle is a filthy stagnated pool; and this character of filthiness is equally applicable to the walks round the city walls and the general avenues. . . .'

I am happy to be able to say with a clear conscience that Carlisle struck me as being very clean and certainly the ditch around the castle is no longer 'stagnated', since, as far as I could see, it no longer exists. It has now apparently been filled in. The castle itself still has the appearance from the outside of an old arsenal, rather than a place of defence. I take it, however, that the War Office has now removed the ammunition. As it was closed during my visit I was unable to enquire.

Thornton then went on to Wigton as 'Mr P. Brown who dined and passed the evening with me, advised me to alter my intended route and go by Wigton. . . . Reached Wigton, after an uninteresting ride of ten miles on a bad road. Wigton is a small wretched town, the inn not extraordinary. . .'. So much for the advice of chance acquaintances. Wigton has not changed vastly.[34]

While there he 'heard there were some famous pointers. I looked at a brace, and tried them on my road to Ouse Bridge, but did not approve of them. I scarcely ever find one pointer in fifty answer my expectations, either for shape, bone, or action, and the different modes of breaking, if they are not whelps, make them irreclaimable; but it only costs a little time and a little money, at least to see such as are recommended, and the greater the opportunity the greater the chance of success; if well-shaped dogs or bitches, they can be bred soon, and they may make gamekeeper's dogs, anything being good enough for people that do not shoot for pleasure'.

What an indefatigable supporter of field trials Thornton would have made on that very principle of 'the greater the opportunity the greater the chance of success'. It is in a way an unfortunate thing that this is very true of field trials. Those who can afford to 'follow the circuit', or travel round all the field trials one after another, are almost assured of some success, for inevitably they will have their lucky days when all goes well. There can be thus a dangerous tendency for the breeders of the winning dogs to be limited to a small number of people and there follows a vicious circle which does no good to anyone. The resultant inbreeding leads to a steady deviation in the type of dog bred and to poorer performances year by year instead of steady improvement. It is to the credit of most people who support field trials that they appreciate this danger and encourage new entries. Yet it is still an expensive pastime.

As an instance I travelled this road from near Edinburgh to Shap, starting at four in the morning to be at the trial by nine. This was not giving my bitch chance to settle down, or being fair to her, and she soon showed me what she thought of that, and served me right. I have in the past travelled several hundred miles to a field trial overnight and returned after it, but this again is simply not fair to the dogs. To do the job properly it is necessary to take the dogs down a few days beforehand and acclimatize them to the new surroundings. Then they have a chance of performing reasonably.

A good example of this that I saw personally was of a dog that had been brought over from Ireland to a field trial in my part of the country, where I was acting as referee. This dog simply did not perform at all, hardly obeying its handler, a well-known Irish judge. The next field trial it entered it won easily, having had time to settle down from its journey.

Odd things can happen in field trials, and if more people were prepared to enter their dogs they would appreciate that point and that they have a chance of winning if their dog is under reasonable control. Unless the average gun-dog owner will enter his dog there is a danger of field trials losing their whole *raison d'être*. It may not be generally realized that there are a number of people who enter field trials but never work their dogs with a gun, simply because 'they haven't the time'. Field trials to them, like shows to another type of mentality, have become simply an end in themselves. This undue emphasis on specialization is a purely modern phenomenon, and in this instance, as showing has done, can only lead ultimately to a separate type of dog bred solely for that purpose. This is already noticeable in some breeds and is clearly undesirable.

The original aims of shows and field trials to produce a better working dog have largely been lost sight of in the competitive scramble for trophies. Yet both are important. The answer is to insist on greater realism in trials so that they are closer to the actual conditions encountered in a shooting day and to refuse a first prize to any dog that does not conform to the breed standards, just as a show winner should be able to prove that it can work.

Returning again briefly to Thornton, we can leave him on the road beyond Wigton disgusted with the pointers he had tried.

Chapter 13

GONE TO GROUND

Though not amongst the most select,
In matters of the intellect:
He had at times some small pretence,
At least to having common sense.

Wigton, via Kendal to Boroughbridge

Beyond Wigton on the road to Keswick Thornton had another of his roadside amours: 'I had not rode above a mile, when I came up to one of the most beautiful and innocent country girls I ever saw: I wished much to get into conversation with her; but found her as coy as handsome. Mr Garrard, perceiving her distress, left us and trotted on, when her coyness diminished and we became more familiar. She permitted me to accompany her *five* miles, which added much to the pleasure I received in this ride, and gave me every intelligence I wished for, answering all my enquiries concerning the gentleman's seats, etc., and I flatter myself we were so well pleased with each other, during this short intercourse, as to feel a mutual inconveniency in parting.'

Either the reader was intended to deduce from this that he was the devil of a fellow, or else it is a genuine account of a wayside interlude. Nowadays, with the spread of TV and films, innocent country girls are scarce indeed, but a snatch of conversation overheard in this part of the country is worth quoting as an example. Two young girls were talking in uninhibited tones over their morning cup of tea.

'Eeh, I did have a time wi' Bert in t' back of bus last night.'
'Why didn't you tell 'im off, like?'

' 'Ow could I, wi' my mouth boonged oop wi' wine gooms?'

Thornton might have found his dalliance with a country maid more than a little difficult under these circumstances.

As it was, when he had finally dragged himself away from this girl it was getting late and it was by the light of the moon that they arrived at the inn at Keswick, 'which we found inferior to most of the Highland inns, a circumstance unpardonable in a country much more frequented'. Of Keswick itself he had little to say beyond 'took a view of the town, a small one, and of little note'.

On the subject of the lake he was more forthcoming: 'Derwent-water ... is as charming a scene as can be imagined; but I am sorry to add, that the original simplicity, which, in my opinion, constitutes its chief beauty, is, in great measure, destroyed by several inelegant houses, as formal as numerous on one of the islands.' What he would have had to say on the subject as regards the present ruination of the countryside it is difficult to imagine. In fact Derwentwater and the Lake District as a whole seem to have been remarkably well managed as regards avoiding any wholesale destruction of views or countryside by new development.

In this connection he mentioned the 'valuable discovery made some years since of a mineral, called black lead, which is the produce of England solely, not being met with in any other part of Europe. It is found in great abundance on the shores of Vicar's Isle ... such was the importance of the discovery, that soon after it was made, it became an object of serious speculation by what methods the whole lake might be drained, an idea being formed that the profits arising from such an acquisition would be prodigious'.

He then quoted a lengthy passage from Dr Campbell's *Political Survey of Great Britain* to explain why this was not done. After some eighteenth-century 'scientific double-talk' to disguise his own lack of knowledge Dr Campbell came to the point: 'the sole mine in which it is found by itself is on Borrowdale, about six miles from Keswick, in the county of Cumberland. It is there called *wadd* . . . the great consumption of it is in two articles; in dyeing to fix blues, so that they may never change their colour, and in pencils . . . the mine is private property, is opened but once in seven years and the quantity known to be equal to the consumption in that space sold at once; and, as it is used without any preparation, it is more valuable than the ore of any metal found in this island.'

The true chemical nature of graphite was only discovered in 1779 and the name 'graphite' given to it in 1789. At this time no one knew whether it was a mineral, or a metal, or what it was. It is found in Siberia, Canada and New York, amongst other places, but whereas normally the ore contains only 20 per cent to 50 per cent graphite the Cumberland graphite contains only 12 per cent impurities and is especially suitable for pencils. Since the turn of the century graphite has been manufactured artificially, and now, with the advent of modern writing processes in the past decade, pencils are gradually going out of fashion.

Few people realize that if it had not been for the discovery of the Borrowdale mine, Derwentwater might at one time have been drained and the natural beauties of the place lost. It is also interesting to appreciate that there was so little demand for graphite in those days that the mine needed to open only once every seven years. I can think of no parallel industrial concern which would be content with operating only at seven-year intervals today.

On this part of the journey I was particularly interested to see a few farmers, or they may have been shepherds, mounted on small unkempt, fell ponies, riding bareback, usually with only a halter. Crossing the fields or by the roadside, accompanied by their sheep-dogs, they were obviously using the ponies as their most economical means of getting about. From the point of view of utility and economy I can imagine that they would be more useful on these hills than either a Land-Rover or any form of utility car. This must be one of the few points that has not changed at all since Thornton's day. The shaggy pony, the shaggy dog and the shaggy rider provide a picture of the fells which is unaltering and timeless.

Thornton's next stop was at Rydal Hall. 'This is the ancient mansion of the respectable family of Le Fleming, who have been resident in the North of England from the time of the Conquest.' Although intending only to stay a few hours, Thornton found that Sir Michael Le Fleming had gone fishing, but had left instructions with a groom to provide him with a horse and show him the way. 'We joined the party, all busy drawing a pool of the river; it consisted of ladies and gentlemen.'

He went on: 'Sir Michael very much admired the horse I rode, I offered readily to sell him, and we had nearly agreed, before I discovered to him that it was one of his own. He paid me some compliments on my seat as a Yorkshireman, and we all laughed most immoderately.' Thereafter he was persuaded to stay for several days.

Rydal Hall is still owned by the Le Fleming family, but it is now an hotel and the present Le Flemings, I understand, live in London. Thus, due presumably to penal death duties, a family connection going back to the Conquest has at last been broken.[35]

In the hall of the hotel there is an oil painting of Sir Michael. If it is at all an accurate likeness he was a fat and somewhat pompous-looking youth. Thornton certainly seems to have regarded him with a certain amount of tolerant amusement. At one point he referred to 'Sir Michael being engaged in justice business and other similarly *pleasant* avocations for a young gentleman'. After a day's shooting he noted: 'Returns of the day; a brace of hares; Sir Michael's shooting quite harmless.' On another occasion he mentioned: 'Overtook Sir M. F., who had seen plenty of game, but had been unsuccessful, which he attributed to his gun being crooked.'

He went after woodcock in the grounds, amidst the rhododendrons and shot two brace and a half: 'They are very plentiful in this part of the country during the season, and are publicly sold in great numbers in the vicinity of Rydal, formerly for sixpence each, but now the *Fly's* from Kendal take them south; they are as much increased in value as other articles of luxury.'

One thing he did not mention about Rydal Hall is the fact that it has a priest's hole. It may be that he was not let into the secret; for it could well still have been a family secret in those days. The exterior of the house has changed quite considerably, having been rebuilt in part, but the grounds still retain traces of what must once have been great charm.

He made several expeditions from Rydal Hall, especially to visit Coniston Water, which he did not consider as beautiful as Windermere. He dated a note he made here 26th October 1784, so that it would seem probable that he visited Rydal on his journey in 1784 with Mr Garrard. Part of his journey, however, is still taken from Pennant, and parts, nearer home, are from memory.

The next point he mentioned in his journey was Ambleside, where he noted the 'Roman Camp, the outline of which is still very visible'. He then passed Lake Windermere and gave a list of the various features of the lakes: 'Grassmere is characterized by mildness; Derwentwater by grandeur; Coniston is elegant, romantic and sublime; but Windermere from its immensity and variety of prospect may justly claim the character of magnificence.' He also noted: 'The great island is little better than a bank of sand, and is now under the despoiling hand of a deformer.' For what they are worth these adjectives are still applicable today and do give some idea of the differences between the various lakes. Fortunately the 'hand of the deformer' does not seem to have been very effective.

The noticeable feature is that the hills around the Lake District are quite different from the Border countryside north of Carlisle and from the dales to the east. They have a knobbliness which is entirely distinct from the sweeping roll of the dales, or the Border countryside. Yet it is not like the ruggedness of the Highlands. It is a completely separate and distinctive form of beauty.

On his way to Kendal he noted: 'Passed by Ings church, a neat, modern building, which is said to owe its foundation to the following event:

'A British merchant of the name of Ings, or Innes, a native of this part of the country, having acquired a very considerable fortune at Lisbon, where he had resided many years; and from whence he had, from time to time, conveyed great part of his property to his relations in England; at length resolved to return to his native country, and having converted the remainder of his effects in Portugal into gold, embarked with it privately on board a vessel bound for England; which was scarcely got out of the harbour when his escape was discovered and a great outcry made from the shore to bring her back; the captain, sensible of his own danger, would have tacked about, and landed him, when his whole property would have been confiscated and his person imprisoned; it being contrary to the laws of Portugal to carry the gold coin out of the kingdom; but providentially, the wind blowing directly contrary, obliged the captain to continue his course, and he arrived safe in England; and built this church in grateful remembrance of his wonderful preservation.'

Although the smuggling of gold is not uncommon today it is extremely doubtful if anyone nowadays considers building a church in return for their safe deliverance. Nowadays the wretched merchant would have merely found that he had got out of the frying pan into the arms of H.M. Customs. The interesting feature of this story is that any law-abiding British subject in those days would have applauded the action wholeheartedly. Now our freedom is sufficiently circumscribed to make it a matter for Interpol, or even for extradition. The honest buccaneering instincts of the British merchant today are confined to the flotation of companies in the City, and from time to time they are liable to find themselves in trouble over that. Either way the Church does not benefit nowadays. The church Thornton mentioned, incidentally, is still there and now looks as if it could do with the guilt money of another uneasy conscience.[36]

Thornton went on to describe Kendal: 'It consists of two principal streets, one about a mile and a quarter long, the other about half a mile. . . . The only public building worth the notice of travellers is the parish church, one of the largest perhaps in Britain . . . very plain within, but kept remarkably clean and neat.'

We arrived in Kendal on a Saturday afternoon and the town was crowded, so that we did not see it to best advantage. My own favourite memory of Kendal relates to an occasion during the war when I had been fishing on Loch Tay and returned South, hitch-hiking from Glasgow. I left Glasgow in a drizzle and my first lift was in a small Austin Seven van. This was driven by a commercial gentleman who apparently made the journey often as he seemed to know every barmaid on the way. Driving at hair-raising speed in the black-out, with dimmed headlights, in a mist over Shap he had me on the edge of my seat, although my night vision is better than most. Then he suddenly braked for no apparent reason and drew into the side, whereupon out of the darkness loomed a convoy of heavy lorries. Finally we arrived safely in Kendal about eleven in the evening.

I approached the police station and asked them to find me a bed for the night. A policeman then directed me to a doss-house for lorry drivers somewhere behind the church. I was introduced to a large room which was completely filled with beds of all conceivable shapes and sizes varying from vast brass double beds to cots. There was no floor space visible.

A small single bed in one corner was pointed out to me and I clambered over the others to get into it after having asked the proprietors to wake me up at six. I slept well and heard nothing, but the following morning, on being awakened by the insistent prodding of a pole, I discovered that every bed in the room was filled with sleeping forms. Duly climbing back to the doorway, without waking anyone, I washed and had an excellent breakfast of new bread, butter and bacon and eggs. The sum total for this and my night's lodging amounted to 2s. 6d. While not exactly recommending this to every traveller, it was certainly not expensive.

Thornton noted: 'The inhabitants of Kendal are very industrious and, from time immemorial, have carried on an extensive trade in fish hooks, for the fabrication of which they are famous; they have also established a cotton manufactory, and expect great advantages from it.' He noted also the irregularity of the buildings, which is probably still one of the most outstanding features of the town today.[37]

From there he pressed on through Kirkby Lonsdale towards
Settle, where he had a dinner engagement at three o'clock. He
rode the next thirty-three miles in two hours and forty-two
minutes, minus fourteen minutes spent feeding the mare at Kirkby
Lonsdale. 'The mare I rode was certainly an astonishing creature;
not fourteen hands high, and mistress of sixteen stone; she won
several trotting matches of sixteen miles within the hour; but her
bottom was her great fort, for it appeared to me, as the ride will
testify, that she varied very little in the two hours and twenty-eight
minutes she was on the road.'

How exactly comparable this is with the boasting of the man
who steps out of his sports car and says airily: 'Got here from so-
and-so in three hours flat. Not a bad old bus, eh?' Methods of
transport may alter but habits remain the same.

His host, a Mr Parker, took him down a peg by giving him the
details of a much more remarkable feat, which Thornton duly
noted:

'September 4th 1780. Giles Hoyle rode from Ipswich to Tiptree,
and back again, for the purpose of obtaining leave of absence for
Major Clayton, to attend the election at Clitherhoe from General
Parker, being sixty-six miles in six hours.

'Sept. 5—He rode with his master from Ipswich to Gisburne
Park; they started at six o'clock in the morning and arrived at
Gisburne Park at two o'clock in the afternoon the day following,
two hundred and thirty-two miles; this he performed in thirty-
two hours.

'7th—Dined at Browsholme, twelve miles.

'8th—Returned to Clitherhoe, five miles, and at ten o'clock that
night he took horse for Lulworth Castle, in Dorsetshire. . . . He
arrived at Lulworth between nine and ten o'clock on Monday
morning the 10th and returned to Clitherhoe on the following
evening at seven o'clock; the whole being five hundred and forty
miles. This he performed in sixty-nine hours.

'N.B. Giles Hoyle kept an exact account of his expences to a
penny during the above time. The weather was very wet and
stormy the whole journey.'

This certainly knocks most endurance records into a cocked hat. Presumably he rode post, although the point is not made clear. It hardly seems likely that one horse could have lasted out this marathon.

Whenever faced with a long journey today, especially during the months from July to September, while the holiday traffic is at its worst, I find that the best method is to travel at night, like Giles Hoyle. The virtues of night travel are that the roads are usually clear of traffic, the lorry drivers are generally considerate and reliable, and a steady speed can be kept up consistently, which is the secret of all long-distance driving.

The biggest danger on the roads today is the man in charge of a car with more power than he can control. In the days of horses, a man with a horse he could not control soon had it made plain to him by the horse. Accordingly, perforce, most people rode horses they could control. Today, unfortunately, this is not the case. A man, or woman, can learn on a simple ten-horse-power car and once having passed the test can then go out on the roads in a high-powered sports model. Even the expert and experienced driver requires a period of mental readjustment on changing from one type of car to another. Too often the inexperienced driver fails to appreciate his own danger before it is too late. Inexperience or exasperation are both dangerous on horseback, but when driving a car they can be fatal. Even though new methods of transport are appearing on the horizon, which in a few decades may make the motor-car seem as dated as the horse and carriage, these two factors will still be all-important. At any speed calm, experienced control is essential for safety.

The Colonel's next stop was at Settle, 'a small town; but possessed of . . . a market place so spacious that it is out of all proportion to its size. The houses here, in general, are low and old. . .'. He also mentioned 'directly above the town, a white rock, not unlike a tower, called Castle-Bar, about nineteen or twenty yards in perpendicular height. I confess I was much pleased with it'.

Settle still has the remains of the large market place, although it is not really apparently so large by modern standards. By dint of very skilful driving we managed to get the car up some tortuous lanes above the market place and inspected the 'Castle-Bar' at reasonably close quarters. It is not by any means spectacular and consists merely of a slight cliff. The lanes, however, are worth investigation in a modern car, if it is desired to test the driver's skill and command of the Queen's English.

On this final day of his 'Tour' the Colonel was back at his old tricks. He started: 'Rose early, wishing to get to Thornville as soon as possible.' (As he did not buy Thornville Royal until 1789 this last part and the start are clearly fabrications, or else part of an expedition after that date.) He then reached Skipton in time for breakfast. There is a slight discrepancy on approaching Skipton, but this may have been due to the difference between the old road and the new.

His description of Skipton was accurate enough as far as it went: 'Skipton is situated in a deep valley, surrounded by lofty hills. . . . It is rather a large market town, and has one spacious street ascending to the castle, which is, however, the only building of any consequence. This edifice appears to be of modern date, on an old foundation, has round towers, and is the property of the Earl of Thanet, but it is not inhabited; it is kept in tolerable repair, but has been unfurnished these five years.'

Apart from the fact that the castle is once more lived in today Skipton has not greatly changed from the picture Thornton painted. It was market day when we were there and the stalls erected along the market place made it seem a good deal smaller than it really is and also made parking next to impossible. Thornton commented on 'the multiplicity of inns in all the towns after Carlisle', but it was not until we reached Skipton that we found this really noticeable.

Beyond Skipton the Colonel began to slip badly once again. Presumably he had reached the stage where he could scarcely be bothered even to pretend any longer. He went straight on, as if Knaresborough was his next stop, as, in practice, it would have been. Then he suddenly introduced 'leaving Burnt Gates, and proceeding towards Pately Bridge . . .'. This is, in effect, a thirty mile detour back the way he had come.

Anyone leaving Skipton, therefore, has the alternative of going straight to Knaresborough, or of taking the route via Grassington and so along to Pateley Bridge. The place he wanted to bring in near Pateley Bridge was the locally famed Brimham Rocks. I confess that I had never heard of these myself and only went to see them because I was determined not to allow Thornton to get away with anything at this late stage.

The drive over the moors from Skipton is a pleasant one. The moors at Grassington and Blubberhouses were where Thornton used to fly his hawks at herons and other birds. In those days, prior to the enclosures, the countryside must have been wild indeed, but no doubt Thornton knew it well from frequent hunting days over that way.

The Brimham Rocks, when we finally reached them, proved to be rather fascinating; something like a freak formation from the Grand Canyon in Colorado, planted down in the middle of the Yorkshire moors. Thornton described them as 'at a distance like the ruins of some great city'. This we thought at first was a considerable exaggeration as we were only looking at an outcrop and not unnaturally were somewhat disappointed. We happened, quite by chance, to go on over the hill and then we realized the truth of his statement. They really are the most surprising rock formation to find in the middle of the moors. At a distance they do resemble 'the ruins of some great city'.

There are large rocks balanced on small rocks. There are rocking stones and hollow rocks and rocks of almost every conceivable size and shape suddenly piled for no very obvious reason in the middle of nowhere. They are presumably of consuming interest to a geologist, but, after a little, we found they began to pall.

From there we headed for Knaresborough. This was his last stopping place and here he mentioned 'that celebrated natural curiosity, the Dropping Well, or Petrifying Stream, which is situated in the Long Walk, close by the river'. Somewhere in the dim recesses of memory I felt that I had heard of this place, but it was

not until we visited it that I realized that it was intimately associated with that remarkable old character Mother Shipton.

Passing through Knaresborough we enquired the way and were
directed down Gracious Street. At the bottom of the hill and over
the bridge we stopped opposite the Mother Shipton Inn. As it was
not quite opening time, although we felt in need of refreshment,
we went towards the well, which was more than adequately
sign-posted.

The walk up to the well is pleasant, along an avenue on the
river bank, marred only by a fine view of the antique gasworks on
the far side of the river. The well itself is a quite remarkable
spectacle. Not particularly edifying, but still remarkable. It is not
in fact a well so much as a slow seepage of water over an overhang
into a pool. Under the fine curtain of water which steadily drips
down are hung the weirdest assortment of articles it is possible to
imagine. I counted two Teddy bears, one top-hat, several other
caps and sundry quite unidentifiable and unsavoury-looking
objects hanging in a row. The water dripping steadily over them in
course of time petrifies them with a coating of stone-like appearance. The final effect is certainly unexpected. A stone Teddy bear
is not without its curiosity value, nor a stone top-hat. The state of
the well, however, full of discarded paper wrappings from sweets
and ice-cream, was not attractive.

Perhaps we were too early and it was not fair to judge the place.
Our immediate reaction was simply that people are pigs. The place
was filthy with litter and the so-called wishing well behind the
petrifying well looked more like a public urinal than anything else.
The provision of waste-paper baskets on a large scale would certainly be worth trying here even if they are not used.[38]

We returned to the inn and washed the taste out of our mouths
while examining some of the accumulated history relating to old
Mother Shipton. She was a remarkable old 'wise woman', the
daughter of a reputed witch, born out of wedlock in 1488 and
brought up 'on the parish'. Mother Shipton seems to have been a
prophet of no mean calibre. Those who believe in her prophecies,
of course, like those who believe in the measurements of the 'Great

Pyramid', manage to read far more into them than was probably intended. There is, nevertheless, no denying that, from the evidence, she was remarkably accurate at times.

What interested me was the way the attraction of the place seems to have waxed and waned. It was at the height of its popularity before the '14–18 War, when a considerable number of the Royal family visited it. Since then the social standing of the visitors appears to have declined, although, no doubt, it still does a roaring trade with bus parties today. Considering that it seems to have been attracting visitors fairly steadily since 1500 this is not a bad record.

Mother Shipton herself is buried near York under a stone with the inscription:

> Here lies she who never ly'd,
> Whose skill so often has been try'd,
> Her prophecies shall still survive,
> And ever keep her name alive.

She apparently predicted her own death accurately, but the one prophecy she made which is most worth recording today is, undoubtedly:

> Carriages without horses shall go,
> And accidents shall fill the world with woe.

As a poet she may have left something to be desired, but as a prophecy in the sixteenth century that was pretty good. Those who believe that the world is standing on the brink of disaster will be delighted to learn that according to Mother Shipton it will not come to an end until 1991.

After leaving Knaresborough, Thornton was almost on his own doorstep. He was unable to avoid dragging in a mention of a silver table, which had been presented to his father by the grateful citizens of the town for his services in raising a company of militia to fight the rebels in the '45. He then ended his odyssey with a panegyric on the beauties of Scotland and a final passage taken from the long-suffering Pennant.

There is no doubt that it was an interesting journey. From a sporting viewpoint, had it not been a question of following the Colonel's time-table as well as his route, it would have been preferable to have made the journey much earlier in the year, or else much later. With the roads as congested as they are today July, August and September are not desirable months to travel anywhere.

As regards Thornton himself this has not been a biography, but I have tried to remain as impartial as possible. Judged only as a writer he was by no means always accurate, but nor was Pennant for that matter. It must be left to each person to make his own assessments of the Colonel's character on the evidence I have given him. He certainly had his weaknesses, but it should be remembered that he was very much the product of his age.

Perhaps he may be allowed a last and very typical quotation: 'It is certain that no pursuit is more congenial to the feelings of an Englishman than foxhunting, which is enjoyed in its highest state of perfection when a fox is well found, after a severe chace over a fine country, topping five-barred gates, leaping fences, and swimming a river or two. In England this is considered a fine day's sport, and the chace concludes with a view and a whoo-whoop, much to the satisfaction of the sportsman.'

If there are any happy hunting grounds I am sure the Colonel is sitting somewhere in the background swapping yarns with others of like tastes. In view of the good 'chace' he provided I am personally prepared to call hounds off and let his memory go to ground once more in Thornville Royal with a final 'Whoo-whoop'.

Chapter 14

WHOO WHOOP

I'll fill hup the chinks wi' cheese.

R. S. SURTEES

I have often felt that the present system of hotel charges required drastic revision and that in fairness to innkeepers there should be some form of sliding scale of charges worked on the reverse principle to tipping. In others words if the overall charge was twenty pounds per week the perfect guest who smashed no furniture, stole no towels and was considerate to the staff would be charged only ten pounds. Those who stubbed out their cigarettes on the carpet, or in their soup plates, or who attempted to browbeat the staff, or alternatively were tiresomely and odiously familiar, would find themselves charged accordingly up to the full amount. In short full payment would be exacted for impossible behaviour. It is only fair that innkeepers should have their means of defence in such cases.

This does not mean that I am advocating that slovenly service should be overlooked, or accepted, as it too often is, without comment. The guest, however, always has his defence to hand. He can leave and go elsewhere and, sooner or later, the poorly managed inn will be out of business.

Recommending inns can be a tricky business. I once recommended an inn to the mother of a friend of mine. On arrival she asked if she could have China tea. The waitress went away with a mystified air and returned to explain:

'We have Plain tea, or High tea, but no China tea.'

Let it be clear that if any similar contretemps arises at any inn mentioned in this list I do not accept any responsibility in the matter. This is not intended as an exhaustive list of inns in England and Scotland, or even of those on this route. With some exceptions it is merely a list of those inns, usually with sport available, at which I, or my friends, stopped, either for a meal or for the night, on one or other of my various excursions round the route. Apart from the minimum rates quoted the information supplied is not generally found in A.A. or R.A.C. books, but it must be fully appreciated that by the time this book is in print it may in many cases already be out of date. As I have pointed out elsewhere, inns can change their character radically for a number of reasons in a very short space of time. In any event other people may well have different views to mine. As Thornton would almost certainly have said in the circumstances: 'Chacun à son goût'.

In order of route:

N.B. All prices quoted are at 1959 rates and no longer applicable:
Boroughbridge. *The Three Arrows.*
Old house converted into a modern inn. Pleasant garden with swimming pool. Inclined to be crowded at week-ends. BB 25s. Weekly 11 gns.

Wooler. *The Cottage.*
Can be recommended. BB 19s. 6d. Weekly 9 gns.

Kelso. *Ednam House.*
Run by Mr and Mrs R. Brooks for the past forty-four years. Overlooks Junction Pool of the Tweed. Public trout and salmon fishing available. Strongly recommended. BB 24s. Weekly 12 gns.

Lauder. *Black Bull.*
Run by Miss Jean Cook, a Crufts Champion Dachshund breeder and judge, also a champion hotelier. Highly commended for comfort, good food and well trained staff. Added to all of which Thornton stayed here.

Edinburgh and Glasgow.

The Station Hotels are probably as good as any. About the only hotels in Scotland where fishing is not available.

Loch Lomond. *The Loch Castle Hotel.*

Mr McCowen is an excellent host. Full marks for efficiency and service. Water ski-ing, motor-boats and fishing available. Good food, good wine, comfortable. BB 32s. 6d. Weekly 16 gns.

Tarbet Hotel. Well placed and comfortable. BB 27s. 6d. Weekly 13 gns.

Crianlarich.

Strategically placed for travel east, west or south. Liable to be crowded during the season. BB 19s. 6d. Weekly 8 gns.

Killin.

There is an inn in Killin. (Also, a little way out on the North Road round Loch Tay, is the Bridge of Lochay Hotel. Caters for skiers especially. BB 21s. 6d. Weekly 10 gns.)

Ardeonig.

Strongly recommended under the late proprietors it is now run by Mr and Mrs R. Cook and has been considerably enlarged. Whether it is now better or worse depends on your viewpoint.

Kenmore. *The Kenmore Hotel.*

Strategically placed at the foot of Loch Tay. Colonel Thornton and R. Burns stayed here. Comfortable, good food and service. Excellent fishing in river and loch. Boats and ghillies. BB 25s. Weekly 12 gns.

Fearnan. *Tigh-an-Loan.*

On North Road. One boat on loch. BB 22s. Weekly 9 gns.

Grandtully.

Good stretch of river Tay. Boats and ghillies. Weekly 12 gns.

Ski-ing on Ben Lawers—January to March. Golf at Taymouth. Fishing.

For Aberfeldy, Dunkeld and Pitlochry see A.A. or R.A.C. books, etc.

Dunkeld. *Dunkeld House Hotel.*
In quiet hundred acre grounds north of Dunkeld it has a mile and three quarters salmon fishing on the Tay upstream from Dunkeld Bridge. Efficiently run by Mrs Miller and strongly recommended.

Blair Atholl. *Atholl Arms.*
Grouse shooting, by arrangement, locally; £5 per day. Trout fishing poor. Food recommended. BB 27s. 6d. Weekly 12 gns.

Dalwhinnie. *Loch Ericht Hotel.*
Trout fishing in Loch Ericht, Stalking by arrangement. BB 23s. Weekly 9½ gns.

Newtonmore. *Balavil Arms.*
Pony-trekking, deer-stalking, fishing, ski-ing, climbing, etc. Mr Ormiston can probably arrange anything legal for his guests. BB 25s. Weekly 10 gns.

Kingussie. *Star.*
Old-type commercial inn with new look. None the worse for that. Fishing by arrangement. Comfortable. BB 22s. 6d. Weekly 10 gns.

Kingcraig. *Suie.*
Run by Mrs MacBain. Some splendid stuffed capercailzies, suitable for nature photographs. Comfortable. Fishing on Loch Insh and Spey. Recommended. BB 21s. Weekly 9 gns.

Lynwilg.
Recently and attractively modernized. Fishing on Spey and Loch Alvie. Recommended. BB 22s. 6d. Weekly 8 gns.

Aviemore. *The Strathspey Hotel.*
A vast tower block owned by Scottish and Newcastle Breweries.
The views from the windows can certainly be magnificent.

The Badenoch Hotel.
Not quite so large, it is run by Tennent Caledonian Breweries.

The Post House Hotel.
This is run by Trust House Forte. For the facilities of this group
see note 18 p.

Coylumbridge Hotel.
Run by Rank Hotels, Ltd., this is not strictly within the Aviemore Centre, but close enough and with most of the same amenities. Sited closer to the ski slopes for what that is worth.

Boat of Garten. *The Boat.*
Specializes in golf and ski-ing. Food good. BB 25s. Weekly
16 gns.

Nethybridge.
Arranges angling courses in conjunction with S.C.P.B. on the
Spey. Encourages ski-ing. Weekly 13 gns.

Grantown-on-Spey. *The Palace.*
As above. Weekly 14 gns.

Craigellachie.
Three miles of fishing on the Spey. 30s. per day. BB 25s. Weekly
12 gns.

Forres. *Queen's Head.*
Old commercial inn. Comfortable. BB 20s. Weekly 9 gns.
Cluny Hill. Family hotel. Well run. Weekly 16 gns.
Park. Comfortable. BB 21s. Weekly 10 gns.
Fishing arrangements can be made through the Moray Estates
on Loch Allan, Lochantutach and Lochindorb.

Elgin. *Gordon Arms.*
Excellent tea and toast. BB 24s. 6d. Weekly 12 gns.

Fochabers. *Gordon Arms.*
Extremely well run by professional young hoteliers Mr and Mrs
C. Pern. Comfortable. Excellent food. Good fishing and shooting
available by arrangement locally. Strongly recommended.

Tomintoul. *Richmond Arms.*
Mr MacNiven is as good a host and sportsman as his father.
Fishing on Avon. Salmon and sea trout. Shooting available locally.
A pleasant Irish air about this inn. Recommended. BB 18s. Weekly
9 gns.

Daviot. *Meallmore.*
Old shooting lodge. Trout fishing. BB 25s. Weekly 10 gns.

Inverness. *Station.*
BB 39s. Weekly 19 gns. Fishing and shooting available by
arrangement.

Flichity Inn.
Out of water when I was there. Out of the way at any time.
(Trout fishing on Loch Ruthaven. Good. 30s. per day.) Weekly
9 gns.

Fort Augustus.
All inns have fishing. Choice from:
Caledonian. BB 22s. Weekly 13 gns.
Inchnacardoch. BB 23s. 6d. Weekly 10 gns.
Lovat Arms. Recommended. BB 22s. Weekly 13 gns.

Glengarry Castle.
Unlicensed, but good views over Loch Oich. Fishing and stalking
available. BB 18s. 6d. Weekly 8 gns.

Invergarry Hotel.

Although Captain Hunt was a P.O.W. there is nothing prison-like about his sporting inn. Stalking and salmon and trout fishing. Reliably recommended. Weekly 12½ gns.

Spean Bridge.

Advertises itself as homely and comfortable. Fishing by arrangement. BB 19s. 6d. Weekly 10 gns.

Roy Bridge.

Proprietor was a professional musician. Now calls the tune of 11 gns. weekly. Fishing by arrangement.

Fort William. *Station.*

BB 36s. Weekly 19 gns. Fishing and stalking by arrangement with the North British Aluminium Company. 12 gns. per day for stalking inclusive of stalker, ghillie and pony. Venison may be bought at market price. The head (as a by-product?) 'may be kept by the guest'.

Airds.

Sea fishing available. Food good. Weekly 9 gns.

Appin. *Creagan Inn.*

Run by Mr and Mrs J. E. MacDonell. Mrs MacDonell was a MacDonald from Skye and has the Gaelic. She can generally arrange fishing through the Glenure Estates and looks after her guests well.

Taynuilt.

42½ lb. salmon caught in 1952. Pleasant inn. Food good. BB 21s. Weekly 10 gns.

Loch Awe Hotel.

Seventy bedrooms. There ought to be one vacant. BB 32s. 6d. Weekly 10½ gns.

Ardbrecknish House.

Particularly attractive position. Good fishing. Used to be gas lit but now has electricity. Dinner by candlelight. Food, wine and service good. Shooting by arrangement. BB 25s. Weekly 11 gns.

Portsonachan.

Thornton nearly stopped here. Good fishing inn. Weekly 15 gns.

Inverary.

There are two inns here. One is larger than the other.

Teviothead. *Teviotdale Lodge.*

Fishing in upper Teviot not up to much, but a pleasant situation. Food. good. BB 22s. 6d. Weekly 10 gns.

Penrith, Cumberland. *Brackenbank*, Lazonby.

Mr R. N. Burton is well known at field trials. Good varied shooting and good salmon and trout fishing in Eden. Good dog-work assured.

Rydal Hall, Westmorland.

Thornton stayed here when it was a private house. It is now owned by the Diocese of Carlisle and run as a conference centre cum hotel. They have been unable to open the Priest Hole. Probably due to being the wrong denomination.

Appendix 1

EXTRACT FROM 'EDINBURGH REVIEW'
1805

WRITTEN BY WALTER SCOTT.

'... The Reviewers of North Britain in common with the other inhabitants of the Scottish metropolis enjoy some advantages unknown it is believed to their Southern brethren. We do not allude merely to the purer air we breathe in our attics and the more active exercise which we enjoy in ascending to them, although our superiority in these respects is well known to be in the proportion of fourteen stories to three. But we pride ourselves chiefly on this circumstance, although "in populous city pent" for eight months in the year the happy return of August turns the Reviewers with the schoolboys and even the Burghers of Edinburgh adrift through the country to seek among moors and lakes not indeed *whom* but *what* they may devour. For some of us do (Under Colonel Thornton's correction) know where to find a bit of game. On such occasions even the most saturnine of our number has descended from his den garnished with the limbs of mangled authors, wiped his spectacles, adjusted his knapsack and exchanged the critical scalping knife for the fishing rod or fowling piece. But we are doomed to travel in a *style* far different from that of our worthy author. . . .

'In fine being accoutred in a rusty black coat and attended by a pointer which might have belonged to the pack of the frugal Mr Osbaldestone (who kept a pack of hounds and two hunters, not to mention a wife and six children, on sixty pounds a year), being moreover, "Lord of our presence, but no land beside" we have in *our* sporting tours met with interruptions of a nature more disagreeable than we care to mention. Hence the various oppressions exercised by us upon the Lairds (A variety of the Squire genus found in Scotland) whose moors we have perambulated has taught us to rail with Jaqcus against all the first born of Egypt. And deeply have often sworn that if any of these gentlemen should be tempted to hunt across Parnassus, or the demesnes adjacent, or should be detected abandoning their only proper and natural vocation of pursuing, killing and eating the fowls of the air, the beasts of the earth and the fishes in the waters under the earth, for the unnatural and unsquire-like employment of writing, printing and publishing, we would then in return for their lectures on the game laws introduce them to an acquaintance with the canons of criticism. Such an opportunity of vengeance was rather however to be wished than to be hoped and therefor Colonel Thornton was not more joyfully surprised when at Dalnacardock he killed a char with bait than we were to detect a hunting, hawking, English Squire poaching in the fields of literature. We therefor apprize Colonel Thornton that he must produce his licence and establish his qualification or submit to the statutory penalty in terrorem of all such offenders. . . .'

CHRONOLOGICAL LIFE OF COLONEL THOMAS THORNTON

His grandfather Sir William Thornton was knighted by Queen Anne. His father was Colonel William Thornton who founded the first militia, raising a hundred men at his own expense against the Scots in the '45. He subsequently became M.P. for York and according to the *Dictionary of National Biography* married the daughter of John Myster, of Epsom, in 1746 and in:

1747 Thomas Thornton was born in London, but in:

1766 Thomas Thornton matriculated in Classics at Glasgow University after previous education at Charterhouse. (Glasgow University was probably chosen as his father held a military appointment there after the '45.)

1769 Colonel William Thornton died. His health had suffered in the '45 when hiding in a damp cellar after Falkirk, where his militia had fought well. Thomas, who had already been commissioned into the regiment by his father, was then appointed Colonel of the West York Militia by the Marquis of Rockingham.

1772 Thornton founded the Falconry Club (probably on leaving Glasgow University, where he had shown a strong interest in field sports).

1778 He won a match on horseback. He is also reputed to have jumped his own height and similar athletic feats. About this time he also became a member of the notorious Savoire Vivre Club.

1781 He was presented with a cup for nine years' management by the Falconry Club.

1782–9 He appears to have been in Scotland almost every year between these dates, although 1784 is probably the main year of the 'Tour'.

1789 He built a house on Loch Alvie in Speyside.

1790 He bought Allerton Mauleverer from the Duke of York for £110,000, having sold his family seat at Thornville. The Duke tried to cheat him out of £5,000 on the purchase price and was ignominiously exposed. Thornton renamed it Thornville Royal.

1791 He bought Boythorpe Hall twelve miles from Scarborough and rebuilt it at a cost of £10,000 renaming it Falconer's Hall as the country there was eminently suited to coursing and hawking.

1794 He was court-martialled and publicly reprimanded for allowing his soldiers to draw him into camp in a triumphal carriage. He maintained that this was at the direct instigation of the Duke of York and wrote a pamphlet giving his side of the case entitled *An Elucidation of a Mutinous Conspiracy entered into by the Officers of the West York Regiment of Militia against their Commanding Officer*, dedicated (*Sans Permission*) to H.R.H. the Duke of York.

1795 He resigned his commission 'in disgust'.

1796 In the middle of the war with France he appears to have openly invited two French commissioners, notably a M. de Senovert, to visit him and took them to London. This drew a protest from the Duke of Richmond on behalf of the Government and an exchange of letters between him and Thornton, who, being a Whig and Francophile, was against the Tory Government and the war with France. He appears to have owned a house in Westminster at this period called, blatantly, 'The Boudoir'.

1800 He made a public speech at York, against the Government.

1801 He was sued by M'Lean, of Edinburgh for goods received and judgment was given against him. He wrote an indignant refutation of the judgment to the papers.

His illegitimate daughter, Thornvillia Diana Thornton, was born. The mother was an Englishwoman, Pamela Duins of low birth.

1802 He made his tour of France during the Peace of Amiens and reference is made to 'Mrs Thornton' who accompanied him. Probably Alicia Meynell, daughter of a Norwich watchmaker.

1803 The programme for a week's sport was publicly announced as: 'Monday, Stag hunting, followed by Coursing. Tuesday, Wolf, Stag and Fox hunting, and Beagling. Wednesday, Stag
hunting and Coursing. Thursday, Wolf, Stag and Fox hunting,
Beagling and Coursing, to meet every day at Falconer's Hall, where
there will be a sportsman's breakfast provided for all the company.'

1804 His *Scottish Tour* was published.

He laid a wager of £1,000 on 'Mrs Thornton', actually Alicia
Meynell, a notable equestrienne in a race against a Captain Flint.
Her horse went lame and she lost.

1805 'Mrs Alicia Thornton' won a gold cup valued at 700
guineas in a flat race against the 'Fred Archer' of the day and is the
only woman listed in the Jockey Club Records as having won a
flat race against the opposite sex.

Thornton sold Thornville Royal to Lord Stourton for £226,000.
He kept Falconer's Hall.

1806 Alicia turned termagant and shamelessly reviled him
publicly. He moved to London and married Eliza Cawston, of
Bundon, Essex, at Lambeth.

He published a pamphlet explaining and exonerating his conduct
in a quarrel with a Mr Burton, who seems to have been abetted
by Alicia.

The sole rights in his *French Tour* were given to an indigent
schoolfellow, the Rev. Martyn, and it was published as at Thornville Royal.

1807 A son, William Thomas, was born in London. Mention
was made in the sporting Press of the Colonel hunting at Boroughbridge.

1808 The East Riding becoming unsuitable for hawking due to
the increasing pace of the enclosures he sold Falconer's Hall and
moved to Spye Park in Wiltshire in a procession several miles long.
He also sold 'The Boudoir' for fourteen hogsheads of claret and
took a house in the Edgware Road.

During this period he seems to have been in financial difficulties,
but he still continued to have considerable sport with his hawks,

his hounds and his guns in Wiltshire and maintained open house in spite of rascally servants and duns.

1814 He visited France with a pack of hounds and returned prior to Waterloo.

1815 He was involved in a scene in a London hotel, Pagliano's, when a huntsman came to claim back wages and was ejected. The case against him was dismissed. He then returned to France and bought an estate, styling himself Duc de Pont and Prince de Chambord.

1817 He applied for naturalization, but merely succeeded in changing his legal domicile.

1818 He made a will in favour of his illegitimate daughter.

1821 He sold his estate in France and moved into lodgings in Paris run by an old servant where he founded a Falconers' Club, primarily devoted to dining, wining and singing hunting songs. The Press reported his death on December 25th. It was suggested that he had spread the report himself, but there is no foundation for this.

1823 Having ordered out his hounds and with his horse waiting at the door, he died suddenly in Paris on March 10th, aged 76.

NUMBERED NOTES ON TEXT

1. Allerton Mauleverer, or Thornville Royal, when Colonel Thornton owned it, was one of the finest Georgian mansions in Yorkshire. In the early 19th century it was almost entirely rebuilt in the worst imaginable gothic taste by the then Lord Stourton. Only two rooms of the old Georgian house remain and little can be told from them. Ironically Old Thornville, where Thornton was brought up remains a very charming period house far preferable to Allerton Mauleverer as it stands. The latter has been a Jesuit training college and there is talk of turning it into a polytechnic. By modern standards it is only suitable for some such institution.

2. Mr Simpson has been succeeded by other tenants of the same name. The Roman pavement is still covered with sawdust with the addition of linoleum on top of that and Sir Henry Lawson Tancred's agent has informed the Simpsons that they may use the shed as an outhouse, hence they are reluctant, understandably, to show it to anyone. At present it is being wasted and is clearly an embarrassment to everyone concerned with it. The logical solution is that the Ministry of Public Building and Works should approach Sir Henry and suggest lifting the pavement by the modern methods available to deposit it in a suitable site at the Roman Town Museum further up the road.

3. The local police inform me that it has now been turned into flats.

4. The underpasses, overpasses, roundabouts and other convolutions of the motorway date this observation irrevocably,

but even in their new road systems and their blocks of sky-scraper flats Newcastle and Glasgow retain their affinity.

5. The factory has now been removed from the old antiquated and rather fascinating premises to a new factory on the outskirts of the town. It is now highly mechanized.

6. In 1970 the road casualty figures topped a hundred thousand. In 1971 they were slightly down, but still were over 98,000. i.e. there has been a steady increase of over a thousand a year.

7. Note the addition of The Black Bull, Lauder, to the list of Inns in Chapter 14. It appears to have been unaccountably overlooked, but is undoubtedly the inn at which Thornton must have stayed.

8. Messrs Hardy's shop is now contained within Dickson's.

9. At long last there is a reasonable motorway connecting Edinburgh and Glasgow.

10. The overpasses, underpasses and other modern road engineering feats connected with the motorway through and around Glasgow are it must be admitted a vast improvement. The skyscraper blocks of flats which have replaced so many of the truly frightful old blocks of tenement buildings must also be accepted as enhancing the city's general appearance. The motorway to the west and its surroundings have also been greatly improved. Dumbarton itself has fresh paint in evidence almost everywhere and there seems to have been a very determined and successful attempt to make the town more attractive.

11. It is worth quoting Thornton here:
'June 29th . . . We soon landed at the romantic Inchermin, the most considerable island on the lake (Loch Lomond) being nearly two miles in circumference, delightfully wooded, and plentifully stocked with deer, besides, what may be thought not quite so pleasant an accompaniment, a few wild *bears*, turned in there by Lord Graham. From the latter, however, we received no injury . . .'

Sir Herbert Maxwell noted in the edition of Thornton's Tour of 1896, which he edited: 'Enquiry of the present owner of Inch Murrin, the Duke of Montrose, has failed to verify the former existence of either bears or boars here . . .'

Despite this damping footnote, it is interesting to note that now Major Patrick Telfer Smollett in conjunction with Mr Jimmy Chipperfield has opened a bear park in the grounds of Cameron House, his home at the southern end of Loch Lomond. If Thornton was correct the wheel has certainly turned full circle.

12. The old inn at Luib is now closed.

13. The Castle is now a private school for the sons of American diplomats, but although the Civil Defence have been disbanded the remains of the 'village' are still to be seen.

14. A Borland Fish Lift has been installed which effectively returns the smolts and prevents them going through the turbines.

15. Old Fascally House is no longer an inn and the road improvements have not yet been completed.

16. In 1959 long hair such as is common today and was common in Thornton's day was almost unknown.

17. Blue hares are amongst the fauna which can now be seen in the Highland Wildlife Park close to Kincraig.

18. The Aviemore Centre was opened in 1966 as a year round holiday and conference centre, the inspiration of the late Lord Fraser of Allander. It contains three main hotels run by a consortium of financial interests, but there are also motels and many other facets of tourism connected with it over which the guiding force is Highland Tourist (Cairngorm Development) Ltd. Everything a tourist in the Highlands or elsewhere could require is offered. There are ski-lifts, indoor skating and curling rinks, indoor heated swimming pools, cinemas, theatres, conference halls, squash, tennis, golf, go-kart racing, bird watching, fishing, shooting, etc. The fact that the new hotels at present form something of a scar on the landscape and stick out like a sore thumb is by the way.

19. With the choice available today there is bound to be one suitable for even the most exacting traveller.

20. Although private enterprise has largely taken over in this

area there are probably more bodies involved than ever and I see no reason to modify this statement.

21. The cost today is liable to be in the region of £1,000 per week.

22. Lt. General Sir George and Lady Gordon Lennox may be strongly congratulated on the reconstruction work they have effected at Gordon Castle. They have restored order out of chaos. The stable block has been turned into a farm building, housing cattle under its battlemented facade. Around the tower a further block of farm buildings have been built on the site of the old 15th century castle in keeping with the castle facade. The tower block itself now has a staircase and with windows white painted presents an impressive appearance. Trees and bushes in shelter belts between the buildings and the grounds in good order complete the transformation from the scene of decay in 1959.

23. These have now been removed. Modern caravans greet the visitor instead.

24. Today there are between 150,000 and 180,000 head of deer. Around 30,000 are shot annually. Taking into account stalkers and other ancillary workers obtaining employment from stalking, as well as those who shoot the deer the figure of those benefiting from them must be much closer to 20,000 or more. Nor must their tourist attraction be overlooked. Although the Deer Commission may have done quite a good job there is little doubt that their unnecessarily bureaucratic approach to their task has not made them popular.

25. This archaic law has now been repealed and no longer applies.

26. This is now part of Glenure Estates owned by Mr Simon Fraser. The sporting facilities are no longer available, but see The Creagan Arms, run by Mrs MacDonell, under the list of inns in Chapter 14.

27. This inquitous imposition has now been removed and automatic traffic lights have been installed. Such enormous queues formed under the old system during the Summer months that it was decided something had to be done to try to speed up the traffic.

28. The village of Dumbeg above Dunstaffnage Castle has been considerably enlarged. The Castle itself has now been renovated and is in the care of the Ministry of Works. The remains of the wartime camp have been removed and the 'Dunstaffnage Marine Research Laboratory', a well kept complex of white buildings by the lochside have replaced them. A notice at the gate states: 'Private: This is a Research Laboratory with no public aquarium or exhibits. The Director regrets that members of the public are not admitted, except on business.' Opposite the Connel Race stands another new building, an inn named 'The Dunstaffnage Arms' owned appropriately by the Captain of Dunstaffnage.

29. The fishing has not been as adversely affected as was feared. The view from the dam above the Pass of Brander and below Ben Cruachan is magnificent.

30. The new Erskine Bridge over the Clyde, a smaller version of that over the Forth with graceful curving lines, has now supplanted the ferry here.

31. The price of land has soared beyond most people's wildest dreams in 1959.

32. Floors Castle is only open to the public on exceptional occasions.

33. The state-owned inns and brewery in Cumberland, around the Carlisle area, have all now been de-nationalized and sold to private enterprise. The particular inn in question apparently had a very good, efficient and well-liked manageress for some years previous to de-nationalization. Until then it provided excellent service, very different from the time of my visit in 1959. Under private enterprise under a landlord ill-equipped for the job it has gone downhill, but this is an exception to the general rule.

34. Like Carlisle, Wigtown has been bypassed by the motorway which now slices inexorably across country.

35. Rydal Hall is now owned by the Diocese of Carlisle, but see list of inns included in Chapter 14. Apart from no longer having the portrait of Sir Michael in the hall there is little change in the use to which Rydal Hall has been put. It is now,

in effect, a Christian hotel well organized by the Warden, the Reverend D. D. Dixon, who knows a good deal about the Le Fleming family history.

36. Ings church and the small cluster of houses round it has now been bypassed by a road improvement scheme. Looking at the old narrow winding road one appreciates how very much better and broader all the roads throughout the Lake District and elsewhere are compared with fifteen years ago, although even so insufficient to meet the requirements of ever increasing summer traffic. The church itself now has a well cared for appearance.

37. Perhaps most noticeable today is the effective, though slightly bewildering one way system throughout the town. Not far beyond the town the motorway once again slices across the country with its concomitant collection of underpasses and overpasses.

38. The well is closed from October to March, perhaps to save the expense of cleaning it.

BIBLIOGRAPHY

Thornton's *Scottish Tour.*
Thornton's *French Tour.* Volumes 1 and 2.
Pennant's *Tours of Scotland.* Volumes 1, 2 and 3.
Notes of a Highland Chieftain. Sir Aeneas Mackintosh.
Sporting visitors to Badenoch. J. M. Bulloch.
Glimpses of Church and Social Life in the Highlands. Alexander
  MacPherson.
Travelling in Moray and N. Scotland over a Century Ago. Alexander
  Newland.
English Social History. G. M. Trevelyan.
Edinburgh Review, 1805
Edinburgh Weekly Review, 1782–4.
Gentleman's Magazine, 1782–4.
Annual Biography, 1824.